CW01671917

ART AND PRINT: THE CURWEN STORY

TATE PUBLISHING

ART AND PRINT: THE CURWEN STORY

ALAN POWERS

First published 2008 by order of the Tate Trustees by
Tate Publishing, a division of Tate Enterprises Ltd,
Millbank, London SW1P 4RG
www.tate.org.uk/publishing

British Library Cataloguing in Publication Data
A catalogue record for this book is available from the British Library

ISBN 978 1 85437 721 0

Distributed in the United States and Canada by
Harry N. Abrams, Inc., New York

Library of Congress Cataloging in Publication Data
Library of Congress Control Number: 2008930169

Designed by Esterson Associates
Printed by C&C
Colour reproduction by DL Interactive Ltd, London

Front cover: Edward Bawden, illustration for *The Choice of a Shipping Agent* 1931 (fig.11, detail, with amendments)
Back cover: Kyffin Williams, *Pontllyfni in Snow* 1974 (fig.110)
pp.2–3: Michael Rothenstein, *Sunrise at 36,000 ft* 1973 (fig.117, detail)
pp.8–9: Claude Lovat Fraser, *'The Spirit of Joy'* (fig.10, detail)
pp.68–9: Alan Davie, *Sleep My Angel* 1961–2 (fig.66, detail)

Tate Publishing would like to acknowledge with thanks the kind support of The Curwen Studio in facilitating this publication

CONTENTS

PREFACE

When, in 1977, in my last year as an undergraduate art history student, I walked contentedly out beneath the portico of the Tate Gallery after seeing the *Artists at Curwen* exhibition, I would have been still more pleased had I known that, thirty years on, I would have the chance to write the book that would succeed Pat Gilmour's excellent catalogue. Gilmour covered the two parts of the Curwen story, the Curwen Press, a general printing company flourishing after the First World War as part of the design reform movement of the time, and its offshoot, the Curwen Studio, a specialist print studio on the French model where artists could use the facilities and expertise to produce their own limited edition images.

The year 2008 marks the 50th anniversary of the Curwen Studio, and the book is a celebration of the remarkable work done under the master printer who started there in 1958, Stanley Jones. It seemed best to give an account of the Studio's parent business, since it is a fascinating story in its own right, with links in ethos and individual personalities, major artists among them. While this book is therefore to some extent a 'house history', it tries to put these activities in context at a time when all kinds of traditional printing are disappearing from view as the result of technical change. There is much fascination in the study of printing methods as an approach to the history of a broad category of art, as well as an area for practice by professionals and amateurs alike. Today, print making and collecting has its own intense following, but this is less easily seen by the gallery going pubic, so that the publication of this book and the concurrent exhibition, although smaller than its 1977 precursor, are a welcome recognition of a wider field. More clearly than in 1977, the Curwen Studio can now be seen as a part of an international movement of artists' printmaking which took many different forms. The sudden growth in limited editions by modern artists after the Second World War was unlike anything before or since. While the productions of the Curwen Press and its associated artists such as Edward Bawden and Eric Ravilious are justly celebrated for their intrinsic Englishness, they should also be seen in a wider context of enlivening the conjunction of text and image, and developing more sophisticated forms of visual communication that were working across Europe in the modern movement period. It could be said that the Curwen Studio began, falteringly, in the Lithographic Studio at the Slade School in the early 1950s, when Stanley Jones, as a student, tried to find out how to print the plates made by his teacher, Ceri Richards. It has been a continuous path of learning and adaptation, and the most recent enterprise of the Curwen Studio, the Print Study Centre at Chilford Hall, aims to provide access to students of all ages to the mysteries and delights of print making, and to encourage art schools, from which presses and print studios have been progressively eliminated over time, to include this activity among the range of choices offered to the artists of the future.

ACKNOWLEDGEMENTS

Discussion of this project began in June 2001, when Jenny Roland approached me to write a history of the Curwen Press and Studio. I remain grateful to her for giving me this opportunity to deepen my knowledge of many aspects of the history of printing and printmaking. Stanley Jones, whom I got to know when I made my first lithograph at the Curwen Studio in 1983, has been a fascinating source of information and insight through the process of research and writing. Brian Webb was involved in the early discussions of the project and has supported its progress in many ways. Peyton Skipwith, collaborator with Brian on a shorter book about the Curwen Press due to be published simultaneously with this one, has shared research findings and ideas.

Carol Unwin, the daughter of Harold Curwen, and David Unwin, her brother-in-law, provided recollections of this self-effacing man, and Merlin Unwin kindly lent archive material from his collection. Robert Scott Simon and Basil Harley described the post-war years at the Curwen Press on several occasions.

I owe much to other scholars and enthusiasts in the field of printing and illustration, including Jeremy Greenwood, Simon Lawrence Tim Mainstone, John Miles, and Peter Sampson.

The British Library, Tate Archive, Cambridge University Library and London Library have been the main research sources and I am grateful for their help. The research notes by Pat Gilmour in the Tate Archive, relating to the exhibition *Artists at Curwen*, 1977, were a valuable source. The Prints and Drawings Department at Tate houses a large collection of Curwen material, and I was helped to view it by Christine Kurpiel. The British Film Institute kindly provided facilities for viewing the BBC2 1982 series, *Artists in Print*, in which Glynn Boyd Harte demonstrates lithography at Curwen.

At Tate Publishing I am grateful to Roger Thorp, editorial director; Nicola Bion, project editor; Sarah Derry, copyeditor; Celia Gibson, picture researcher; and Simon Esterson and Sara Martin, designers. I would also like, as ever, to thank my wife, Susanna, for getting the spirit of joy, not only into printed things, but into life in general.

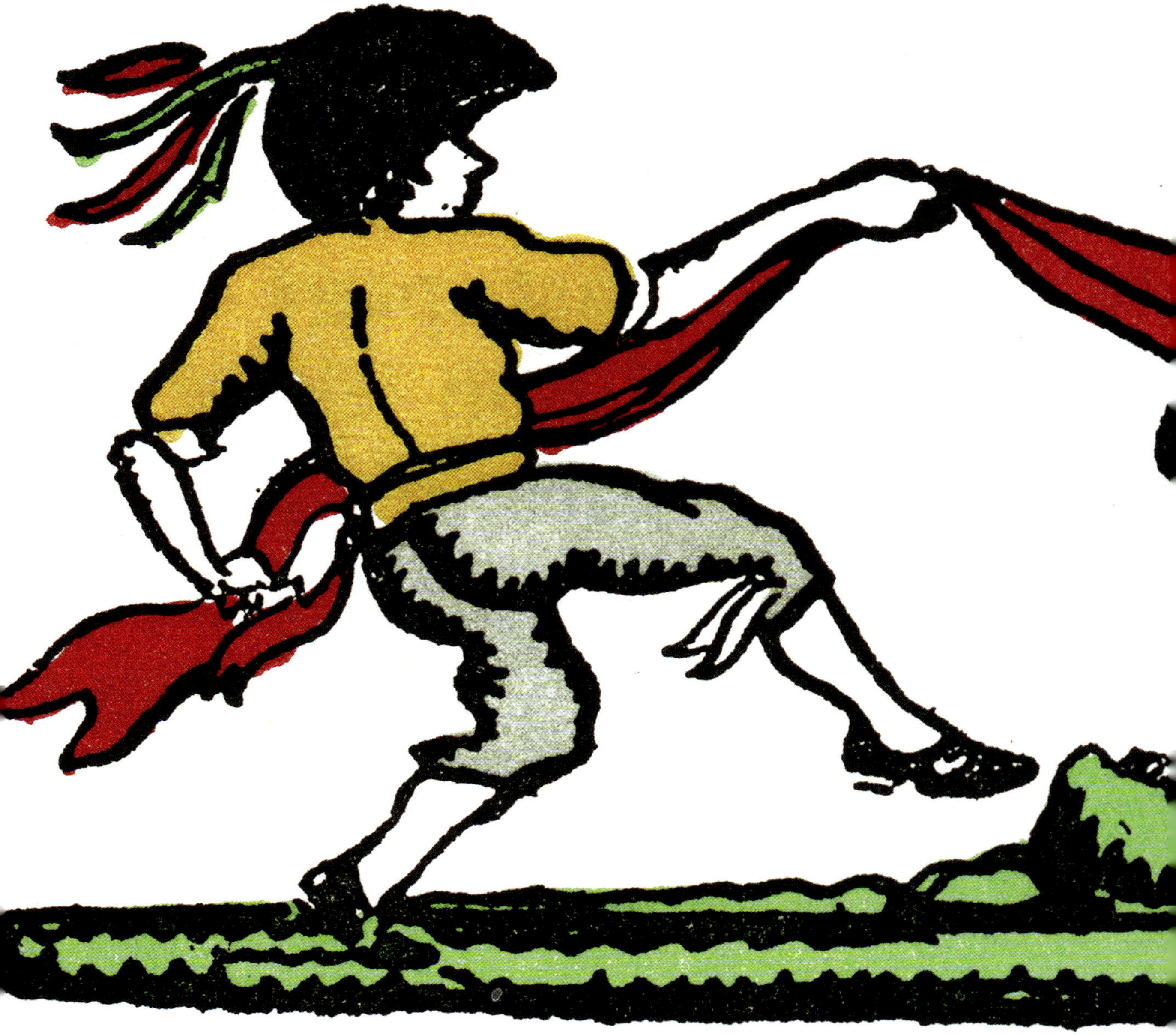

THE CURWEN PRESS

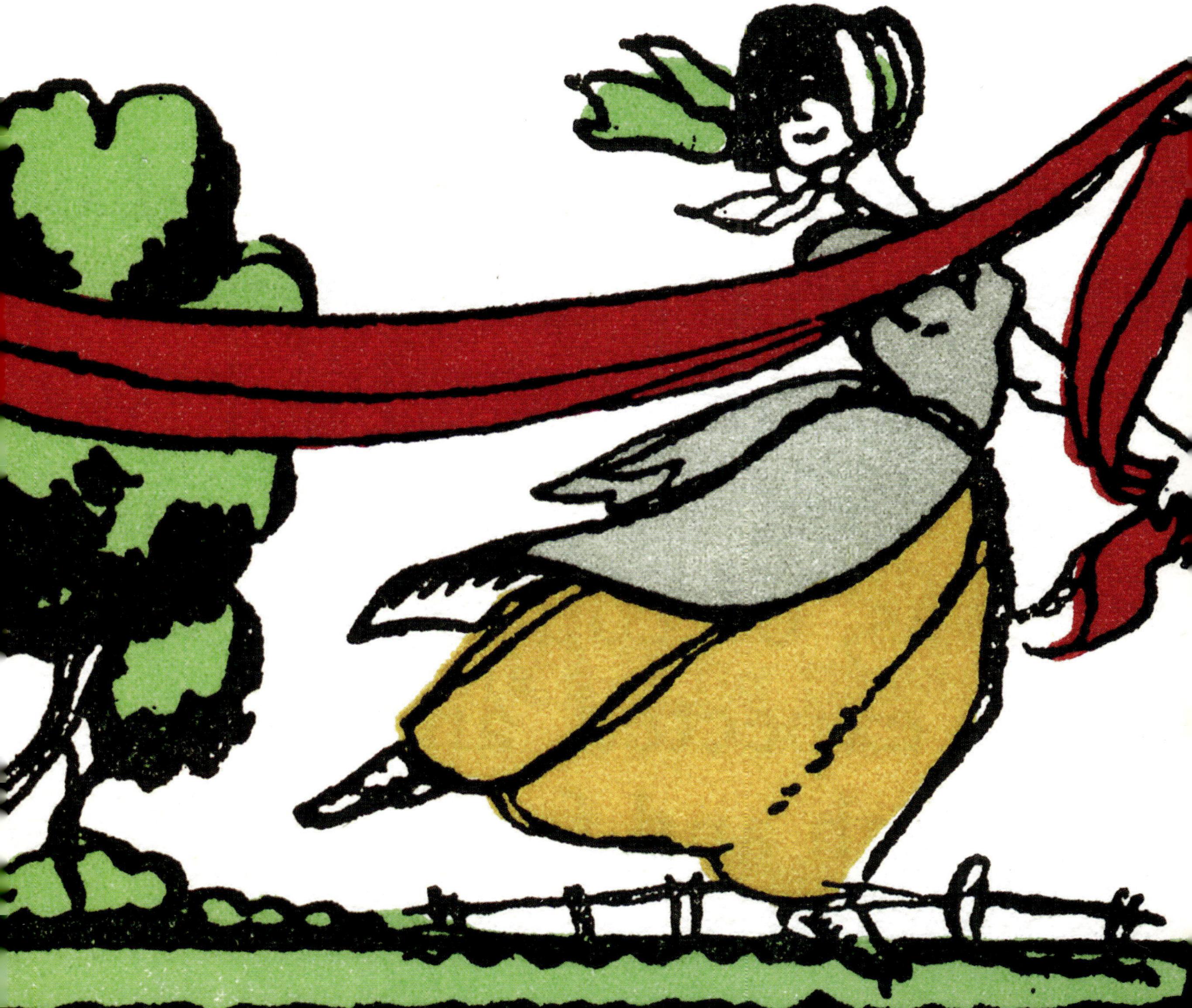

1
Sarah Glover
(1786–1867)

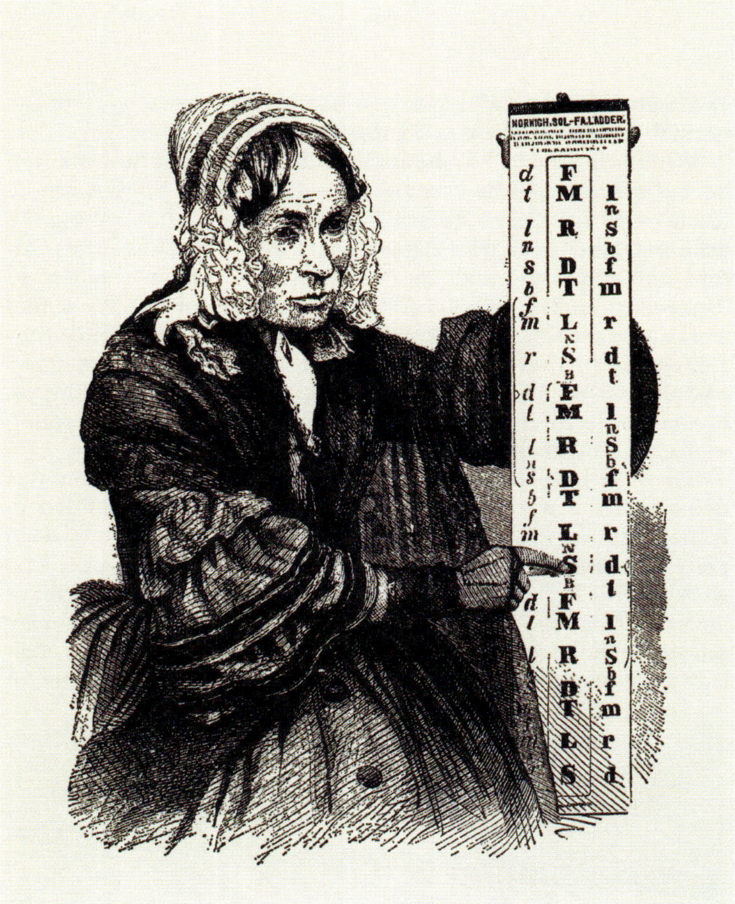

Curwen's Tonic Sol-Fa and *Mrs Curwen's Piano Method* were names familiar in Britain from mid-Victorian days onwards, and may still not be entirely forgotten. The founder of the Curwen Press was the Revd John Curwen, whose work was celebrated in a BBC programme early in 2008. He was a minister of the Congregational Church, born in Heckmondwike, West Yorkshire in 1816. His father was a minister before him in this, one of the principal non-conformist sects to emerge from the religious dissent of the seventeenth century in England.

In the Congregational Church, Christianity was practised in a self-governing and self-funding structure independent of the Church of England, with an emphasis on personal commitment to holy living and salvation. With the rise of the Industrial Revolution, these sects found a new rationale, and Congregationalists, Quakers and Unitarians became the new aristocracy of cities such as Birmingham and Liverpool in the nineteenth century, in their roles as responsible employers, active citizens and public spirited charitable givers.

John Curwen was a preacher by vocation and an industrialist by accident. He viewed singing as a way of bringing people of all sorts together for a heart-warming activity without dangerous consequences. As a result of an appointment to a chapel in Stowmarket in 1841, Curwen got to know Sarah Glover of Norwich (fig.1), who had invented a way of writing and reading music that was simpler to learn and cheaper to reproduce in printed form than conventional notation. Miss Glover was

2
Hand signs representing notes of scale, devised by the Rev. John Curwen, 1870

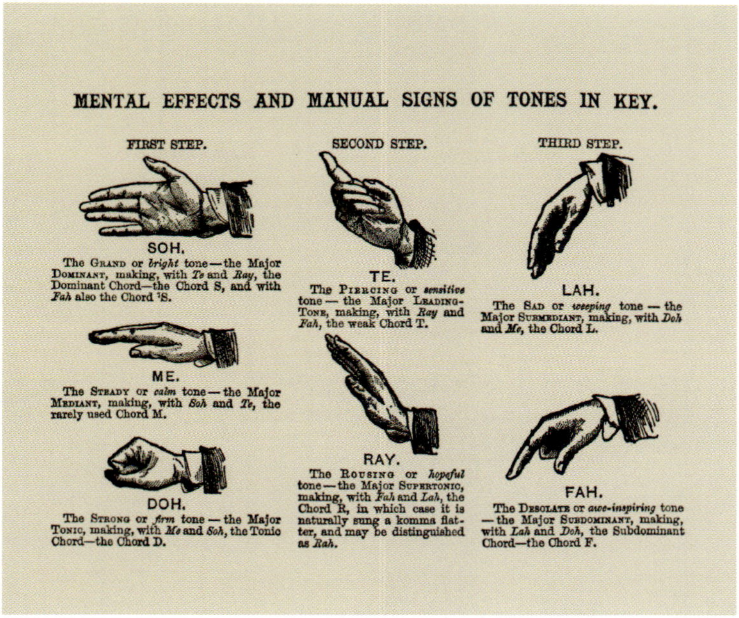

fifty-six years old when she met John Curwen, and was delighted when he popularised her invention, known as the 'tonic sol-fa', simplifying it somewhat in the process (fig.2). Three years later, Curwen was appointed pastor of the Independent Chapel in Plaistow, Essex, a rural area on the fringes of London, about a mile north of Silvertown and the Royal Docks. The village was soon to be swallowed up by rows of houses and light industry, its population rising from 2,000 in 1841 to 80,000 in 1891. At Plaistow, Curwen established a school next to the chapel, and in 1863 both buildings formed the beginning of the future Curwen Press site (fig.3), when Curwen decided he should print his tonic sol-fa materials himself, including a monthly magazine with a circulation of 180,00, *The Reporter*. Having had a breakdown from overwork, Curwen resigned his ministry in 1864 and devoted himself to his musical activities, joined by his wife and two sons, who carried on the business after Curwen's death in 1880.

Curwen's sons John Spencer Curwen and Joseph Spedding Curwen were in their father's mould, social idealists and abstainers from alcohol. Operating as J. Curwen and Sons they established a sound business in which the printing works' output was almost wholly devoted to the publishing enterprises of the company. They looked to Germany for the latest technical developments in machinery, and in 1895 Spedding Curwen took his fourteen-year-old son Harold to Leipzig, where Curwen music covers were then being printed. Soon, the Curwens acquired the necessary lithographic equipment to do

3
The Curwen works at Plaistow, 1896

4
Advertisement in the *Imprint*, no.1, January 1913

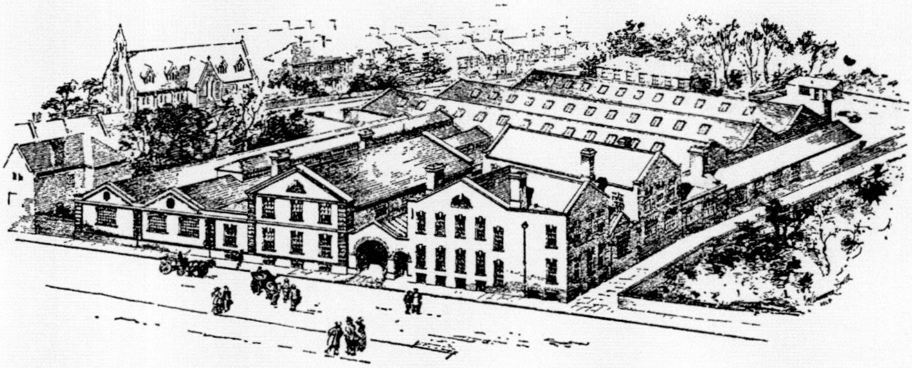

this type of work at Plaistow. Improvements were technical rather than aesthetic, however, for the printing trade was initially resistant to the revival in design and quality of production associated with William Morris and the Arts and Crafts movement.

Harold Curwen

Harold Curwen joined the company in 1908 after a progressive education at a new public school, Abbotsholme in Derbyshire, which broke away from conventions of dress, hierarchy and curriculum. At school he became a fine cabinet-maker and metalworker, and then spent a year at Plaistow before spending most of 1906 in Leipzig with the music printers, Brandstetter. In Leipzig, the centre of German book printing, the effects of the English typographical revival, involving figures such as William Morris, Emery Walker and Edward Johnston, were beginning to be felt, especially through the publisher Insel, whose work was noticed by Curwen. On returning to England he spent a year studying calligraphy with Johnston at the Central School in London, before joining the family firm. In his early years he put his leisure time into the Boy Scouting movement, founded in 1907. Photography, sailing and winter sports were his other recreations, and he joined a regular group of visitors to Lenzerheide in Switzerland before the First World War. Here he met his first wife, Rose Blanche Wenner, and they were married in 1912, although she died soon after the birth of their daughter Isobel in 1916.

At Plaistow, the two sons of John Curwen were beginning to think of retirement, leaving Harold and his cousin Kenneth Curwen in line of succession. There were also worrying signs of a decline in profits, and a lack of diversification in a business that was both a printer and publisher, directing its whole output towards a specialised market. Harold's name is prominent in a full-page

HAROLD CURWEN OF THE

CURWEN PRESS

has studied under one of the editors of this Magazine, as well as under other leaders of the movement for improving the style of commercial printing.

THE STAFF OF THE

CURWEN PRESS

has been trained so that it is able, with the present-day materials, to produce the best results in artistic and forceful Catalogues, Show Cards, Pamphlets, Labels, etc., and also in the printing and binding of beautiful books of every description.

Mr. Curwen requests permission to call at your address, or to send examples of his work executed at

THE CURWEN PRESS,

Plaistow, London, E.

'Phone: EAST 1737 (3 lines).

66

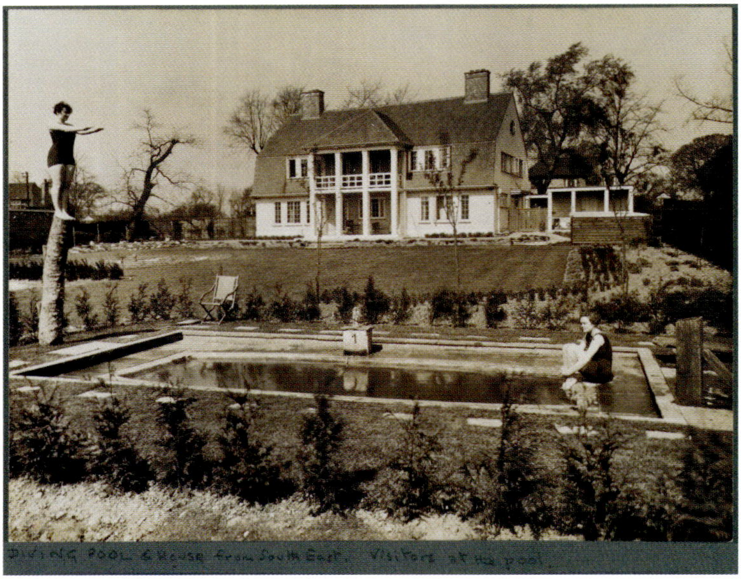

5
Harold Curwen's house, Mansard, Loughton Hill, Essex, designed by Edward Maufe in 1927, represented the taste of the DIA founders

advertisement in the *Imprint*, the magazine launched in 1913 by a group of enthusiastic artists, designers and printers (fig.4), announcing that 'Harold Curwen of the Curwen Press has studied under one of the editors of this Magazine, as well as under other leaders of the movement for improving the style of commercial printing.' It goes on to solicit orders for 'artistic and forceful Catalogues, Show Cards, Pamphlets, Labels, etc., and also … the printing and binding of beautiful books of every description.' In joining the revival of fine commercial printing, Curwen established the basis for his future success.

The religious backgrounds of Curwen's contemporaries in the design reform movement were sublimated into an essentially Ruskinian mixture of aesthetics and social service. The humblest trade cards, catalogues and press advertisements mattered at least as much as the finely printed book. The idea of reforming the visual world from the bottom up was part of the Arts and Crafts agenda, and believing that the struggle need not be in vain, the younger generation accepted machine production and tried to mould it to their standards. In most cases, design meant stripping away superfluous ornament before structuring the remaining information.

In 1914, before the outbreak of war, a party of British manufacturers and educationalists visited Cologne for the annual exhibition of the Deutsche Werkbund, a trade association dedicated to design reform, and they were deeply impressed by what they saw. In March 1915, despite hostilities with Germany and to encourage British manufacturers to higher standards, the Board of Trade organised an exhibition of the best German industrial goods in London, and in May, members of the Cologne party, with others, founded the Design and Industries Association. Harold Curwen was one of the original 200 members (fig.5). It was through the DIA that Joseph Thorp, a journalist with a

6
Curwen Sans., drawn by Harold Curwen in 1911, and produced as metal type in 1928

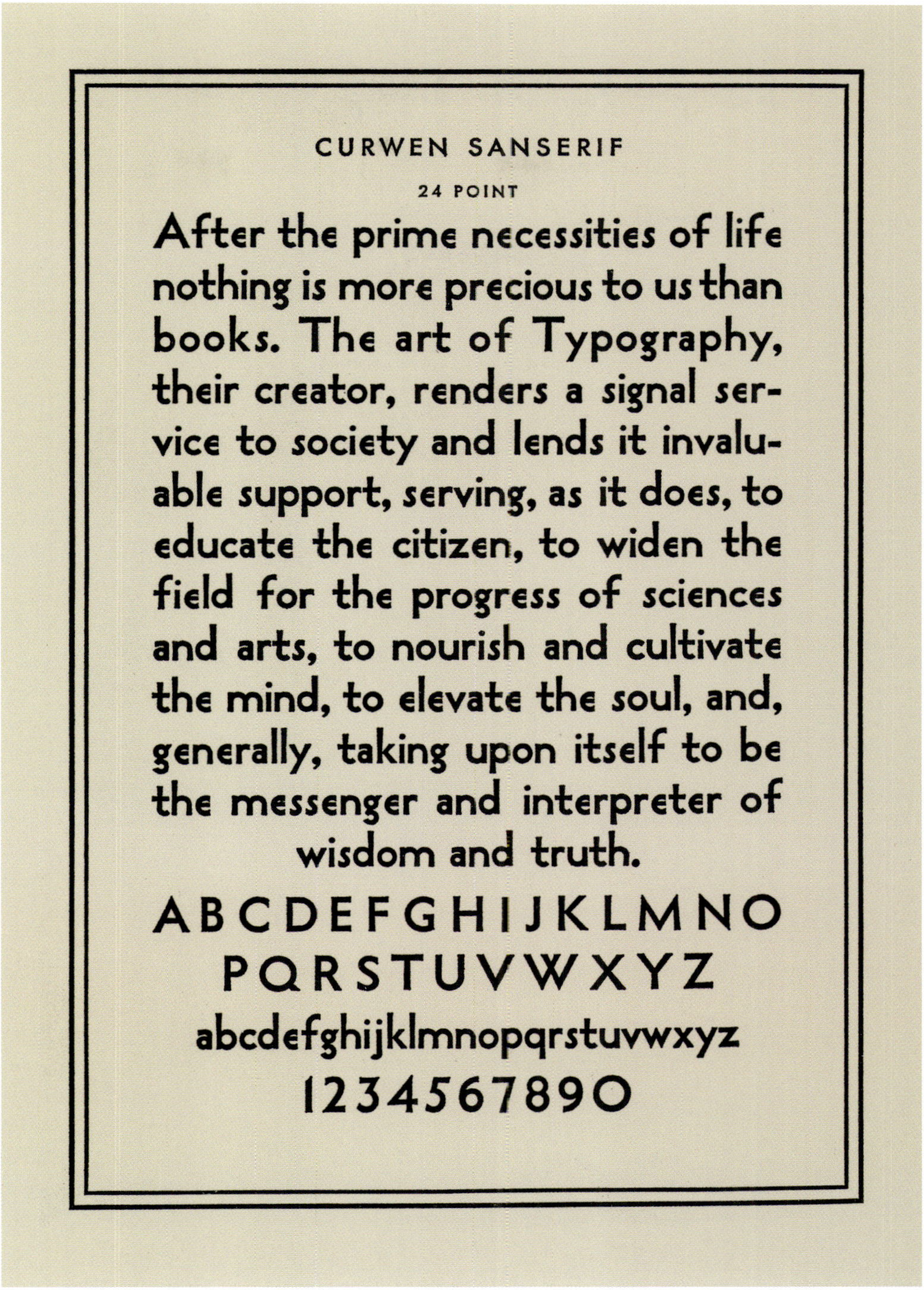
CURWEN SANSERIF

24 POINT

After the prime necessities of life nothing is more precious to us than books. The art of Typography, their creator, renders a signal service to society and lends it invaluable support, serving, as it does, to educate the citizen, to widen the field for the progress of sciences and arts, to nourish and cultivate the mind, to elevate the soul, and, generally, taking upon itself to be the messenger and interpreter of wisdom and truth.

ABCDEFGHIJKLMNO
PQRSTUVWXYZ
abcdefghijklmnopqrstuvwxyz
1234567890

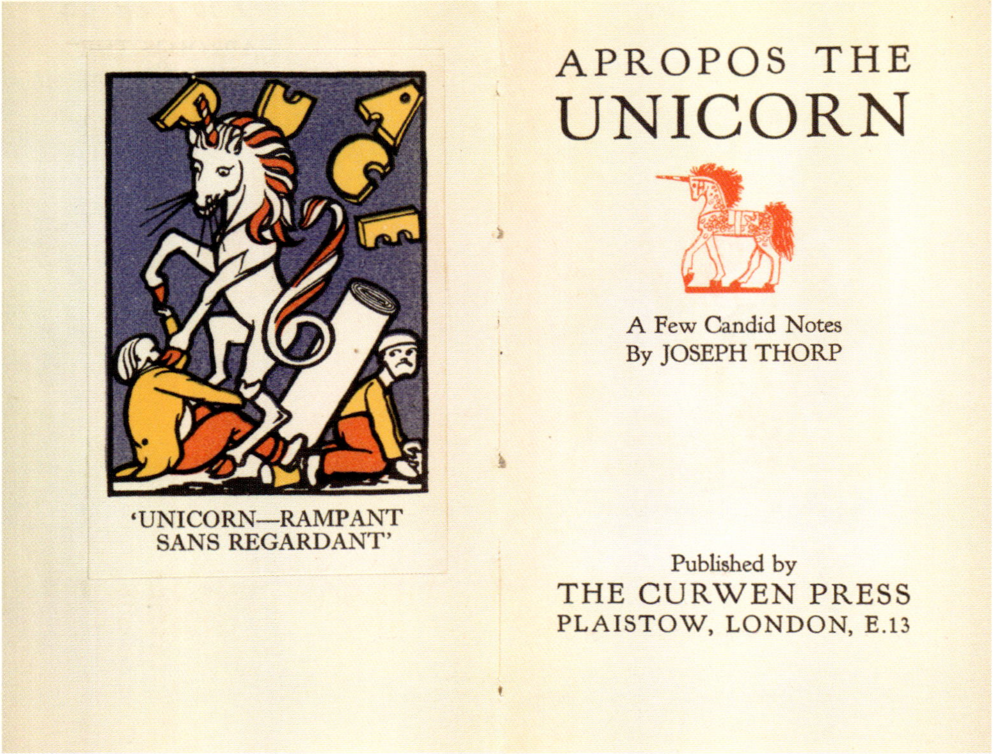

7
Promotional booklet by Joseph Thorp, 1920. Frontispiece drawing by Macdonald Gill

background in printing, got to know Harold Curwen and began to act as his publicity agent (fig.7).

The war also gave Curwen the excuse he needed to offer large quantities of old metal type for munitions making. As Herbert Simon, a later director and historian of the company wrote, 'He could sell off at a figure well above book value all the horrors which the firm had collected since its foundation. The range of faces was reduced to a half dozen, the best that could be had at the time, including Caslon, Imprint and Plantin.' It was a bold step, and older members of staff were in despair at the loss of old friends. The West Ham Corporation Tramways, furious at receiving their note headings in Caslon Old Face, a gracious font whose use since the 1720s had never completely died out, cancelled their account, but new customers came to fill their place.

Thorp was responsible for bringing to Curwen the idea of using artists as an integral part of the Press's identity. He proposed a unicorn as a device for the Press, a modern equivalent to some of the printer's devices from the Renaissance, and commissioned his old school friend Paul Woodroffe to draw it for line-block reproduction, the first of many interpretations (fig.8). More significant, however, was the Press's new association with the young artist Claud Lovat Fraser, who was introduced to them by Thorp. Fraser had returned from the Battle of Loos in 1916, weakened by gas and shellshock, and was persuaded to join the DIA. Although still enrolled in a non-combatant role until 1919, he had the leisure to produce a stream of drawings, some to commission, others simply for the pleasure of drawing, but nearly all intended for printing. Around 1919, Fraser's work became almost a trademark of the Curwen Press. His widow wrote that he and Harold Curwen 'understood each other perfectly, and shared many tastes in common; and both had the

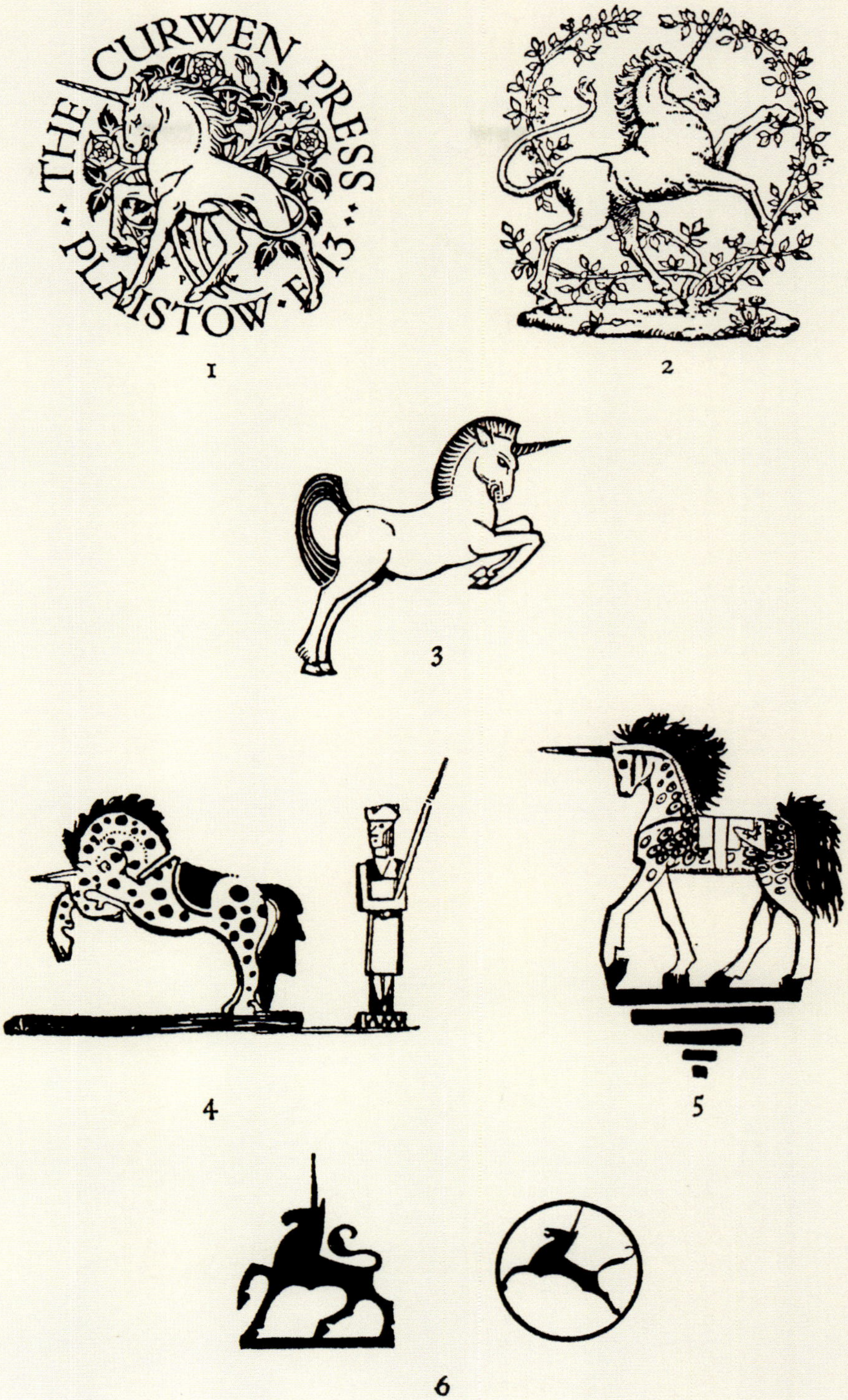

8
Curwen Press unicorns.
1 Paul Woodroffe,
2 Percy Smith, 3 Eric Gill,
4 and 5 Claud Lovat
Fraser, 6 Aldo Cosomati

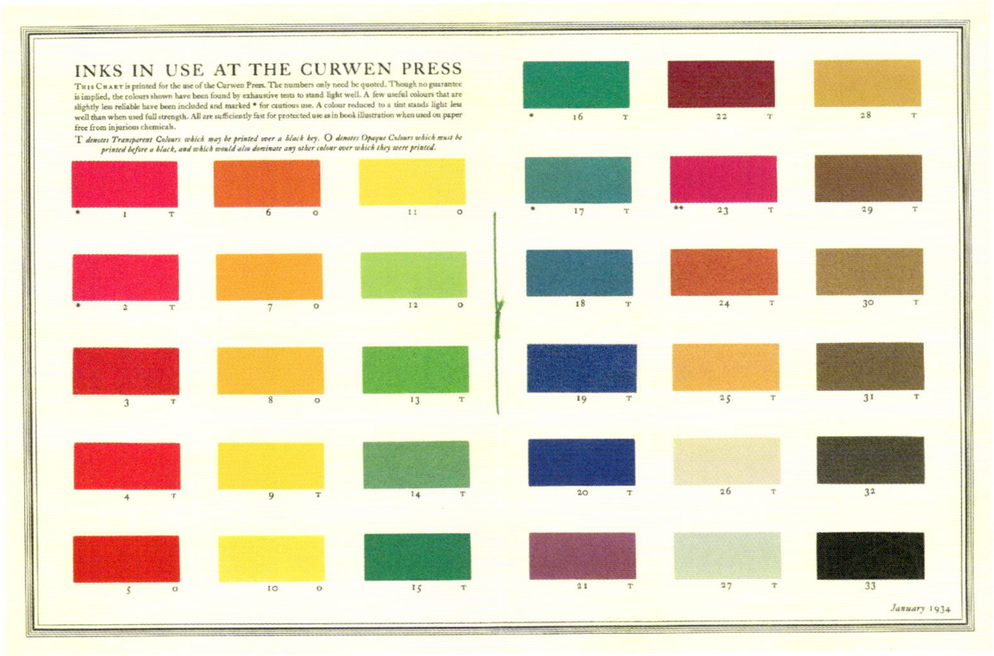

9
Coloured inks in use at Curwen, from the *Curwen Press Newsletter*, no.6, 1934

same fierce integrity in regard to work … From their first meeting, Lovat worked continuously for the Curwen Press, designing printer's ornaments, Christmas cards, letter headings, advertising booklets and display cards, and many other kinds of advertising material.'[1]

Fraser used coloured inks to hand-colour the black-and-white images reproduced from his drawings, in a typical range of crimson, gamboge, turquoise and purple. This was a reversion to the hand-colouring found in Regency children's books and was part of a European movement associated with the avant-garde in Vienna and Paris. Fraser drew 'colour separations' so that colours could be overlaid, printed one at a time in specially mixed tones and thereby retaining the clarity and brilliance of hand-coloured work. At the Curwen Press, an extra effort was made to find strong but non-fading coloured inks (fig.9) appropriate for this type of work, and in the 1920s, since there were no papers available bright enough for Harold Curwen's needs, he printed plain sheets that could then be used as cover papers or backgrounds for type. The most famous self-promotional leaflet of the time, which soon became a byword for the Curwen Press in the immediate post-war years, was the one that urged 'Get the Spirit of Joy into your printed things', beneath a couple of Lovat Fraser dancers, out of doors, wind-blown in breeches, bonnet and crinoline (fig.10).

For Harold Curwen, all aspects of the process contributed to the quality of the end product. Relationships in the workplace were important, and Curwen was one of the first companies to reduce the six-day working week to five.

Advertising in the 1920s

Harold Curwen played a significant part in the transformation of newspaper and magazine advertising from hard selling to more subtle forms of brand reinforcement. The Curwen Press would sometimes deal

10
Curwen Press leaflet from 1920, illustrated by Claud Lovat Fraser

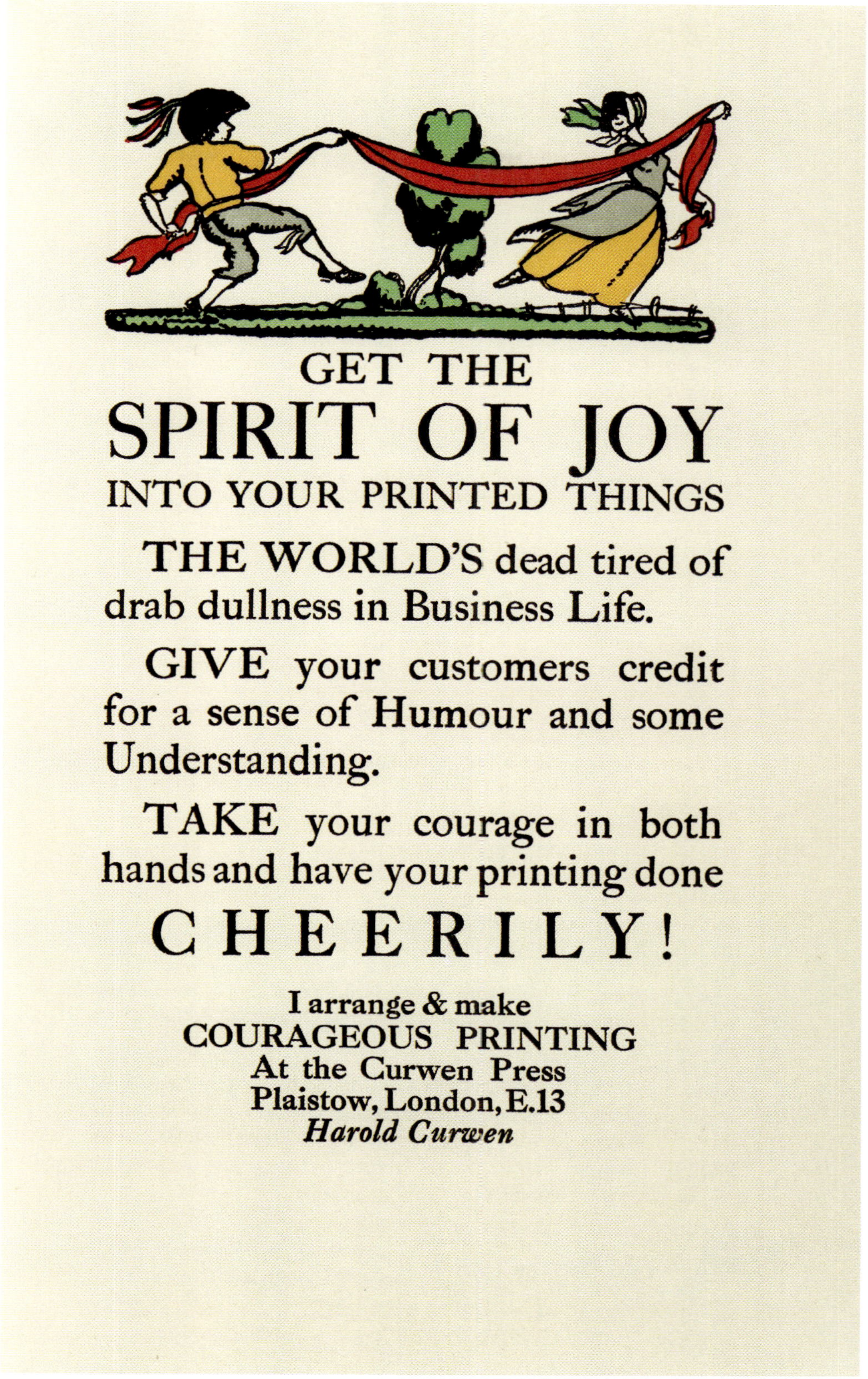

11
Edward Bawden, illustration for *The Choice of a Shipping Agent*, for Thomas Meadows and Co. Ltd., 1931

with the advertising agencies that were emerging in the 1920s, such as Crawfords or Stuarts, but it could also provide the same services directly for the client, bringing together copywriter and illustrator, and creating the physical artwork that combined text and image and could be supplied to newspapers in the form they required for reproduction. In the case of booklets and posters, the printing would be undertaken in house, while press advertising could be supplied in line-block form with typesetting for use on newspaper presses. The impact of the Curwen Press on the newspaper-reading or poster-viewing public in the 1920s was considerable, and its standards of charm and humour were widely imitated.

Sometimes pure typography was used, with quantities of white space that caught the eye better than a busy panel, but more often, there was an element of illustration as well, often making an oblique suggestion. Curwen was pleased to help fine artists to earn a living, and there was a considerable crossover between those who worked on advertising commissions and those who were offered more prestigious book illustration jobs.

One of Joseph Thorp's methods of promotion was to tell through advertising a story about the product and the company that made it, a style still familiar today in advertisements for Jack Daniels whisky (fig.11). This allowed 'exclusive' brands to appear more accessible, and satisfied the DIA's aspiration to public education. Harold Curwen recognised the abilities of Francis Bruguière, an avant-garde photographer based in London who had risen to prominence around 1930 through his abstract photographs and films. Bruguière's photographs for *Match Making* (fig.12), a Bryant and May brochure of 1931, used the avant-garde techniques of double-exposure, close-ups and diagonal rotations to create patterns and puzzles from the match-making process, as well as depicting some of the attractive match girls commanding complex machinery, with a lithographed cover by Paul Nash (fig.13) and a text by E.P. Leigh-Bennett, typeset in a large font with narrow margins to set it apart from an ordinary booklet of this kind. The words are a jocular account of production and sales, appealing to the consumer or investor, and evidently intended to resist foreign competition at a time when Ivar Kreuger, the infamous Swedish 'match king', was taking over the industry. *Commercial Art* magazine described a Bruguière brochure for Gestetner, the makers of duplicating machines, as 'designed to be a trifle puzzling, and to intrigue one to look inside – a symbolic treatment of the machine itself.'[2] It is perhaps significant that several of the companies that went to Curwen for their printing design also patronised modern architecture. Thus Crittall's built some of the earliest flat-roofed houses in Britain at Braintree and Silver End in Essex, while Gestetner were the developers of the Highpoint flats in Highgate by Berthold Lubetkin, originally intended, like Silver End, as housing for their workers.

London Transport printed a number of posters at the Curwen Press (fig.15), while Curwen designed much of their press advertising, with line images by Bawden and Ravilious.[3] Harold Curwen enjoyed

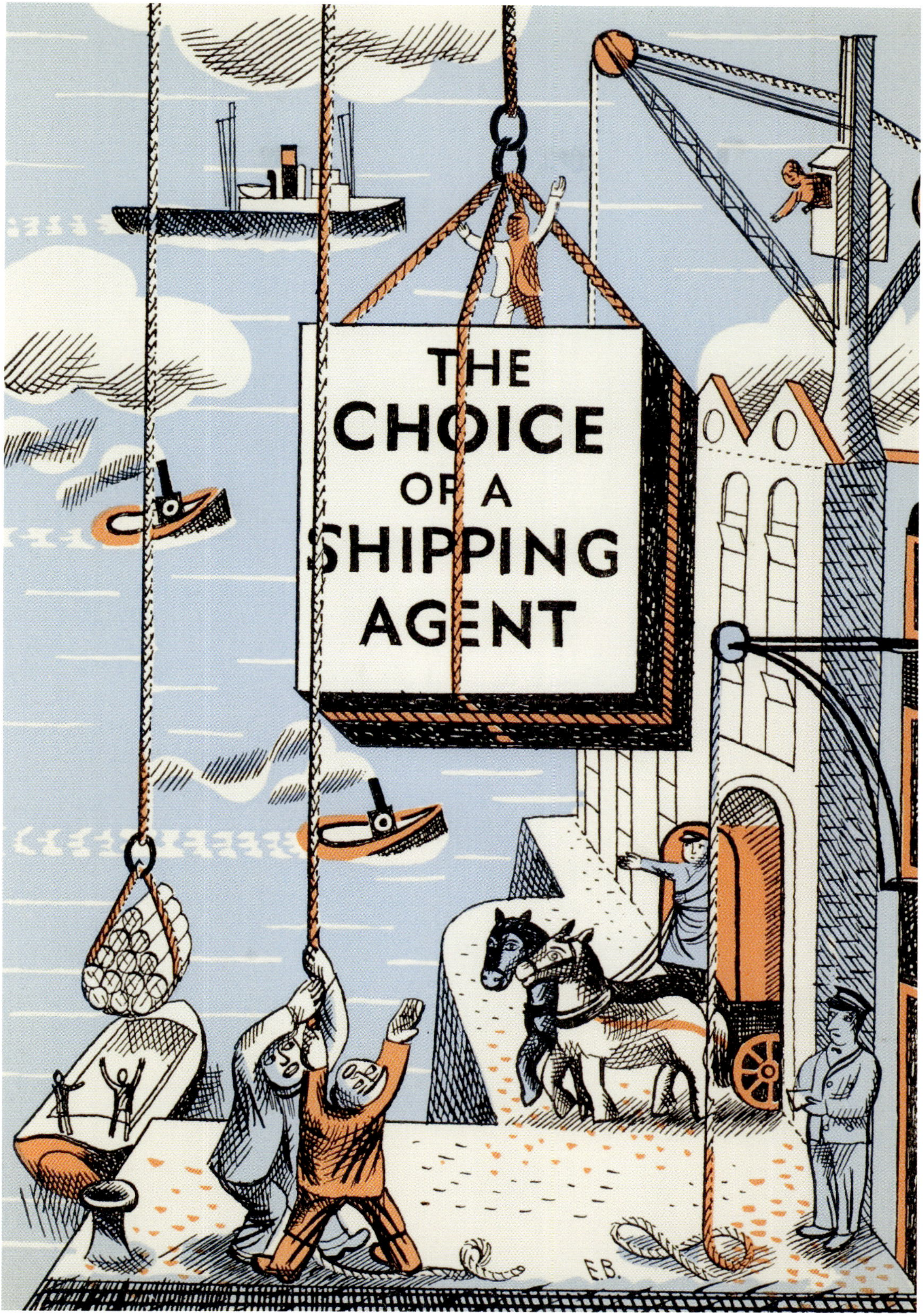
THE
CHOICE
OF A
SHIPPING
AGENT
E.B.

12
Match Making.
Photograph by Francis Bruguière, 1931

13
Match Making brochure for Bryant and May, cover by Paul Nash, 1931

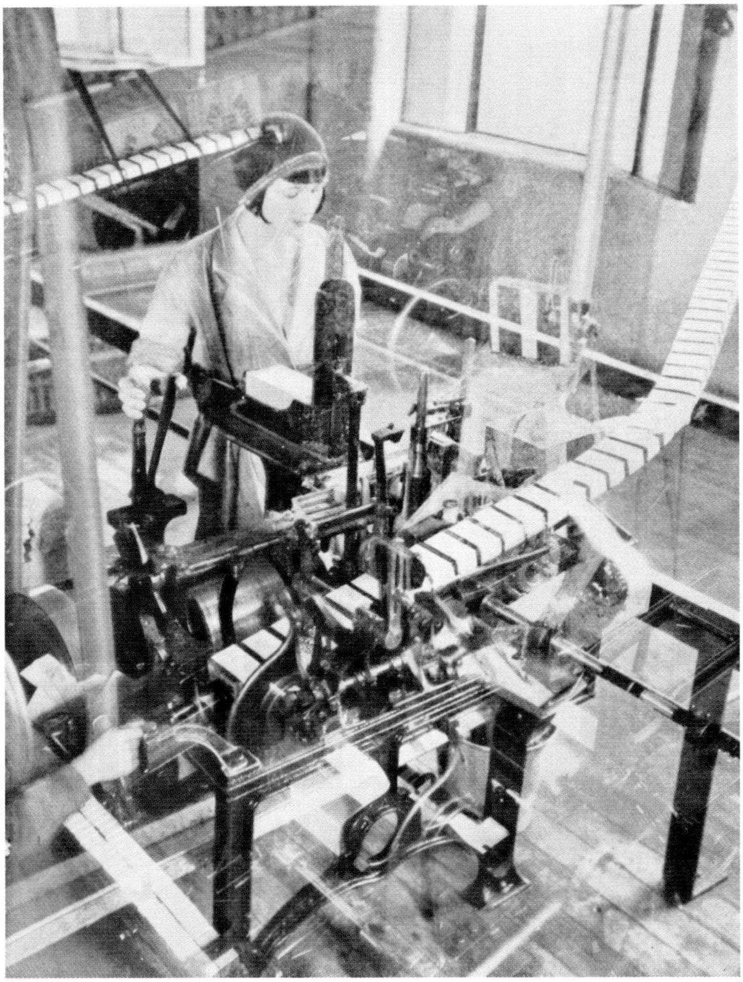

designing transport timetables, whether for Imperial Airways or London Transport, introducing a convention of 'leading' or a blank line between every five lines of text to give the eye guidance in a long list. He also worked on the design of automatically printed tickets for London Transport, as well as printing some of the famous posters commissioned by Frank Pick and Christian Barman. Well into the post-war period, the Curwen Press continued to produce posters such as Bawden's *City* of 1952.

Oliver Simon

The 'coup de foudre' or thunderclap is a French metaphor for a sudden transforming experience. This seems to happen frequently in the lives of people associated with printing. Oliver Simon was passing the window of the bookseller Henry Sotheran in Piccadilly in 1919, where, as he later recalled 'an astonishing window display of sumptuous, dazzling, richly decorated books caught my eye and arrested my steps. I felt compelled to enter and make inquiries and was told, for the first time in my life, about William Morris and the Kelmscott Press, and of the Kelmscott Chaucer in particular, which held a place of honour in the window.' Leaving the shop, Simon knew that his vague career plans following wartime service in Gallipoli and Palestine (which he apparently rather enjoyed) were suddenly clear. He would not follow the family cotton trade, nor banking nor forestry, but 'it was plain to me I *must* become a printer.'[4]

Oliver Simon grew up in Manchester, where his father was a cotton merchant with aspirations to scholarship in his spare

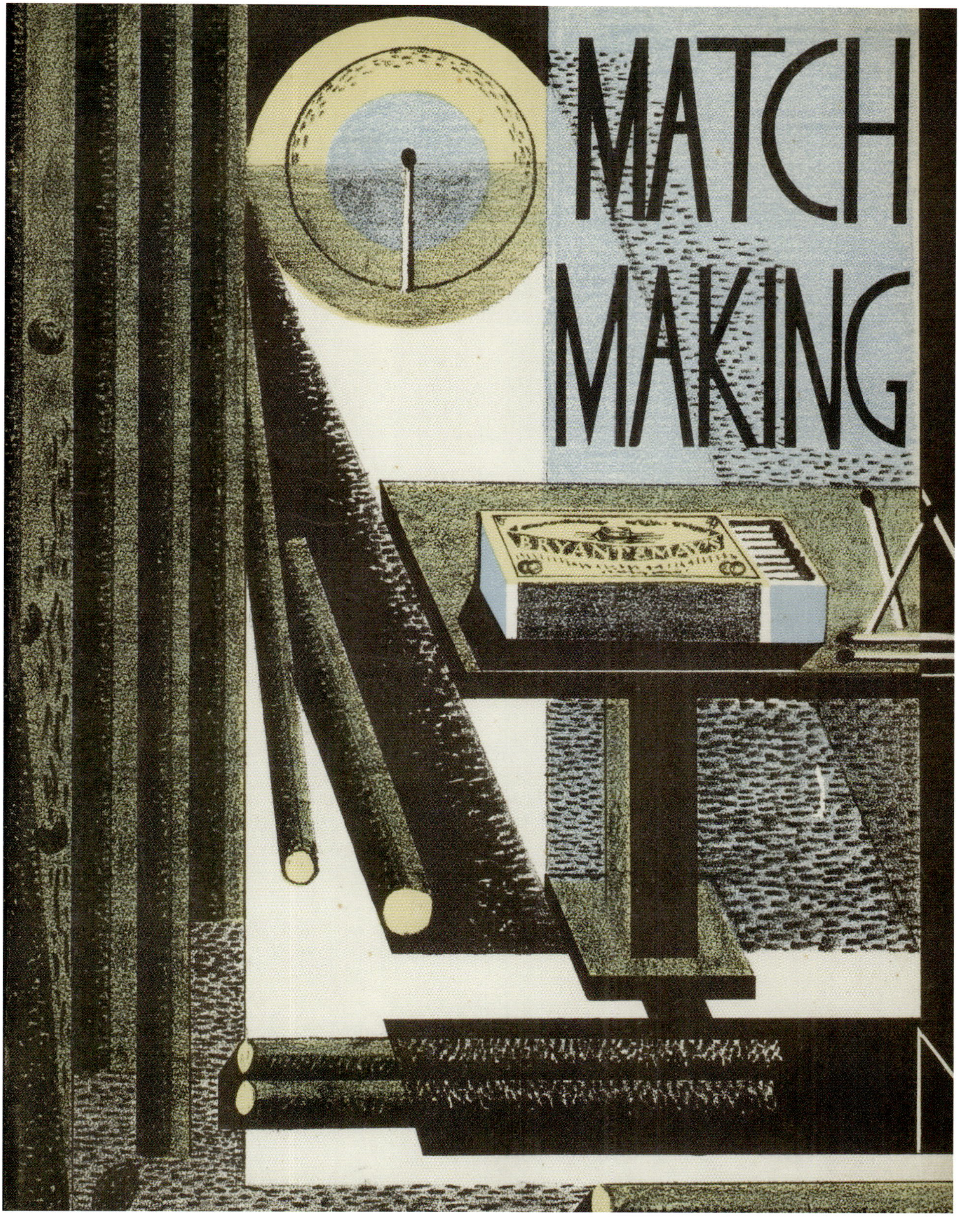
MATCH
MAKING

14
Claud Lovat Fraser,
The Luck of the Bean-Rows, 1921

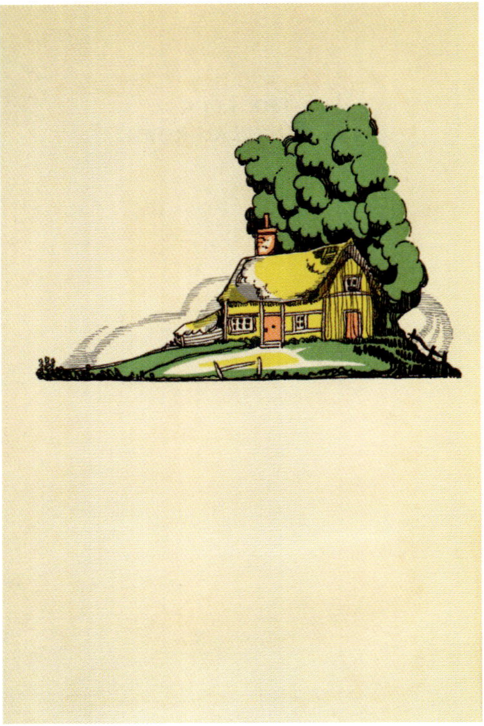

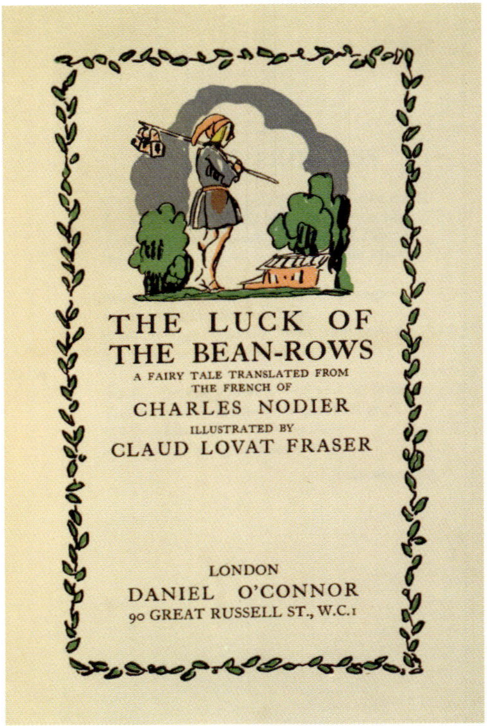

time. His mother, also of German origin, came from Bradford. All three of her brothers were concerned with the visual arts, two of them, William and Albert Rothenstein (who changed his name to Rutherston during the First World War) being prominent both as artists and as educators. William Rothenstein, appointed principal of the Royal College of Art in 1919, was one of the most influential figures of his generation. By a chain of connection via Rutherston, Lovat Fraser and Thorp, Oliver Simon joined Curwen in 1920.

His enthusiasm was for book printing, which Curwen had not previously attempted on any scale. Although the presses were adequate, and Curwen also had a bindery, neither was on a large scale, and rates of pay for workers in book printing in the London area were higher than those of printers outside London, so that when competing for tenders, it was important to offer some special compensatory advantages to clients willing to appreciate them. The Lovat Fraser craze enabled Simon to bring his first large book-printing order to Plaistow, after spending some time visiting publishers to ask for commissions. A small publisher, Daniel O'Connor, produced a French fairytale, *The Luck of the Bean-Rows* (fig.14), with Lovat Fraser illustrations, in a slim volume with harlequin-patterned paper sides for Christmas 1921. He had 20,000 copies already printed, but was so sure of its future success that he urgently commissioned a further 30,000 and went out of business soon afterwards. It is a delightful book, but understandably still not expensive to buy second hand. Much Curwen book printing, while specialising in illustrated texts, tended in future towards poetry and limited editions rather than the mainstream market.

Soon Simon was putting his own character into the books printed at Curwen, a restrained classicism based on precision in every part of the work, but especially in the

15
Albert Rutherston (with Claud Lovat Fraser), *The Good Fairy*, London Underground Poster, 1922

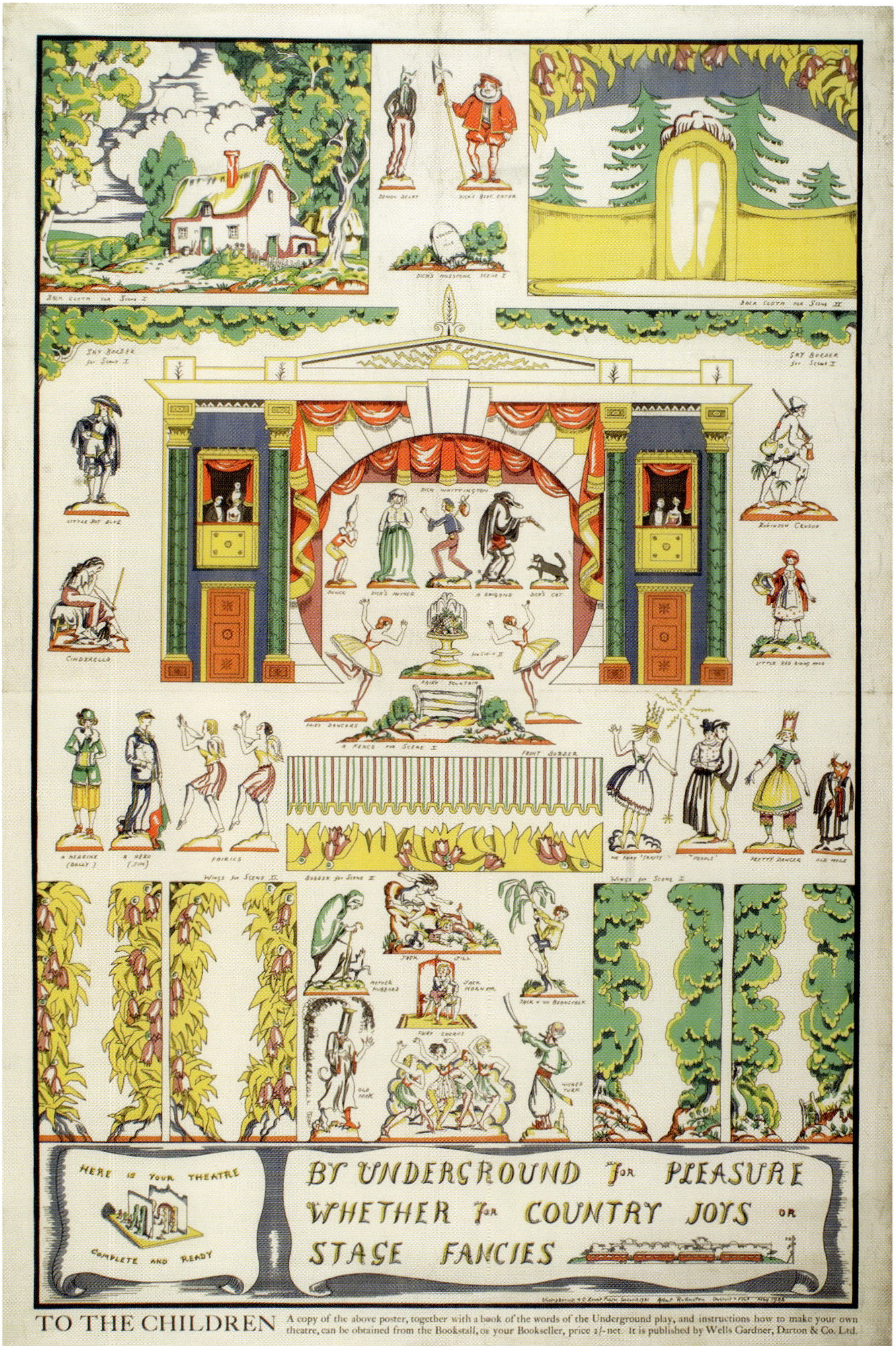

16
Paul Nash, 'And God said let the waters be gathered together', *Genesis*, Nonesuch Press, 1924

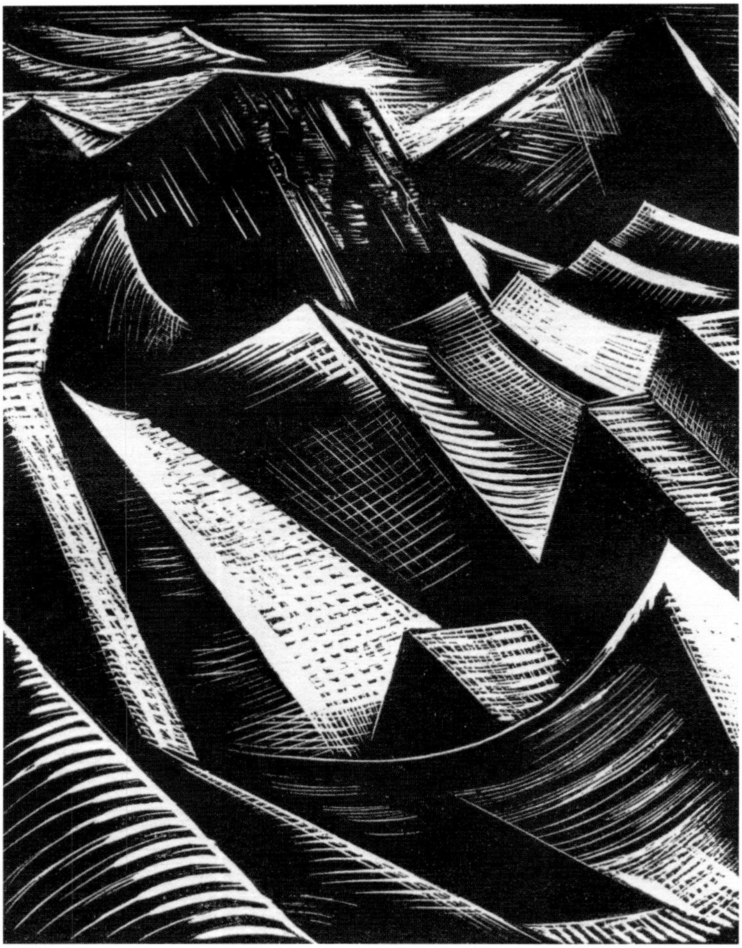

selection of appropriate typefaces, a discreet use of ornaments, and a taut quality of spacing both in set-pieces such as title pages and in the setting of continuous text. While working concurrently, Harold Curwen and Oliver Simon were therefore responsible for different if overlapping parts of the output from Plaistow. Curwen was a printer with a strong interest in design, while Simon represented a new kind of designer, the typographer, being in addition a mixture of patron and cultural impresario. There was a commercial basis to the work he undertook, but it was a conscious form of cultural mission, going far beyond profit and loss. As his brother Herbert Simon wrote, 'Curwen was essentially a "works" man with the strict disciplines normal to factory life. Oliver made his empire in Bloomsbury where, in the judgement of the ordinary man of business, an almost startling Bohemian way of life held sway.'[5] Holbrook Jackson explained how, 'without appearing to be doing much more than circulate more or less silently, among the art and literary haunts of London, he brought grist to the Curwen mill in the form of new ideas, typefaces, ornaments, and above all personalities.'[6]

The result of this combination of two dissimilar people with shared ideals was to make the Curwen Press an agent of cultural change of a new kind.

Simon visited Francis Meynell, founder of the Pelican Press, and they worked together closely on many of the books that Meynell published when he founded the Nonesuch Press in 1923. Nonesuch represented a new model in the world of fine book publishing, since there was no

17
A Specimen Book of Pattern Papers Designed for and in use at the Curwen Press, 1928

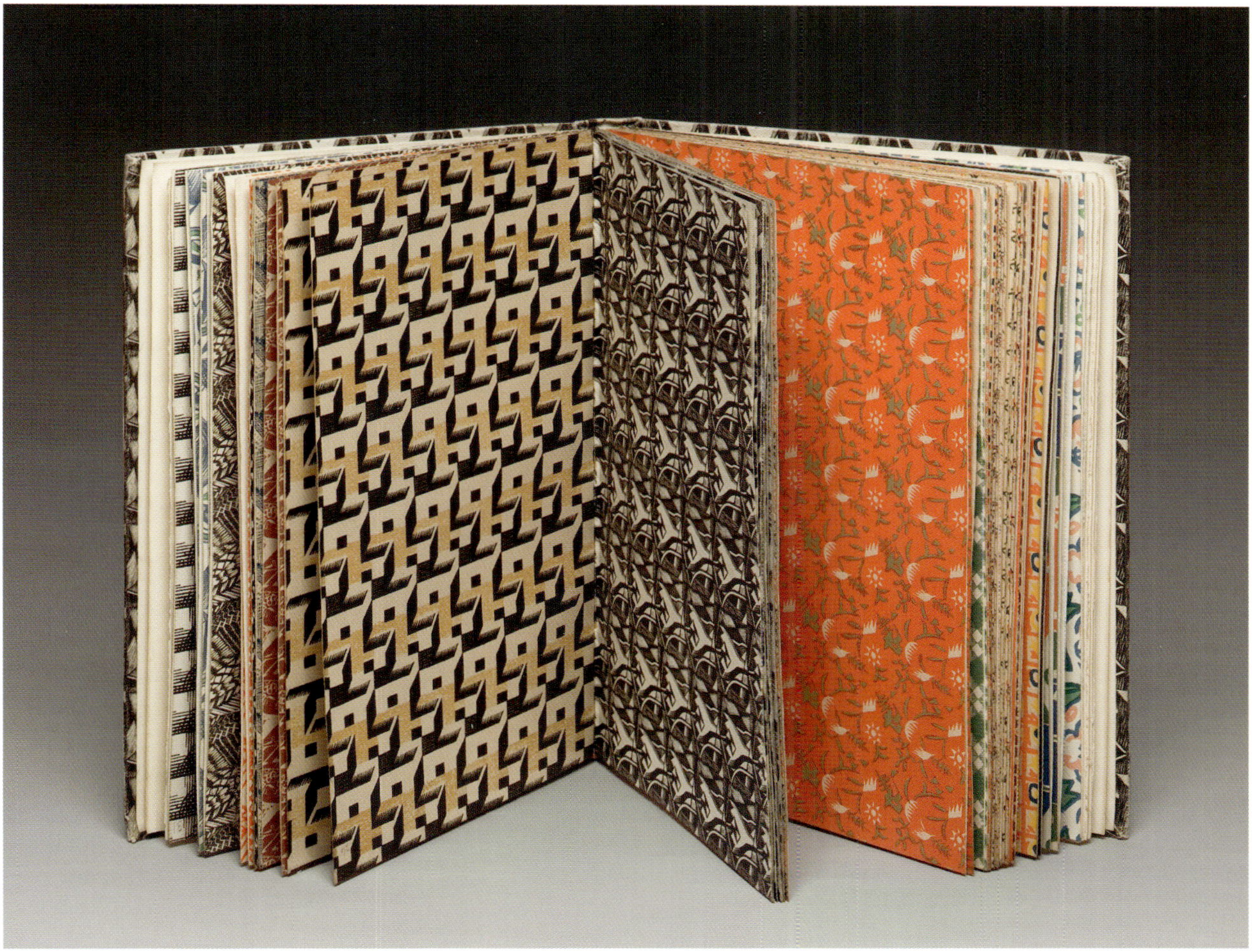

18
Edward Bawden, *Pottery Making at Poole*, 1925

emphasis on anything hand made.
The editions were limited, but in larger numbers than normal, and the prices proportionally lower (fig.16). Each book was designed as a self-sufficient entity, taking its character from the text, so that there was no obvious 'house style'. Simon felt as Meynell did about the acceptability of machine production under strict artistic control, and his books became a means of showing mainstream publishers that higher standards were possible at little extra expense. As a result, the quality of the average book in the 1920s rose sharply, and an increasing number of printing houses, including the two University Presses of Oxford and Cambridge, reached standards of design and production equivalent to Curwen.

A considerable number of artists in England wanted to work in illustration, usually in conjunction with other forms of practice, including oil and watercolour painting, and in some cases mural painting and textile or ceramic design. This was partly the legacy of the Arts and Crafts movement and its influence on art school curricula, and partly the result of the artists' difficulty in making money by other means. Many artists liked the idea of being useful and France provided a precedent with the International Exhibition of 1925 in Paris demonstrating how artists could bring a fresh eye to design tasks.

Commissioning artists

Talent-spotting for artists was shared between Harold Curwen and Oliver Simon. They looked for artists who drew more in outline than tone, since half-tone reproduction was never used, and line work with much cross-hatching lacked clarity in reproduction. The freshness of an original idea must be kept, and Curwen wrote: 'We need a more direct method and a quicker working. So often the first rough sketch for a design is much better than the design itself.'[7] Since people looked at commercial illustration in a hurry, drawings done at speed were more suitable than the laboured efforts often produced by students. Wood engravings were an alternative, a medium popular in the 1920s and intrinsically designed for reproduction in print. The work of Thomas Bewick set a standard for sensitivity and graphic clarity that was interpreted by Eric Ravilious and others.

Paul Nash, a friend of Lovat Fraser in the final years of his short life, was possibly the single most significant, if not prolific, of the artists associated with the Curwen Press. He had a positive belief in the value of artists working in the commercial sphere, for their own good and for the good of public taste. He believed that the spontaneity of the artist's touch should be retained through the industrial process, including precision of colour matching. He was thus a demanding collaborator, but found at Curwen the standards he expected.

In 1932, Nash gathered some of his occasional writings as *Room and Book*, published by Oliver Simon's small imprint, Soncino Books, and launched with an exhibition of modern art and design at the Zwemmer Gallery. Nash made the argument in favour of the artist getting a foothold in the printing world:

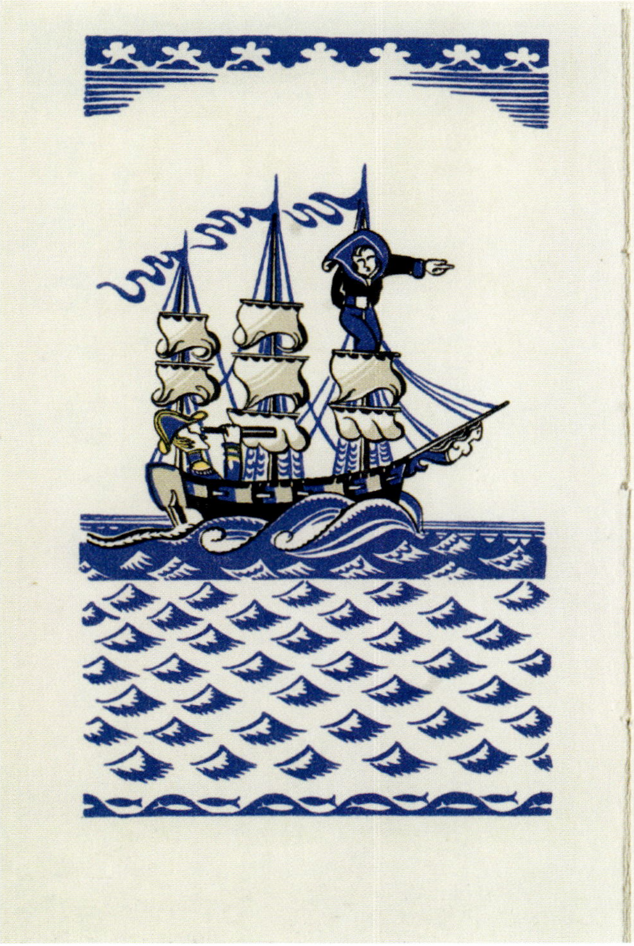

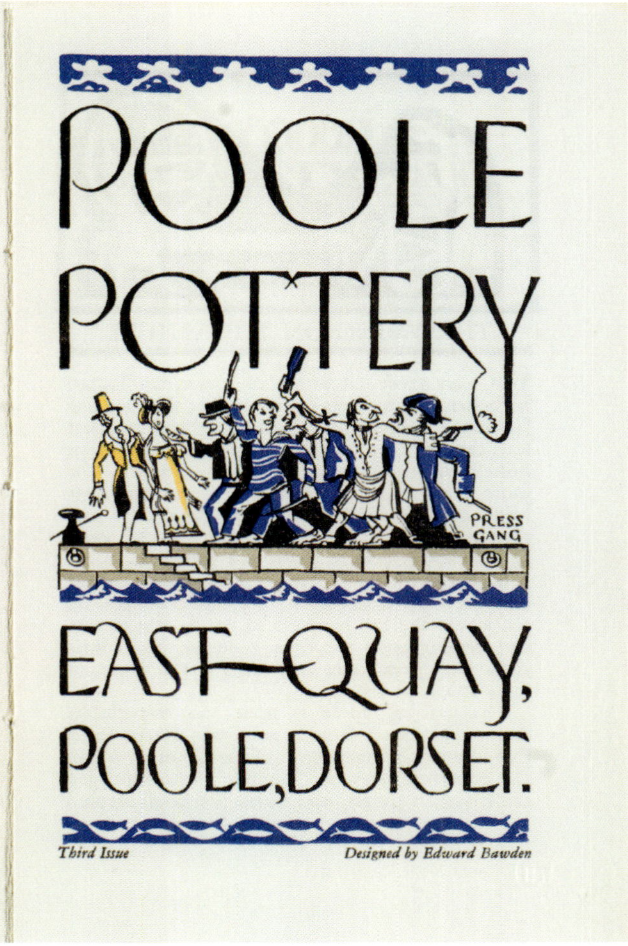

POOLE POTTERY
PRESS GANG
EAST QUAY, POOLE, DORSET.
Third Issue
Designed by Edward Bawden

19
Edward Bawden,
Knole Park wallpaper,
lithograph from linocut
original, 1929

If he is able to show a knowledge of inks, papers and types, this will gain the printer's respect and slightly frighten the publisher. The artist should then have the situation in hand. To be just, the artists often have only themselves to thank if their work is not satisfactorily produced, but not always.[8]

Nash was a generous friend to younger artists, using his influence to help them get work at Curwen and elsewhere. Owing to his single year of teaching in the Design School of the Royal College of Art, a younger generation of artists were introduced to Curwen from the group of students that Nash later described as 'an outbreak of talent.' These were most notably Edward Bawden, Barnett Freedman, Eric Ravilious and Enid Marx, who had already formed something of a group at the college. Marx spent the late 1920s and 1930s printing textiles by hand as her main activity, and her results were both witty and avant-garde. She also made wood-engravings for many purposes throughout her long life, and one of her earliest commissions, in 1925, was for one of the range of Curwen Press *Pattern Papers*. These repeat-pattern sheets were a long-lasting sideline for Curwen, inspired by sketches by Lovat Fraser based on Italian patterns and including examples by the main artists associated with Curwen Press, together with others less well known but all skilled at the task. In 1928 a sample book was published, with sheets folded in four and an introduction by Paul Nash, who himself designed three of the patterns (fig.17).

Edward Bawden's art was linear and witty, even when abstract. Pat Gilmour noted that his list of payments was twice as long as that of any other artist working for Curwen. He could make Poole Pottery (fig.18) come alive in a brochure in 1925 as well as designing tiles for the pottery itself. He made human figures and animals lively even if frequently un-lifelike, while he also designed typographic borders, headpieces and other ornaments for regular use by the Curwen Press. Bawden drew with clear lines, keeping his shading strokes open enough to allow for clean printing, which also helped to give force to his images. At other times he worked with an engraver's burin directly onto copper plates, with a strong sense of controlled design, developing from the style of the French engraver Jean-Emile Laboureur who was popular in the 1920s.

For his own research, Bawden designed wallpapers (figs.19 and 21) using linocuts, a medium that was explored by a small group of avant-garde London artists in the 1920s such as Cyril Power. Bawden's designs were illustrative but far from naturalistic, slightly reminiscent of Victorian pictorial repeat patterns seen through a modern eye. The Curwen Press put these into production by lithographic transfer, retaining the broken 'starved' inking of the hand-prints, and they were retailed (never in large numbers) through the company Modern Textiles. Later, in the 1930s, Bawden designed a further range of wallpapers of a slightly more conventional design that were a protest against the preference of design-conscious people for plain, painted walls.

At the Royal College, Bawden made friends on his first day with Eric Ravilious. Both had been placed in the Design School

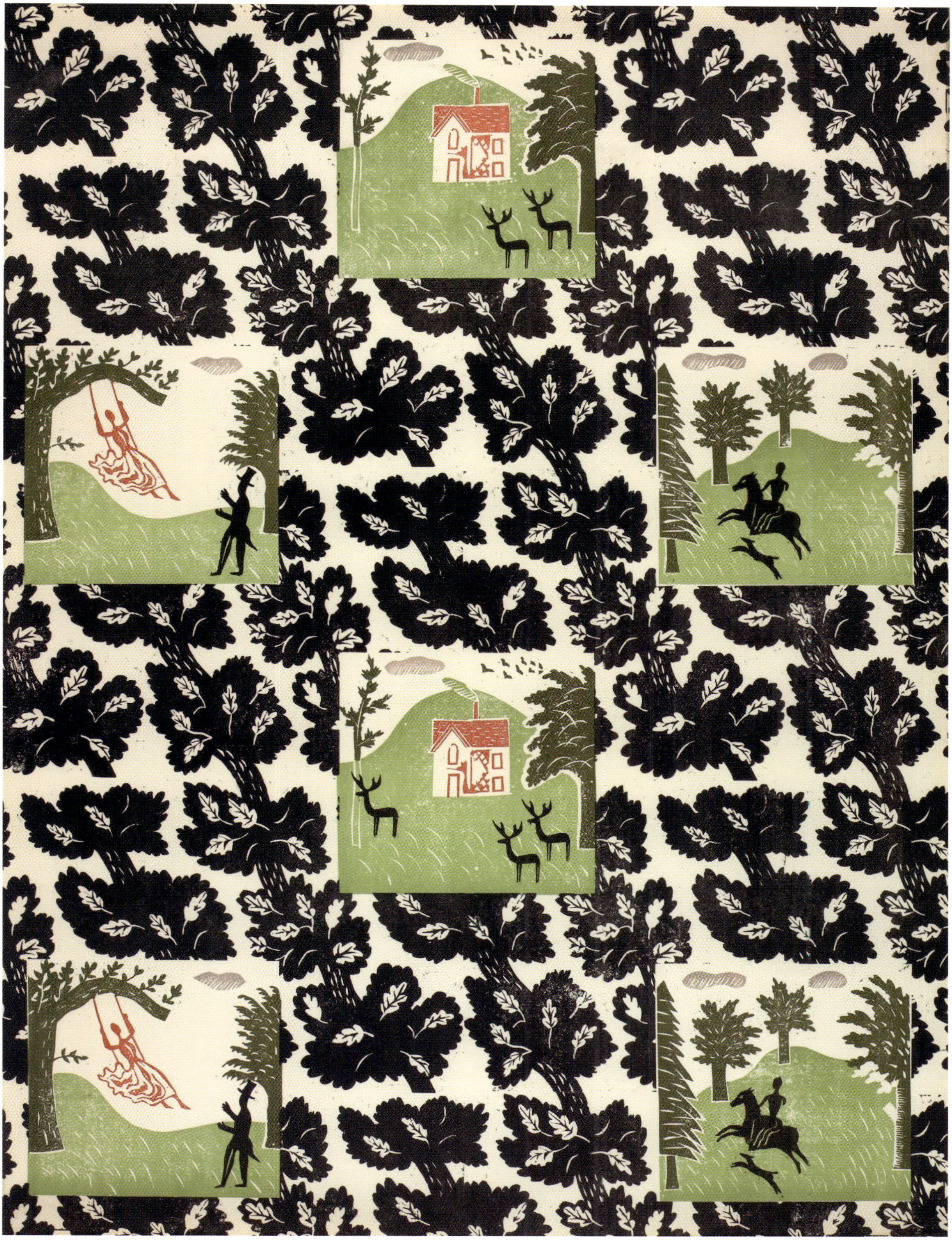

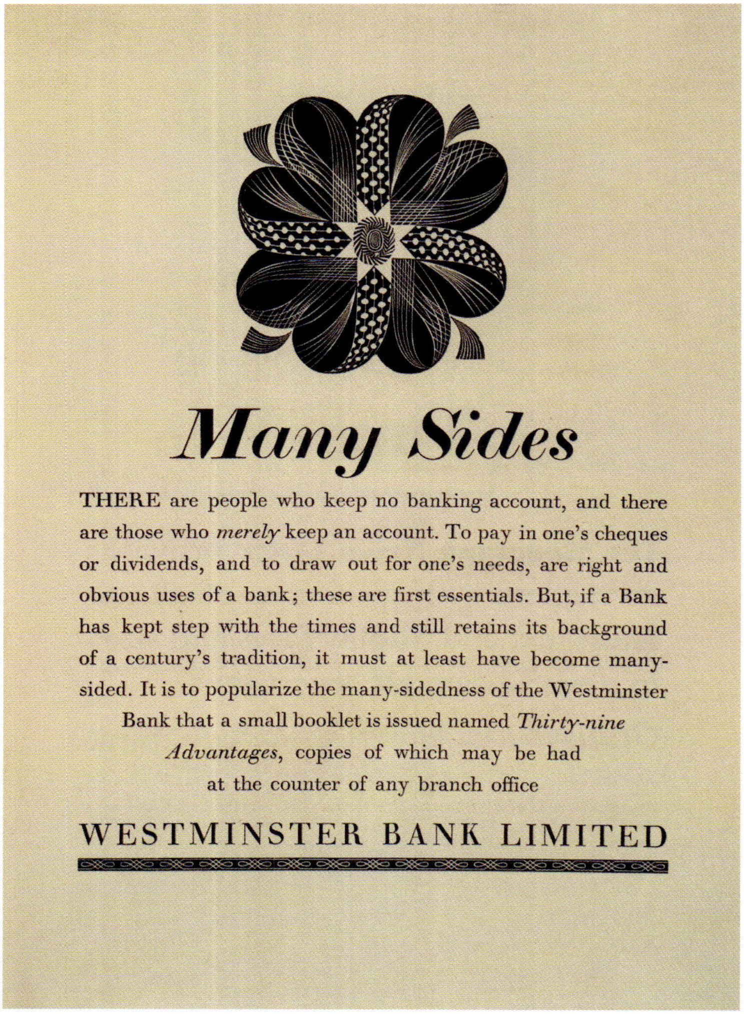

20
Eric Ravilious, Stock wood engraving for Curwen Press, 1934

of the College by the Principal, Sir William Rothenstein, partly because he realised that their relatively modest family backgrounds would require them to make their own livings, which as Fine Art students might be more difficult. Like most students, they taught themselves, benefiting from the close proximity of the Victoria and Albert Museum, where they absorbed drawing and decoration of many periods, especially Elizabethan, with its stylised classicism, naive perspective and attention to surface detail. Ravilious found an affinity with more imaginative subject matter than Bawden, but they collaborated happily on murals for Morley College in Lambeth between 1928 and 1930.

Ravilious specialised in wood engraving and was commissioned by the Golden Cockerell Press, run by the artist Robert Gibbings and one of the most enterprising of the new private presses of the 1920s, although the assumption that private press books must be printed on rough hand-made paper did not suit the delicacy of his work. Ravilious was less enthusiastic about jobbing work than Bawden, although the Curwen Press commissioned decorative ornaments from him with characteristic radial patterns like stars or sunbursts that became 'stock blocks', available for use on various occasions (fig.20). He made some of his most enchanting images for a 1935 Curwen Press promotional booklet for Southern Railway, *Thrice Welcome*, with a special pattern-paper cover to celebrate the Jubilee of King George V (fig.22).

For a few years, Ravilious and Bawden shared Brick House in the Essex village of Great Bardfield, while Ravilious later

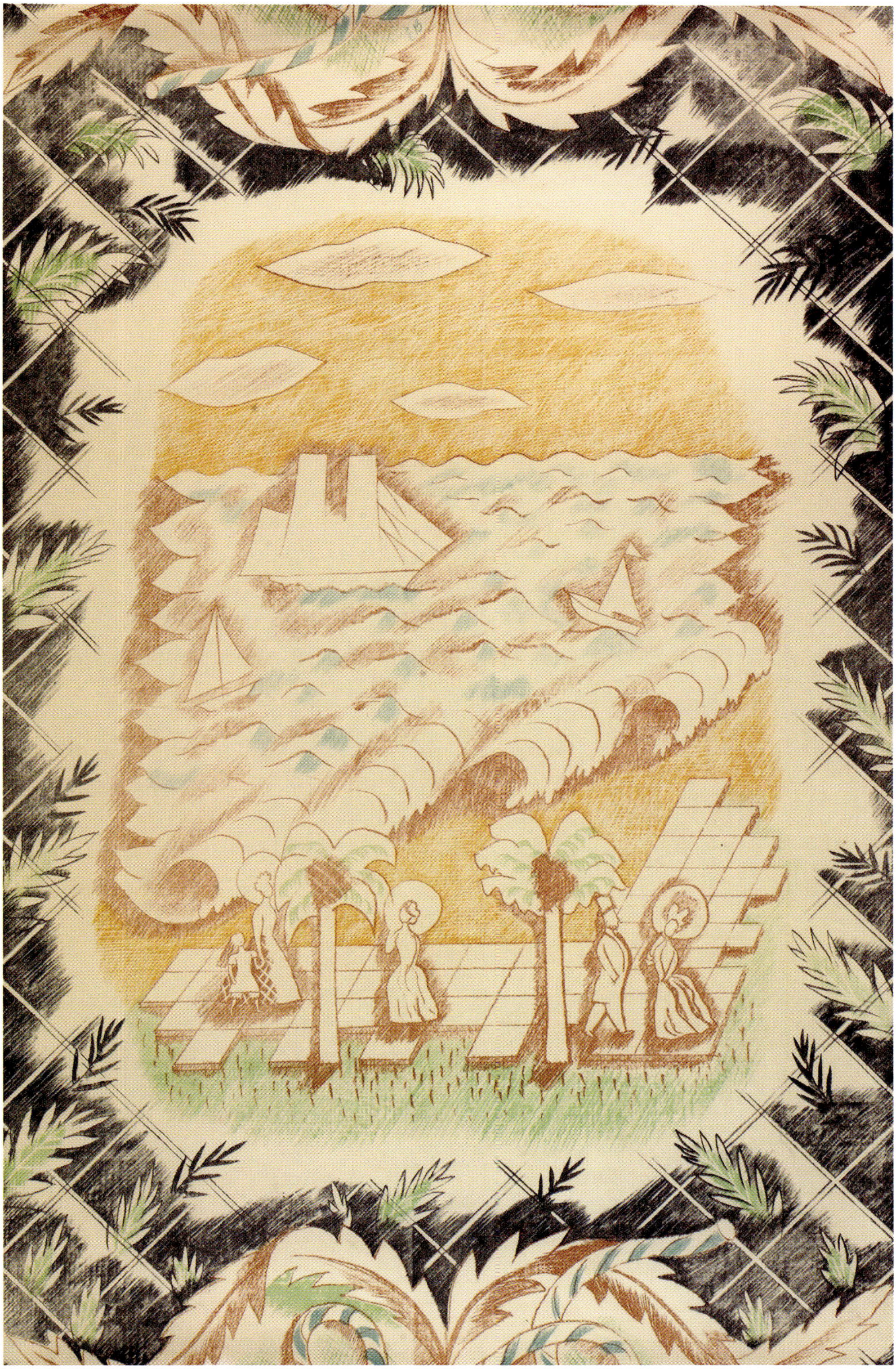

21
Edward Bawden,
Riviera wallpaper,
lithograph from linocut
original, 1929

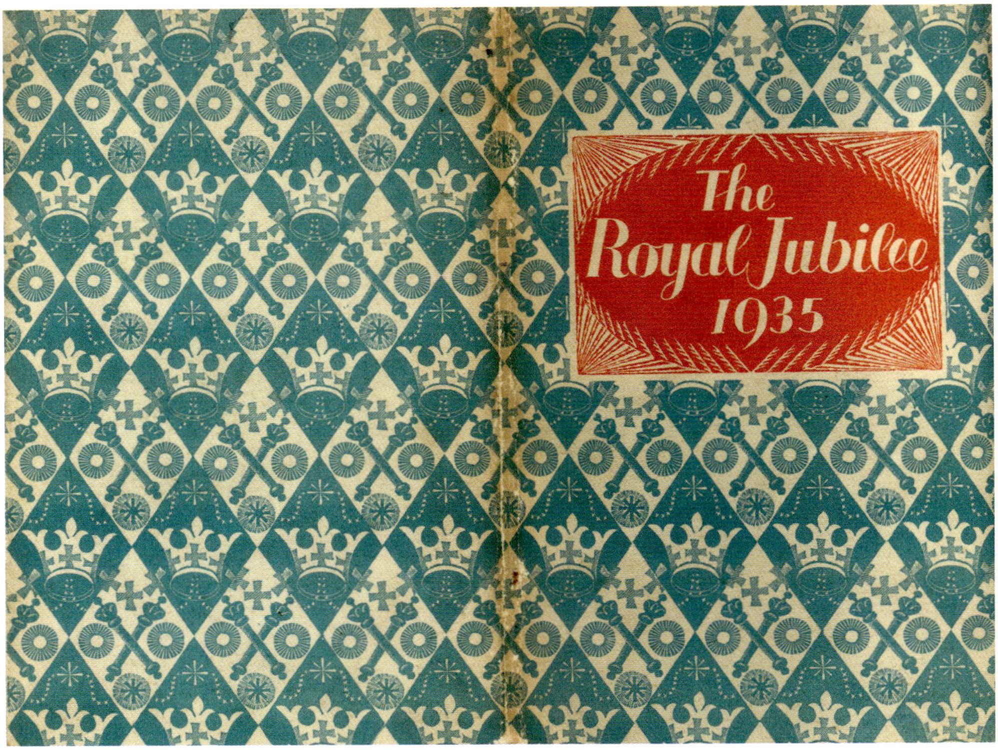

22
Eric Ravilious, *Jubilee* pattern paper, used for *Thrice Welcome* booklet for Southern Railway, 1935

moved to a neighbouring village. Their presence made a nucleus for a group of artists who liked the area and its bright clear light, within commuting distance from London. The fact that the Curwen Press lay on the near side of London was propitious. Harold Curwen and others connected with the press lived in Essex, and this encouraged social contacts between them that enhanced Harold Curwen's pleasure in making it feel like a family enterprise.

Another Royal College artist was Barnett Freedman. Born in 1901 of Russian immigrant parents in the Whitechapel Jewish community, he was ill for long periods as a child but became talented and largely self-educated in art and music. Freedman went to the Royal College on a scholarship, and was one of the first of his generation to learn how to draw lithographic images on stone and plate, becoming the undisputed master of the lithographic book jacket, poster or illustrated book between the wars, with a quirky style suggestive of the Victorian period in its careful drawing, decorative lettering and crowded texture, without being pastiche. His prints had to be drawn with a different stone or plate for each colour, the tonal blending and overlapping of colours coming close at times to the subtlety of oil painting. This was part of the technical know-how developed as a result of the collaboration between artists and printers, including, in Freedman's case, Thomas Griffits, the acknowledged master of hand-drawn lithography, who presided not at Curwen, but at the London businesses of Vincent Brooks Day and Sons, and afterwards at the Baynard Press, who operated in friendly rivalry to Curwen.

If work was done on stone (as Freedman preferred because of the extended range of techniques it permitted), it would be transferred onto zinc plates for printing, as with Freedman's illustrations for George Borrow's *Lavengro* (fig.23), an early Victorian tale of gypsies printed in two

23
Barnett Freedman, illustration for George Borrow, *Lavengro*, Limited Editions Club, New York 1936

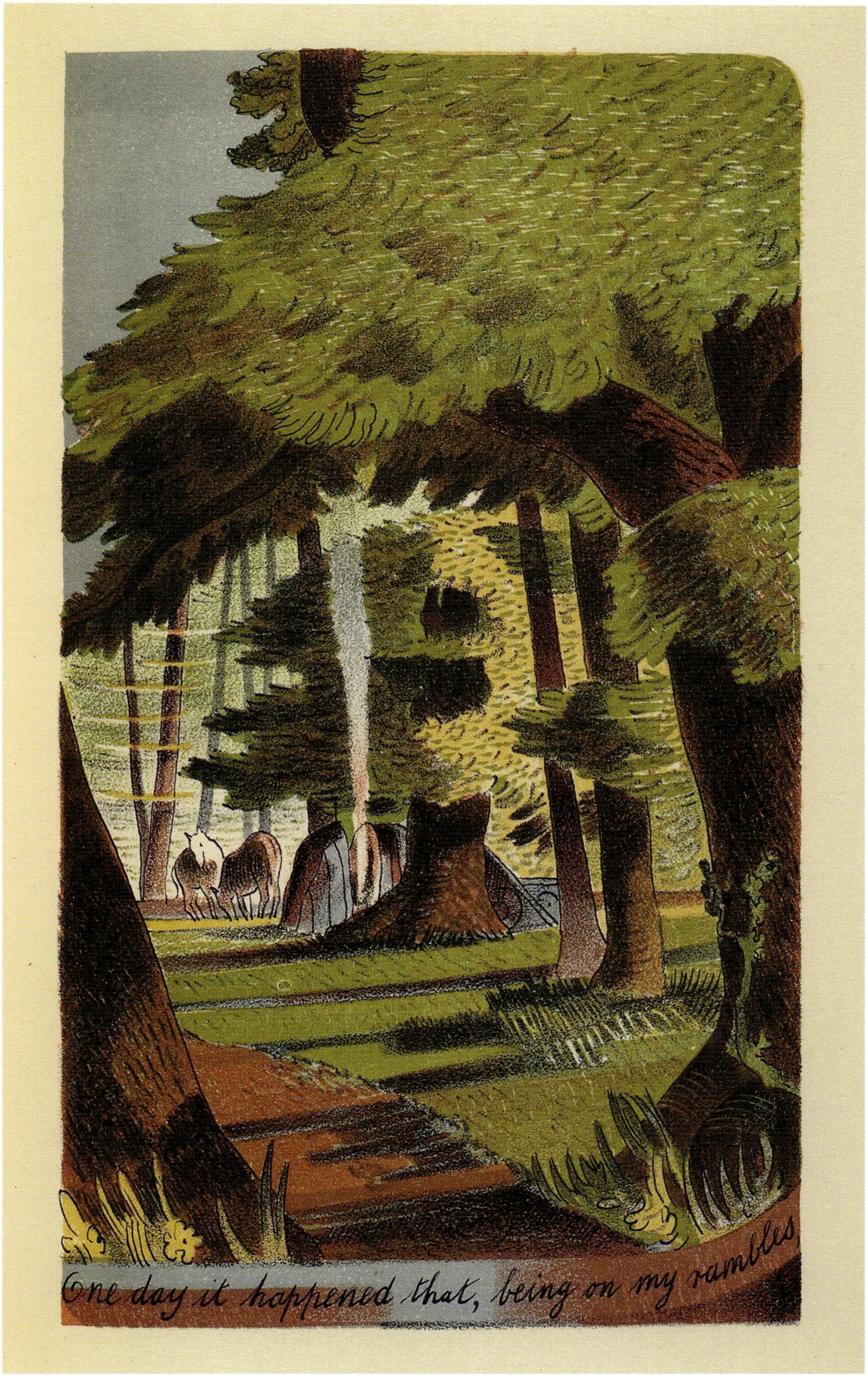

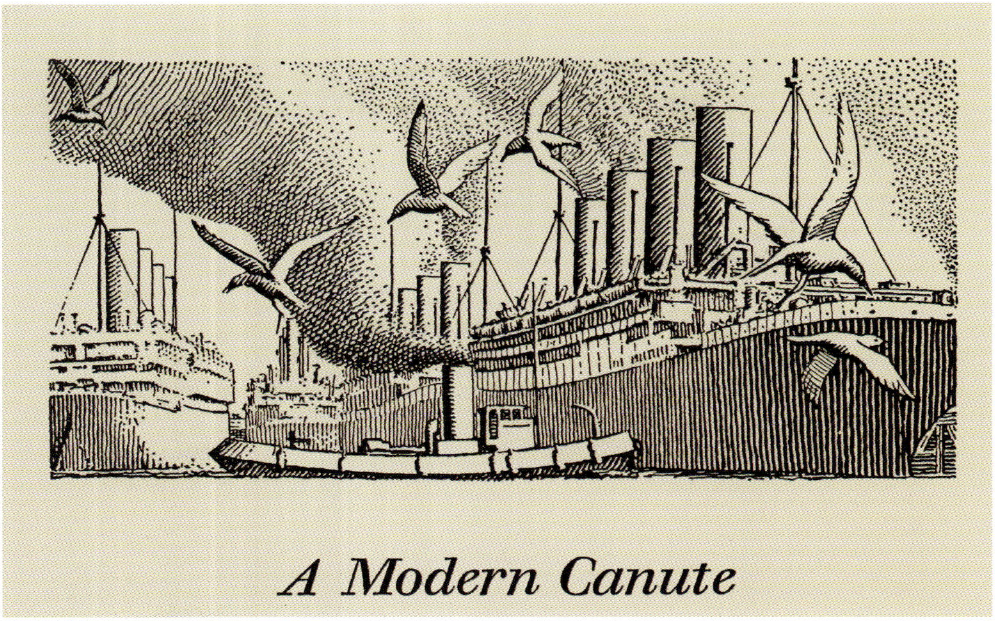

24
Thomas Poulton, illustration for *Over the Points*, Southern Railway magazine, 1929

volumes at Curwen for the American publisher George Macy's Limited Editions Club in 1936. Freedman's plates for this book were his first to develop a full colour range. More often, for reasons of economy, he worked with two or three colours only, bringing his designer's eye into operation to create a sense of richness, often by selecting a coloured paper as a background.

Other artists have been more or less forgotten, but among them, Thomas Poulton is worthy of mention. All his work appears to be in the form of line drawing with a pen, carefully made to avoid 'infilling' with ink in closely hatched areas. He approached his subjects in a rather literal way, compared to Bawden, making illustrations for Izaak Walton for Nonesuch, and for the first edition of *The Week-End Book*, Nonesuch's one mass-market product. Poulton's prolific range of headpieces for the Southern Railway magazine *Over the Points* (fig.24) made between 1929 to 1932 have a slightly hypnotic character similar to some of the illustrations of the American artist Rockwell Kent. The magazine, with text by E.P. Leigh-Bennett, was an example on a grand scale of informing the customer about the 'secrets' of a business, since it was distributed to travellers of this otherwise rather unheroic sector of the pre-nationalised railway system. After 1932, the illustrations were done by Victor Reinganum, a Hungarian artist with a more avant-garde style who continued to produce excellent work after the war.

Albert Rutherston, already mentioned as a friend of Lovat Fraser, produced work that was delicate to the point of whimsicality, with typical 1920s maidens amid floral decorations. He used the same colour line-block technique as Fraser, without the same clarity and strength. On one occasion, the Curwen Press handled illustrations by Stanley Spencer for a Chatto and Windus almanack, but was not responsible for originating the

25
Paul Nash, illustration to Siegfried Sassoon, *Nativity*, Ariel Poem no.7, Faber and Gwyer Ltd., 1927

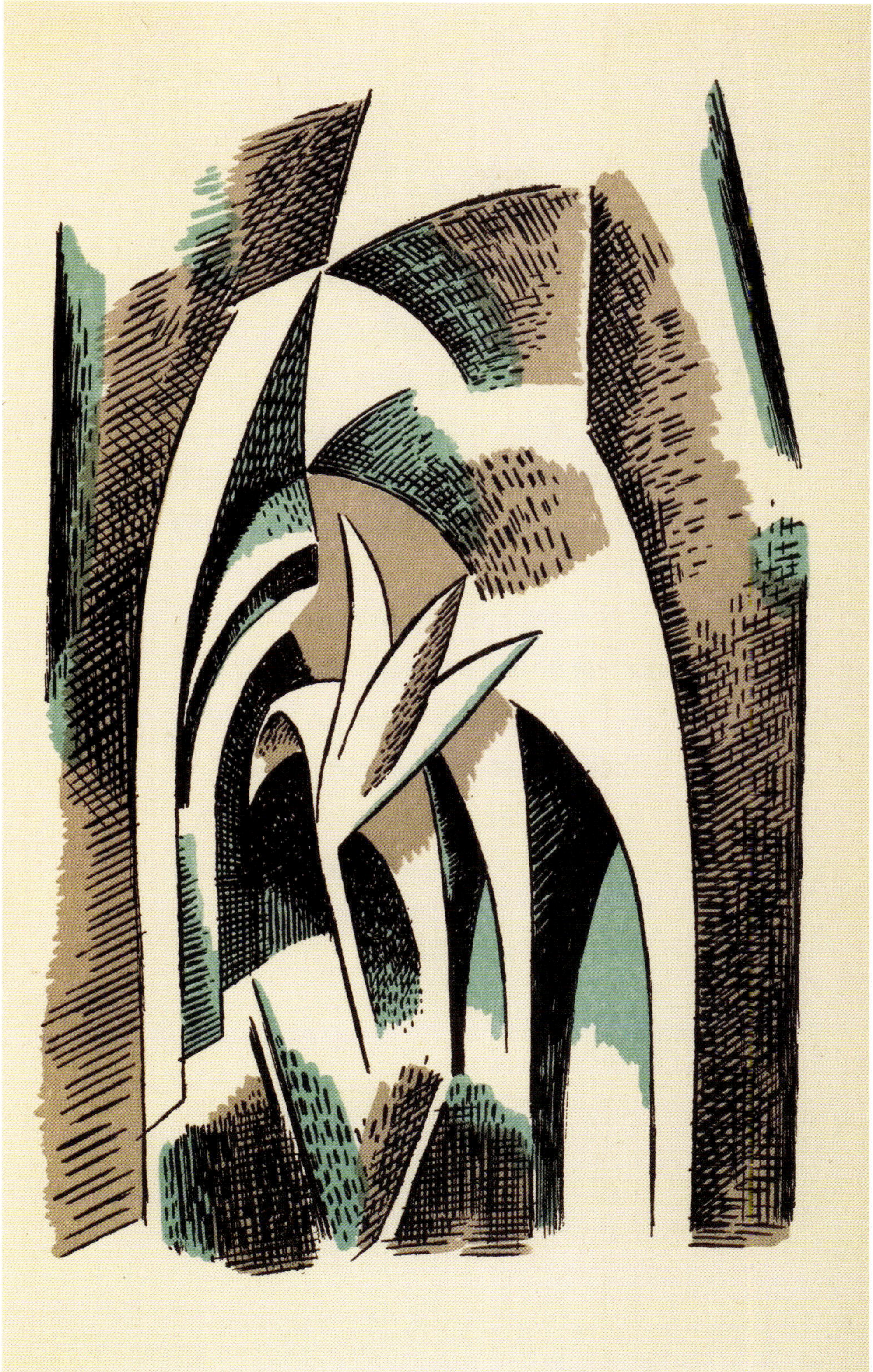

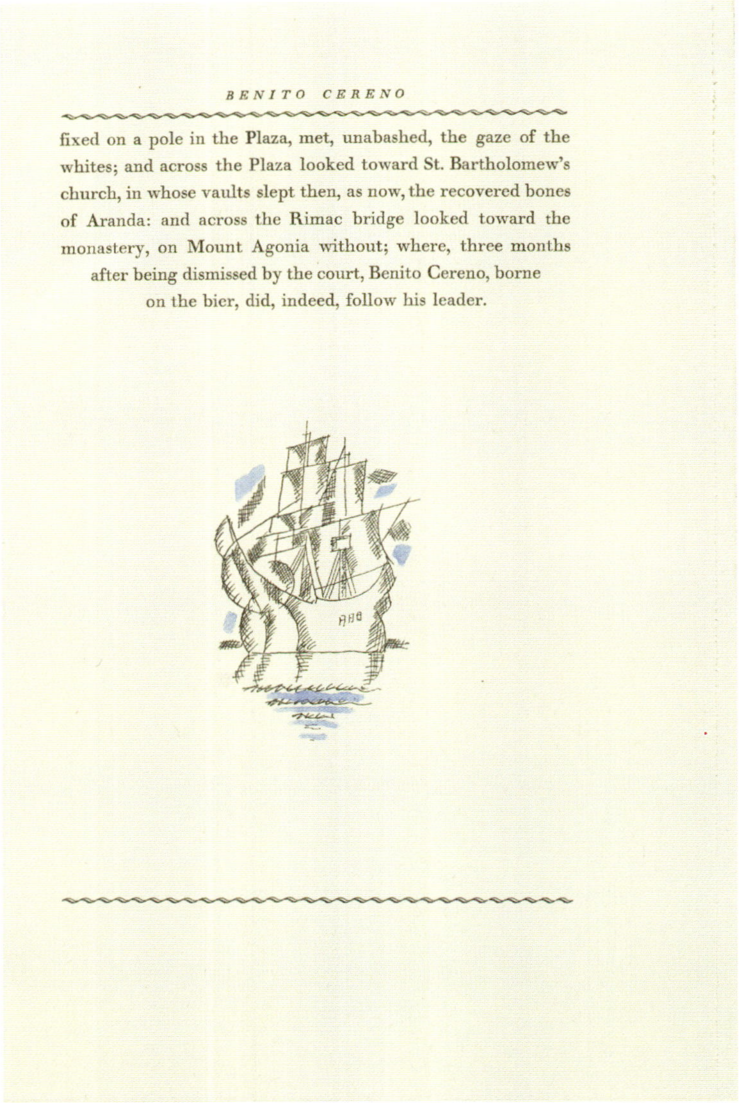

BENITO CERENO

fixed on a pole in the Plaza, met, unabashed, the gaze of the whites; and across the Plaza looked toward St. Bartholomew's church, in whose vaults slept then, as now, the recovered bones of Aranda: and across the Rimac bridge looked toward the monastery, on Mount Agonia without; where, three months after being dismissed by the court, Benito Cereno, borne on the bier, did, indeed, follow his leader.

26
Edward McKnight Kauffer, illustration to Herman Melville, *Benito Cereno*, Nonesuch Press, 1926

commission, which was Spencer's only work for a book.

An enterprise that depended on creative interchange between printer and publisher was Ariel Poems, commissioned by Faber from 1927 onwards and printed by the Curwen. A single poem was printed (usually for the first time) in a simple pamphlet, with a title page, full-page illustration and colophon, in a coloured paper wrapper that usually carried a further image. Since the poems were meant as an alternative to a Christmas card, many have a seasonal slant, including the most famous, T.S. Eliot's *The Journey of the Magi*. The matching of poet and artist was an interesting challenge. Eliot, a director of Faber, was always accompanied by the work of his friend Edward McKnight Kauffer. Other artists included Bawden, David Jones, John and Paul Nash (fig.25), Ravilious and Rutherston. The poems, which were revived after the war with a second series printed by the Baynard Press, were typical of the 1920s quest for the light and informal, but not without some depth of content and meaning.

Francis Meynell commissioned many of the same artists as Curwen, including McKnight Kauffer, who decorated a car body for him with Cubist patterns, and whose illustrations for Herman Melville's 1855 novella *Benito Cereno* (fig.26), published by Nonesuch Press in 1926, were designed to be coloured by hand with stencils, a specialism that Harold Curwen started in imitation of French 'pochoir' work that had ascended from the realm of 'l'art populaire' and 'Imagerie d'Epinal' to modern chic in Paris. With this method, colour could be

27
Edward McKnight Kauffer, illustration to Arnold Bennett, *Elsie and the Child*, Cassell and Co., 1929

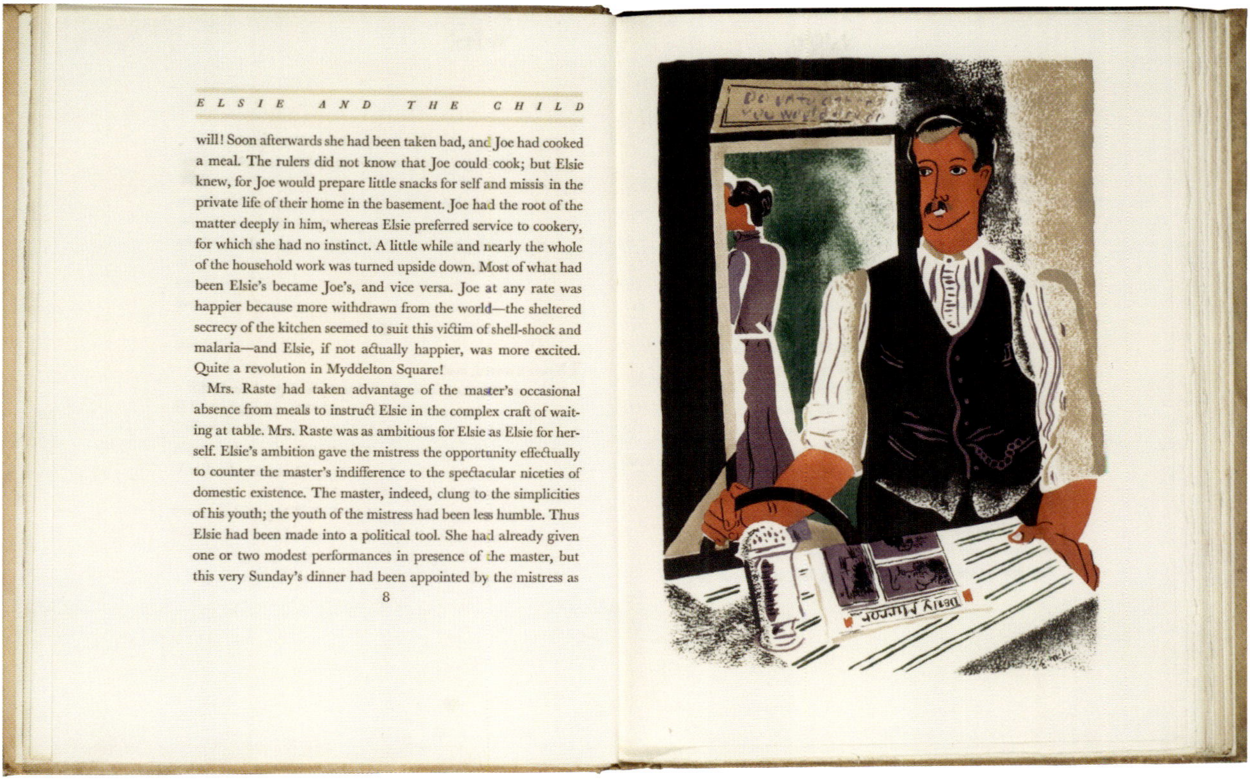

E L S I E   A N D   T H E   C H I L D

will! Soon afterwards she had been taken bad, and Joe had cooked a meal. The rulers did not know that Joe could cook; but Elsie knew, for Joe would prepare little snacks for self and missis in the private life of their home in the basement. Joe had the root of the matter deeply in him, whereas Elsie preferred service to cookery, for which she had no instinct. A little while and nearly the whole of the household work was turned upside down. Most of what had been Elsie's became Joe's, and vice versa. Joe at any rate was happier because more withdrawn from the world—the sheltered secrecy of the kitchen seemed to suit this victim of shell-shock and malaria—and Elsie, if not actually happier, was more excited. Quite a revolution in Myddelton Square!

Mrs. Raste had taken advantage of the master's occasional absence from meals to instruct Elsie in the complex craft of waiting at table. Mrs. Raste was as ambitious for Elsie as Elsie for herself. Elsie's ambition gave the mistress the opportunity effectually to counter the master's indifference to the spectacular niceties of domestic existence. The master, indeed, clung to the simplicities of his youth; the youth of the mistress had been less humble. Thus Elsie had been made into a political tool. She had already given one or two modest performances in presence of the master, but this very Sunday's dinner had been appointed by the mistress as

8

28
Paul Nash, illustration to Sir Thomas Browne, *Urne Buriall* and *The Garden of Cyrus*, Cassell and Co., 1932

put in the page with greater sensitivity than any mechanical method, and Curwen recruited young women from his bindery to learn the technique. The process was economically viable at the time owing to the favourable imbalance between printing wages and the price that collectors were willing to pay for unusual books. *Benito Cereno* was stencilled in transparent watercolour washes, as were most of the products made in the stencilling workshop, including page decorations by Bawden and others. Entirely *sui generis*, however, were the illustrations by Kauffer for a novella by Arnold Bennett, *Elsie and the Child* (fig.27), a sequel to his popular novel of London shopkeeping life, *Riceyman Steps*. These were stencilled in gouache without the printed line usually provided to give a structure to the design. Paul Nash wrote: 'the triumph, to my mind, in this reproduction of a drawing from *Elsie and the Child* is the strict realisation of the texture of the original. To obtain this the same brushes have been used by the stencillers as those used by Mr. Kauffer. This was obviously the only way to do the job thoroughly, yet how many printers would be as thorough?'[9] This was a limited edition, published by Cassell, a mainstream imprint with a young director, Desmond Flower, who was willing to experiment.

In 1932, Cassell published *Urne Buriall* and *The Garden of Cyrus* (fig.28), two texts by the seventeenth-century philosopher-poet Sir Thomas Browne, with illustrations by Paul Nash. These were stencilled in watercolour onto a printed collotype image, which conveyed the tone and texture of Nash's paintbrush and watercolour.[10] The illustrations were some of his most striking, complementing and penetrating the meaning of the text in modern terms and creating affinities between abstraction and the mysticism of the words.

Stanley Morison, a major figure in the printing revival in England, became an important figure in Oliver Simon's life after their first meeting in 1921. The following year, Morison and Simon were the principal agents in forming a new publishing society whose main product was an annual journal of printing, the *Fleuron* Its seven issues each consisted of a substantial hardback book rather than a magazine in the accepted sense. 'Fleuron' was the French name for the 'printer's flowers', a style of arabesque ornament produced in small units that could be assembled to make borders and panels much used in the seventeenth and eighteenth centuries, and revived almost to the point of mania by members of the printing revival around 1920. The aim of the society was to extend the influence and grounding of fine printing on a commercial basis. They commented both on old type designs (a research speciality of Morison's) and on current work, although some members of the movement became dissatisfied with the degree of historical reference, initially masking an essentially modern effort. The resolution of this conflict within a few years was arguably of universal benefit. The best examples of the past, extending even into the early nineteenth century with its 'modern' typefaces such as Didot and Walbaum, were thoroughly absorbed and remained as a standard against which to judge any new directions.

known? or whether there be not more remarkable persons forgot, then any that stand remembred in the known account of time? Without the favour of the everlasting Register the first man had been as unknown as the last, and *Methuselahs* long life had been his only Chronicle.

Oblivion is not to be hired: The greater part must be content to be as though they had not been, to be found in the Register of God, not in the record of man. Twenty seven Names make up the first story,[1]

(1) Before the flood.

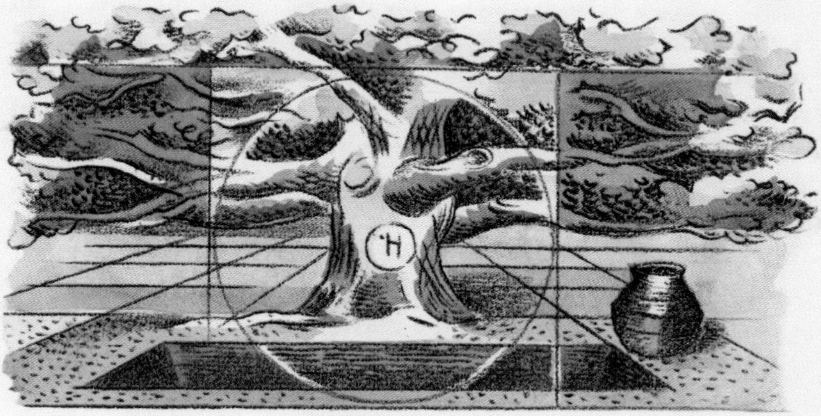

and the recorded names ever since contain not one living Century. The number of the dead long exceedeth all that shall live. The night of time far surpasseth the day, and who knows when was the Æquinox? Every houre addes unto that current Arithmetique, which scarce stands one moment. And since death must be the *Lucina* of life, and even Pagans[2] could doubt whether thus to live, were to dye. Since our longest Sunne sets at right descensions, and makes but winter arches, and therefore it cannot be long before we lie down in darknesse, and have our light in ashes.[3] Since the brother of death daily haunts us with dying *memento's*, and time that grows old it self, bids us hope no long duration: Diuturnity is a dream and folly of expectation.

(2) *Euripides.*

(3) According to the custome of the Jewes, who place a lighted wax candle in a pot of ashes by the Corps. *Leo.*

E

29
Edward Bawden, *Homage to Dicky Doyle*, stencil coloured line block print, from *The Curwen Press Miscellany*, 1931

Lithography

Lithography was the last of the three major printing processes to develop, coming after relief printing (the most basic kind, used for metal type and for images cut in wood) and intaglio (the method in which the lines below the surface of a metal plate contain the ink, and this is transferred to paper under high pressure in a 'rolling' press.) The name derives from the stone on which the first images were made, and which has continued in use as a drawing surface, although grained metal plates were introduced as an alternative.

When Harold Curwen took charge of the lithographic printing at Plaistow in 1913 the technique was already over a hundred years old, but still the exception in printing rather than the norm. Lithography was used for colour printing throughout the nineteenth century but acquired a dubious reputation in the form of the 'chromolithograph', often used for cheap and gaudy images dripping with oil in an attempt to match the quality of oil painting. Lithography was used to produce the posters of Henri Toulouse-Lautrec and Jules Chéret in Paris in the 1880s, which were editioned for collectors as well as posted in the streets. They were an inspiration for printers, and showed the value of the medium for painters. At Curwen, the presence of litho presses for music printing conveniently offered opportunities for use by artists, whether for working on posters or on smaller images for which the particular qualities of lithography were desirable. In 1912, Harold introduced offset printing, in which the ink is picked up from the plate by a rubber impression roller, and then transferred to the paper, a more versatile and delicate method than direct printing, and suitable for high-quality colour work. For an artist drawing an image, it has the benefit that the image does not need to be drawn reversed as if in a mirror.

Artists often drew on transfer paper in their studios, or left the trade 'artists' at the press to redraw their original images as a series of 'colour separations', a skill that only comes with practice. Although the trade artists were skilled, there was a feeling that the authentic mark of the original artist's hand should be preserved, especially since lithography offers a wide range of mark-making in pen and ink, crayon, brush, diluted wash, in isolation or in combination. Compared to the various engraving and etching techniques, however, lithography is harder to learn without tuition from experts, and harder to produce from a private studio, owing to the amount of equipment required. In order to achieve the ambition of 'autolithography', increasingly used in the 1920s for children's book illustration, the artist must draw his own plates and understand how they would be printed. As Barnett Freedman, the leader among the artists who mastered lithography between the wars, wrote in 1936, 'The artist … must become entirely immersed in the whole gamut of production, finding out for himself, by experiment and failure, all about the paper, ink, the temperature of the printing works, as well as the "temperament" of the machine minder and the printing works manager! – surmounting a hundred difficulties which are inevitable when an artist co-operates with the world

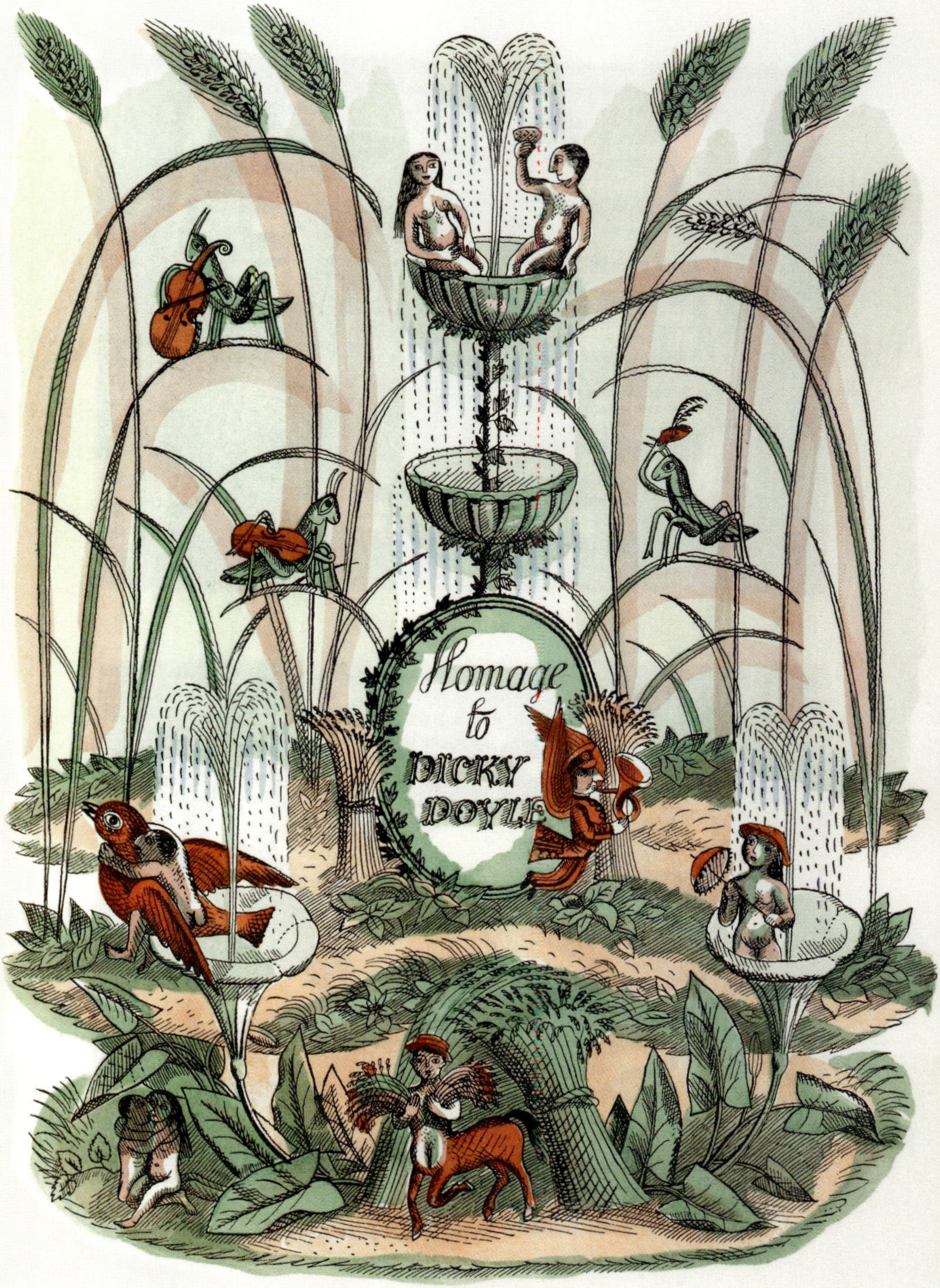

Drawing by Edward Bawden

30
Barnett Freedman, series of 'progressive' proofs showing the build-up of colour in lithography, from *Signature*, no.2, 1936

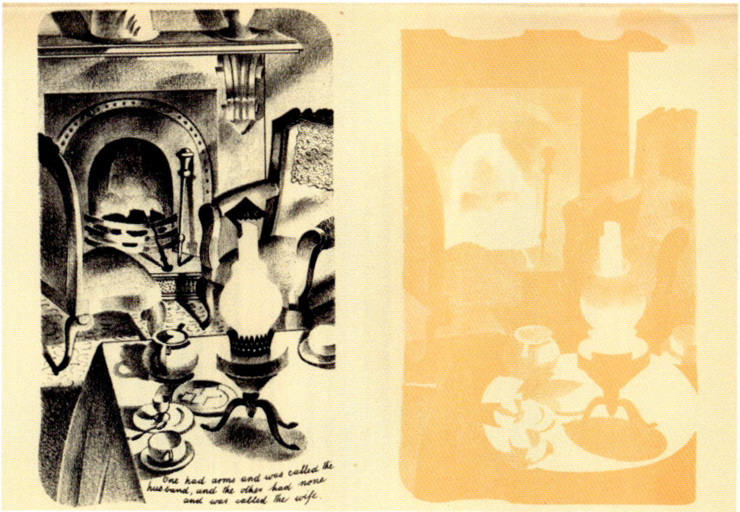

at large' (fig.30).[11] Harold Curwen was one of a handful of printers who encouraged artists to try out the medium at his expense, and this experience prepared the ground for the creation of the Curwen Studio in 1958, to meet the needs of a new kind of artists' print publishing.

The heyday of publishing at Curwen

The management and business structure of J. Curwen and Sons altered in 1933. The economic situation was worrying for all businesses, and the company made a loss in 1931–2, although there had been occasional loss-making years before.[12] To make matters worse, Harold Curwen's cousin Kenneth, who managed the music publishing side of the business, chose this moment to make a heavy but ill-advised investment in Synchrophone, a device for producing sound for films from long playing records that was doomed to obsolescence. As a result, the two branches split, and the works at Plaistow became The Curwen Press Ltd on 1 March 1933, with Oliver Simon's brother Herbert, who moved from Birmingham and his previous printing job at the Kynoch Press, as a director. New shareholders included some of Herbert's business friends in Birmingham, such as Robert Best of the lighting manufacturers Best and Lloyd, and Michael Hope of Hope's Windows. The poet and art patron Edward James also invested £900.[13]

Herbert Simon, three years younger than Oliver, while highly sympathetic to the artistic interests of his brother, brought experience in business management. Some reorganisation took place and the first AGM of the new company noted: 'It is now

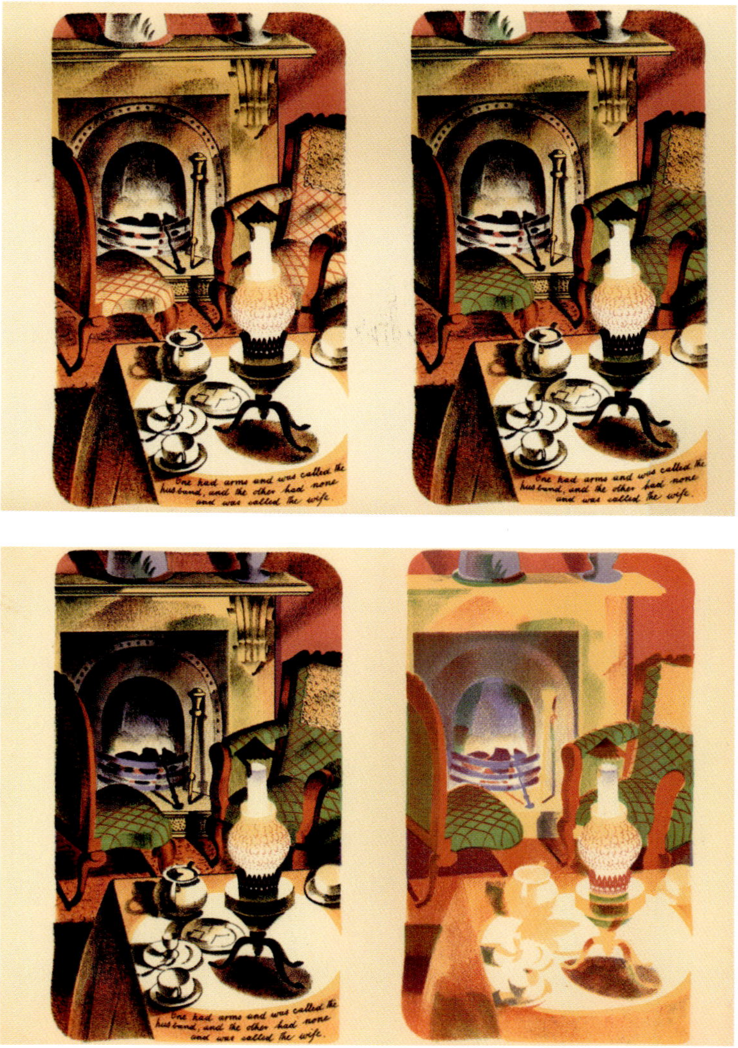

possible to handle larger types of work and to do so without impairing the quality for which Curwen Press is famous.'[14] The lithographic department also expanded, and in 1936 Oliver Simon reported that a new machine for posters was installed, and 'with our staff of lithographic artists, we are now in a position to give an excellent service to our customers. I am glad to say that the orders for lithography have shown a striking increase.'[15] Harold Curwen, overcome perhaps by the strain of this sequence of events, began to experience nervous disorders, so that his role gradually diminished until he retired from active involvement in the company shortly before the Second World War (fig.31).

Oliver Simon's personality is crucial to understanding the emotional and intellectual temper of the Curwen Press in its heyday. There was a hedonistic side to him, and Curwen printed the magazine *Wine and Food* for the eponymous society founded by André Simon (no relation), which tried to lure the thinking Englishman to appreciate and demand better quality. Another of Curwen's clients in the 1930s was the Pavilion Hotel, Scarborough, a stylish establishment favoured by artistic and stage folk run by Tom Laughton, the brother of the actor Charles Laughton, where guests were lured by publicity drawn by Edward Bawden (fig.32). With Hubert Foss, the music publisher for Oxford University Press, and others, Simon founded the Double Crown Club in 1923 as a dining club for people involved in printing and illustration. From the beginning, this included printers, scholars and artists, as it still does, and

31
Harold Curwen

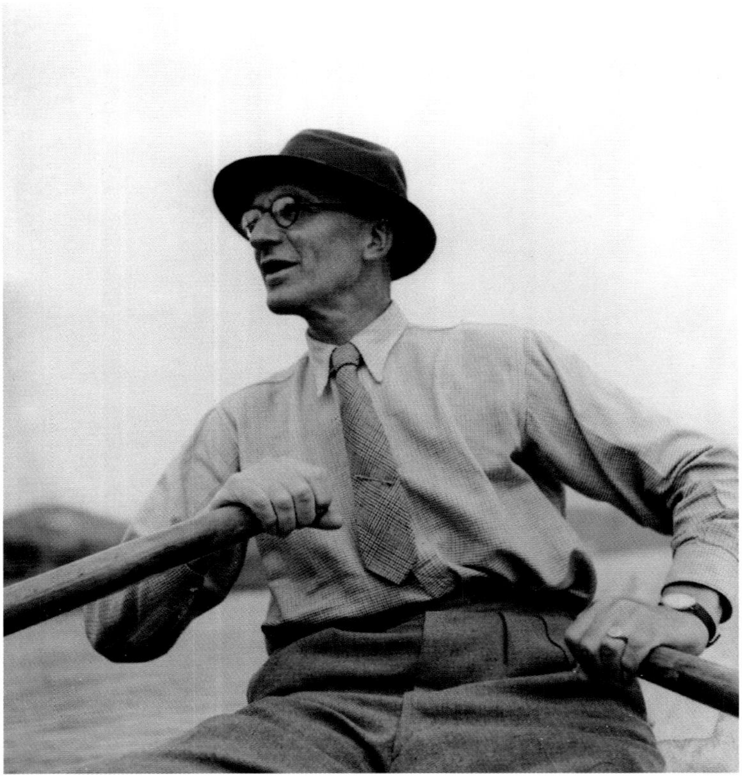

while the meetings, at restaurants such as Kettners in Soho or the Café Royal, were not frequent, they helped to form lasting bonds. At each dinner, a paper would be read and discussed, and a specially printed menu (fig.33) would await the members and their guests. Many of these were printed at Curwen, with illustrations by the Press's regular artists. Simon was also devoted to cricket, and artists such as Ravilious and Lynton Lamb were recruited to play for the Curwen Press side, which he captained.

Oliver Simon's typography was generally conservative while his taste in art was modern. Printers and graphic designers in Britain were predictably suspicious of 'the new typography' as promoted by Jan Tschichold in his book of 1926, and preferred a cool, more neoclassical look that Tschichold himself soon adopted.

The major illustrated books produced at Curwen in the late 1930s reinforce a sense of nostalgia, but fragmented through a modernist lens. Thus the lithographs by John Nash (brother of Paul) for Adrian Bell's country book *Men and the Fields* (Batsford, 1938) are representative of his fresh look at the geometry of trees and fields, and this was one of the first popular general books to use autolithography. John Farleigh's lithographs for *Old Fashioned Flowers* by Sacheverell Sitwell (Country Life, 1939) were a conscious recreation of luscious nineteenth-century botanical colour plates, appropriate to the 'wax fruit' era of 'amusing' interior decoration in the 1930s (fig.34). Eric Ravilious's *High Street* (Country Life, 1938), although presented as a children's book with a text by J.M. Richards, was closer in reality to the later

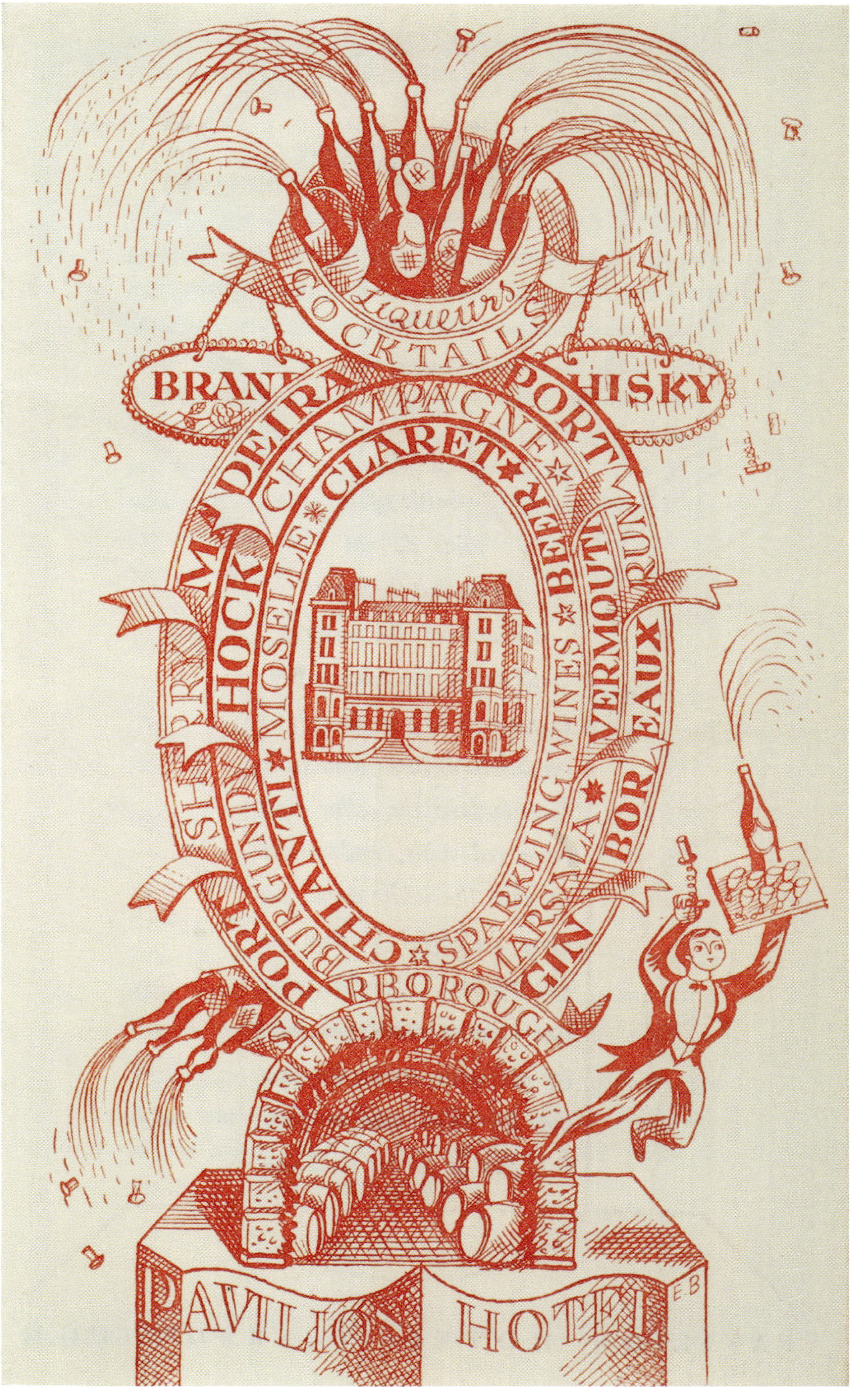

32
Edward Bawden, wine list for the Pavilion Hotel, Scarborough. Lithograph from copper engraving original, 1933

33
Eric Ravilious, menu for the Double Crown Club, 1935

34
John Farleigh, illustration for Sacheverell Sitwell, *Old Fashioned Flowers*, Country Life, 1939

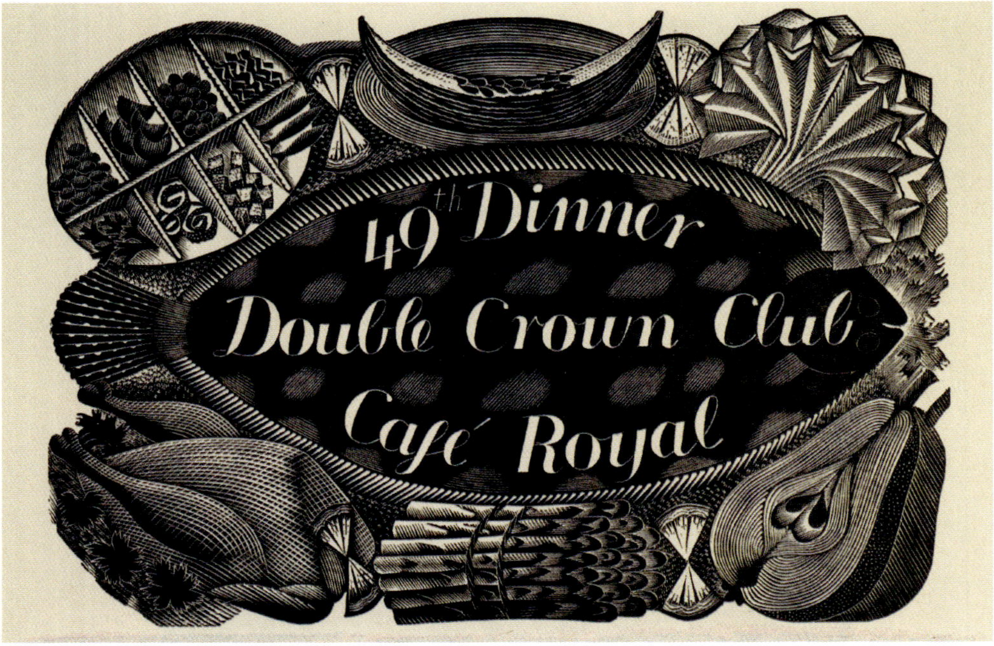

twentieth-century concept of an 'artist's book', in that Ravilious invented the project and chose the subjects for his lithographs (fig.36). The most lavish of this collection of books, John Piper's *Brighton Aquatints* (Duckworth, 1939), was not lithographed, and although the aquatint plates could not be printed at the Curwen Press, they printed the text pages, in Walbaum on pale blue laid paper (fig.35). *Brighton Aquatints* is a fascinating example of a book that sits at the provocative borderline between modernism and nostalgia so typical of the time.

Oliver Simon's tastes were reflected in his choice of artists for books, ephemera and as contributors to the magazine *Signature*, which he edited from 1935 to 1955 (with an interruption during the war). Described as 'A Quadrimestrial of Printing and the Graphic Arts', *Signature* continued the work of the *Fleuron*, in that both magazines aimed to embrace the printing professional and the general reader, whether aesthete or collector. The *Fleuron* had been taken over by Stanley Morison in 1926, with the two final issues produced at the Cambridge University Press. The year 1935 was culturally significant, signalling a shift among English artists and intellectuals away from the polarised politics of the Depression years towards a sort of stoic resistance to the deteriorating international situation that involved a greater openness to many kinds of culture and less insistence on dogmatic forms of modernism.

Oliver and Ruth Simon lived in Downshire Hill, Hampstead, close to many of the most progressive modern artists, collectors and thinkers of the time. Oliver's conservative typography did not necessarily appeal to all of them, and Ben Nicholson referred to him as 'The Pope'. *Signature* was, however, European in its outlook, reflecting the arrival in London of émigrés such as the type-designer Berthold Wolpe. Jewish artist Réné Ben Sussan, originally from Salonika but resident in Paris, was

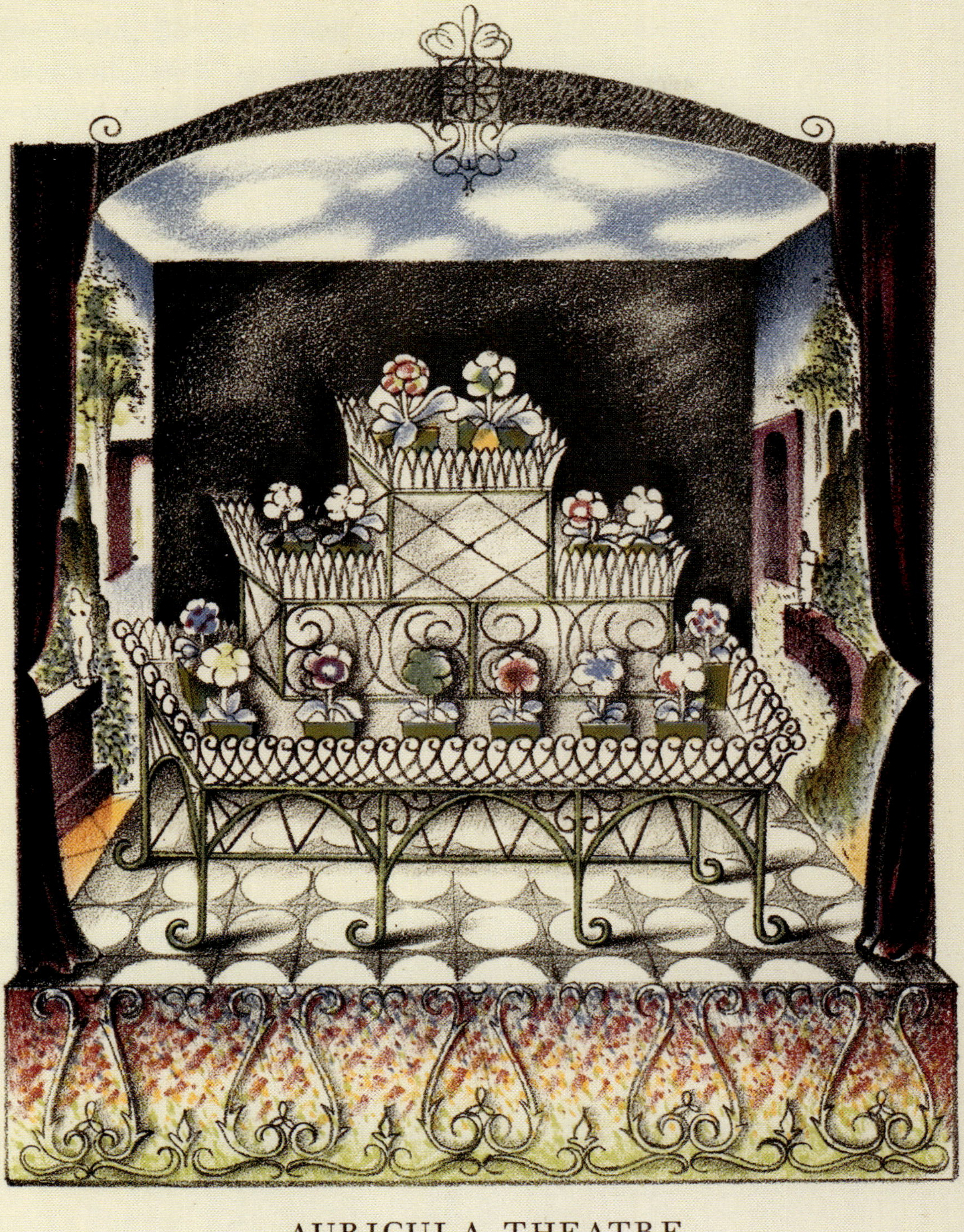

AURICULA THEATRE

35
John Piper, *Brighton from the Station Yard*, from *Brighton Aquatints*, Gerald Duckworth Ltd., 1939

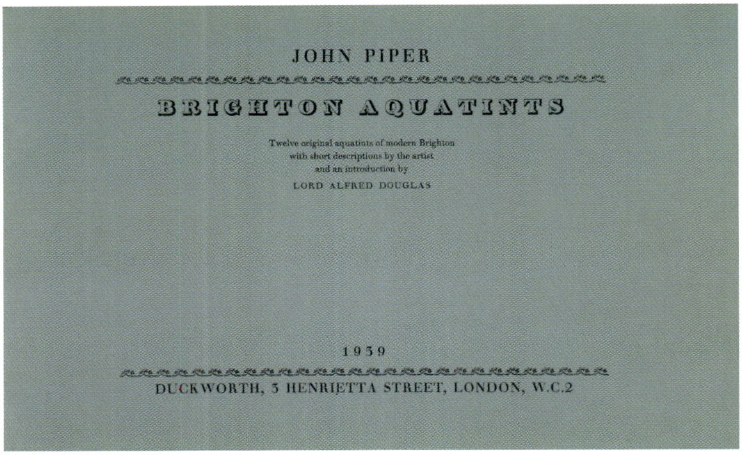

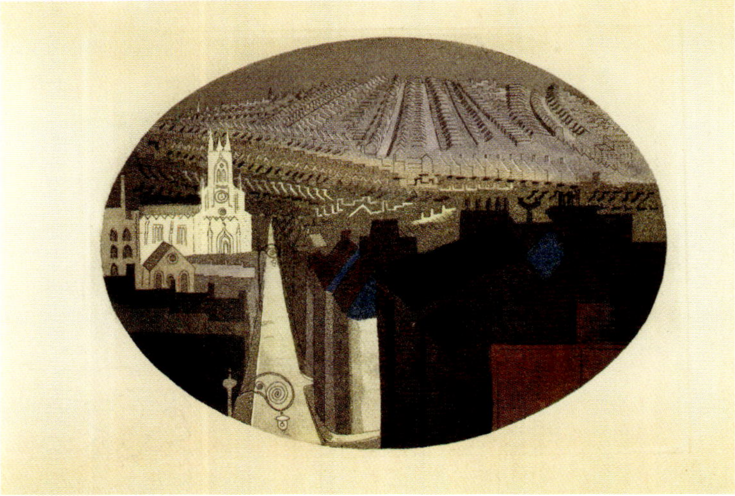

involved in Curwen Press productions. Simon wrote how 'on meeting him, I quickly discovered he had great integrity and a delicious wit, supported by a humorous glint in his eyes.'[16] *Signature* reflects in other ways Simon's interest in the intellectual and cultural aspects of his own Jewish origins, which had an added significance in these years. In 1930, the Soncino Press published a lavish illustrated edition of *The Haggadah* by Ben Sussan and Albert Rutherston, and a collection of speeches and letters by Albert Einstein, *About Zionism*, in the same year.

Each issue of *Signature*, with its limp wrappers of roughly textured paper and a purely typographic cover, contained four or five articles and some book reviews, historical discussions of type and illustration, occasional polemics on advertising design and related matters, and visual surveys of contemporary artists. In many cases, these were 'Curwen' artists such as Ravilious, Freedman, Bawden or Marx. Freedman himself wrote a long and thoroughly researched article on 'Lithography: A Painter's Excursion', signalling the new investment at Curwen in lithographic plant and a desire to encourage artists to use it. There were many fold-out pages of illustration or type, and examples of varied printing techniques, including lithography and engraving, bound in, either as part of the editorial content or as advertisements.

Arguably the most important articles in *Signature* were those by artists on more general themes, especially two by Graham Sutherland (fig.37), 'A Trend in English Draughtsmanship' (no.3, July 1936) and

36
Eric Ravilious, *The Grill Room*, illustration to J.M. Richards, *High Street*, Country Life, 1938

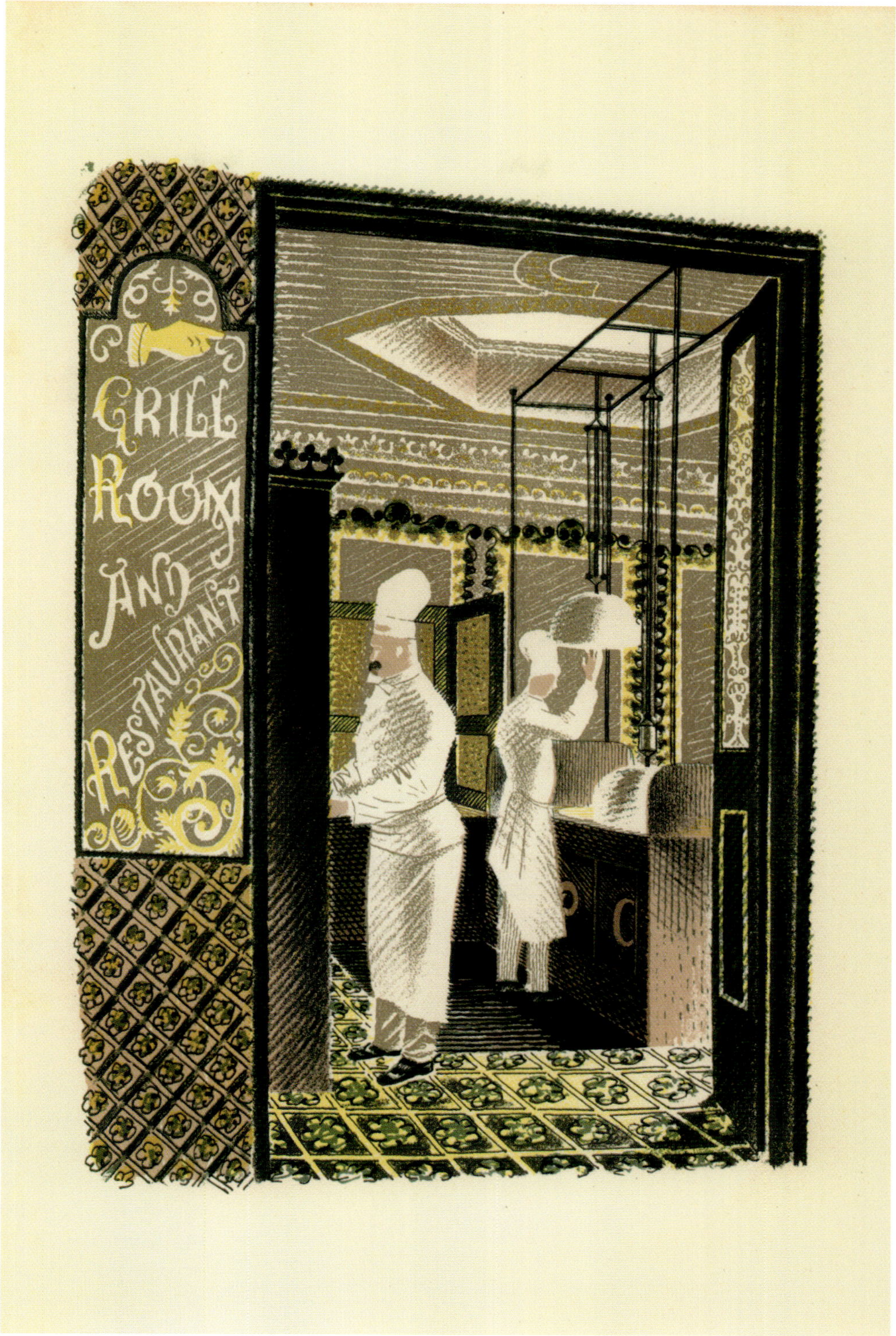

37
Graham Sutherland,
Clegyr-Boia, etching
and aquatint, frontispiece
to *Signature*, no.8, 1938

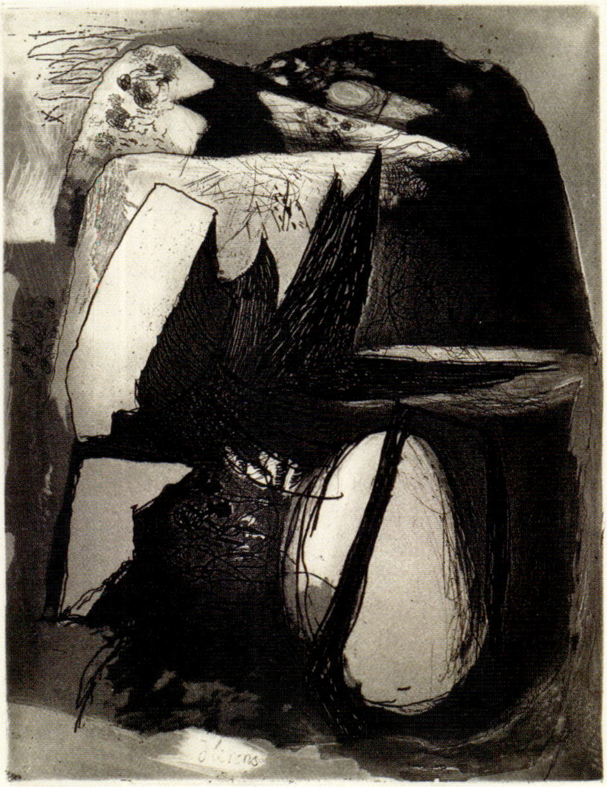

'Graven Images: Line Engraving and the Illustrated Book' (no.6, July 1937), which were important among the limited number of published statements by him. Simon (fig.38) and his wife Ruth met Sutherland and his wife Kathleen shortly before starting *Signature*, and the two couples developed a firm friendship. Sutherland later wrote that Simon 'was of immeasurable help to me in every possible way, encouraging me to write and reproduce my work in *Signature*. He was also the first person to bodily take my work around 1933 or 4 to various collectors, physically carrying the work himself. We spent several holidays together ... He was not only a great typographer but also one among the very few patrons of great intelligence.'[17] Sutherland did commercial design work to support himself in the early 1930s, including lithographic posters for Shell. In 1939, he illustrated Shakespeare's *Henry VI*, Part I, for the Limited Editions Club, with monochrome lithographs of figures against dark backgrounds, quite unlike any other work of his.

Simon met John Piper early in 1937, and an intense friendship ensued. Piper, who at the time was writing more often than Sutherland, as well as participating with his wife, Myfanwy Evans, in the magazine *Axis*, contributed 'Aspects of Modern Drawing' to *Signature* (no.7, November 1937), and his panorama of Cheltenham was accompanied by a text by John Betjeman, one of their earliest collaborations. Sutherland and Piper were the same age as Ravilious and Bawden, but their developed style did not emerge so early. They were more consciously intellectual and 'engaged',

38
Brian Robb,
Oliver Simon, 1955

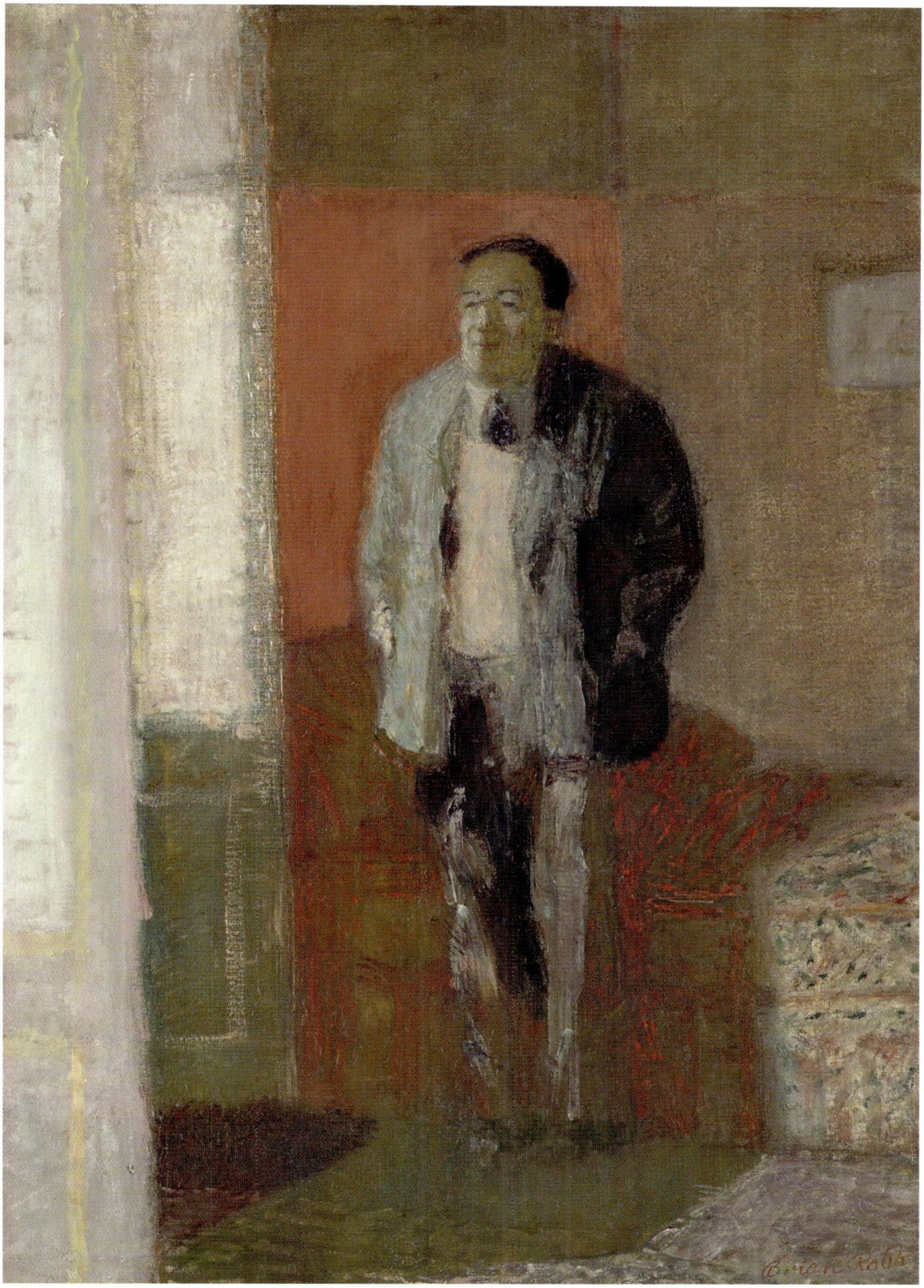

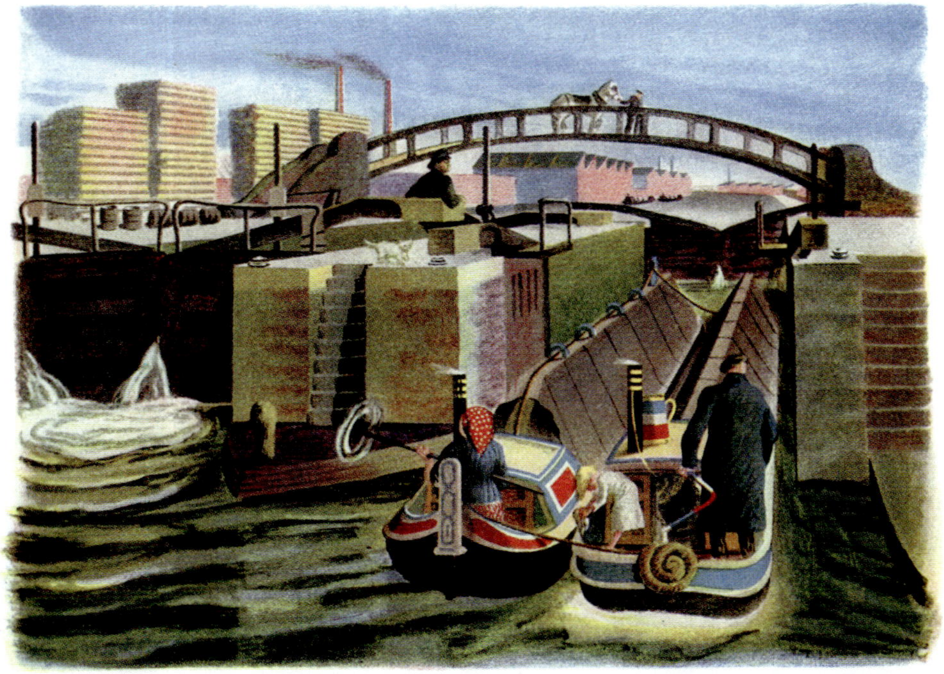

39
Lynton Lamb, *Grand Junction Canal*, 1938

especially in opening up new spaces between tradition and modernity. Their romantic inclination had been foreshadowed by Paul Nash, who supported them, and like him, they practised a sharp but poetical form of artistic criticism unlike anything seen before in England. Simon became their particular champion for a few years until, in a development he somewhat resented, they were promoted to greater heights by Kenneth Clark, in company with Henry Moore, whose drawings were illustrated in Sutherland's first article.

These artists belonged in the category that Clark called 'English imaginative artists', although they were also identified, perhaps misleadingly, as neo-romantic. Their articles in *Signature*, allied with a long piece on Samuel Palmer by Geoffrey Grigson (also a close friend of Piper at the time and a fellow inquirer into the essence of romanticism), stand out as moments when a change of direction in art can be discerned.

Robert Wellington, the manager of the Zwemmer Gallery, where a number of Curwen artists showed their work, had originally introduced Oliver Simon to Sutherland, and collaborated with Piper in launching a series of large poster-like prints in 1937 under the name Contemporary Lithographs, produced and printed at the Curwen Press (fig.40).[18] These were widely noticed at the time as a noble effort at improving the quality of art in schools (for which they were aimed), but while not commercially successful, they had several other significant effects. The prints were drawn as colour separations by the artists themselves, working on the stone at Plaistow, although in some cases it seems that they received substantial help from Curwen's trade artists.[19] They were a further stage in Curwen's campaign to convert more artists to using lithography, drawing on the collaboration of the skilled printers at Plaistow. As Lynton Lamb, the artist for *Grand Junction Canal* (fig.39), recalled:

40
Lithographs for Schools, brochure for Contemporary Lithographs Ltd., 1937, illustrating *Landscape of the Megaliths* by Paul Nash

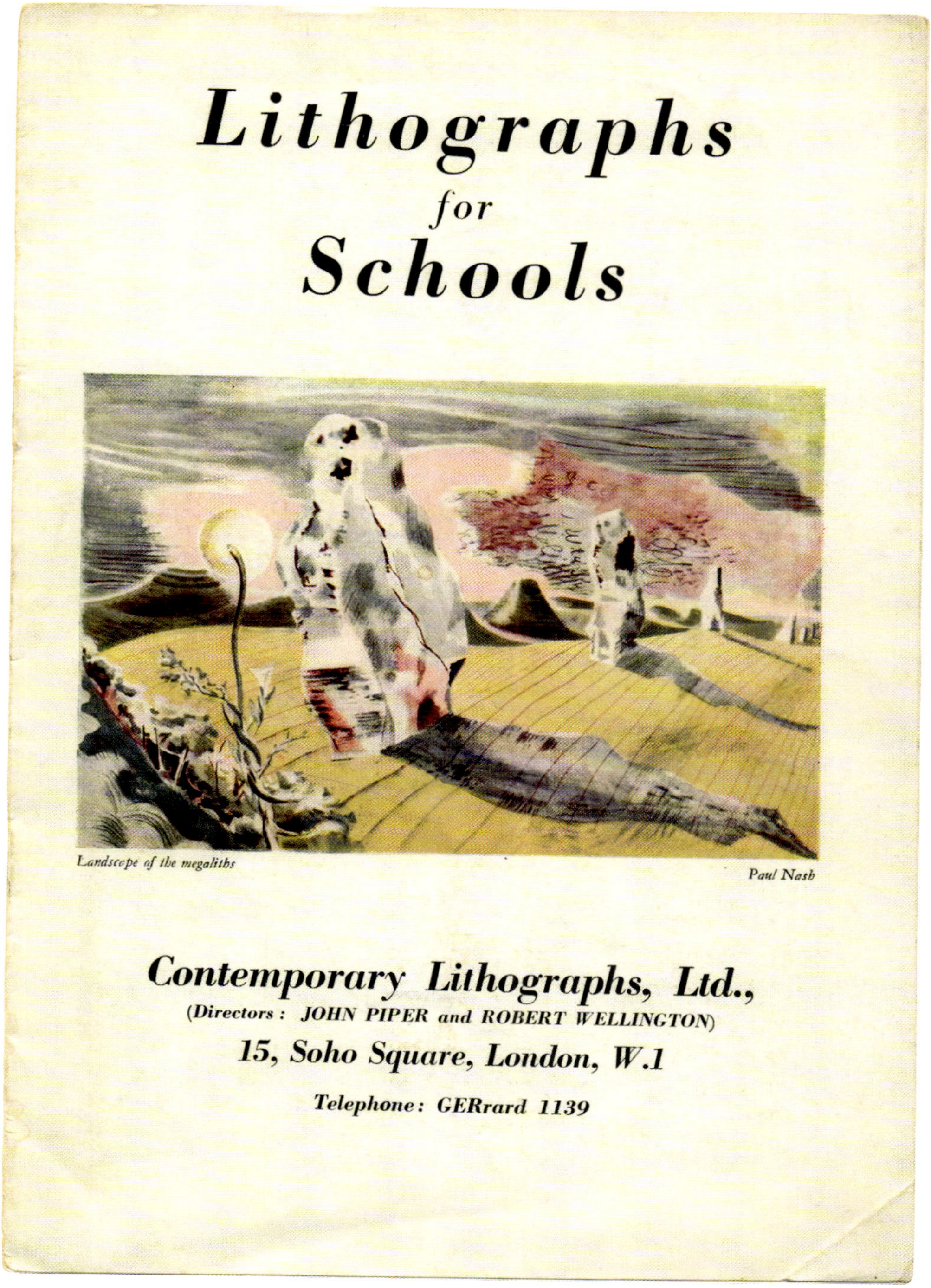

Lithographs
for
Schools

Landscape of the megaliths

Paul Nash

Contemporary Lithographs, Ltd.,
(Directors: JOHN PIPER and ROBERT WELLINGTON)
15, Soho Square, London, W.1
Telephone: GERrard 1139

41
John Piper, *Abstract Composition*, 1938

> I have the happiest memories of North Street, Plaistow in the 1930s. It was bliss in that dawn to be alive: artists flocked, like herring gulls following a plough, to work and watch each other work at North Street ... As a new boy among the delights of print making, I owed much to the kindness and lively interest of Harold Curwen, Oliver Simon, and seasoned members of their staff, who had been told to help us. I remember in particular, a splendid example of the old school of litho draughtsmen, known to me affectionately as Wally Gapp.[20]

Many of the familiar Curwen names were contributors to the Contemporary Lithographs series, including Paul Nash, with a print of the prehistoric stones at Avebury, Eric Ravilious with *Newhaven Harbour* and Edward Bawden with a transferred linocut of Braintree Market. Sutherland contributed an oddity, *The Sick Duck*, an anthropomorphic subject consciously aimed at children, with the surrealist gesture of a family portrait of an egg framed on the wall of the room. For the second series, Piper made an abstract (fig.41), and Edward Ardizzone contributed *The Fat Lady* to the series as well as recording his impressions of Plaistow for the *Curwen Press Newsletter* (fig.42) and making lithographs for *The Local*, a book about pubs (fig.43). The idea of a popular series of large prints persisted in post-war schemes such as Brenda Rawnsley's School Prints in the 1940s, the Guinness Lithographs and the Lyons Lithographs, with an overlapping cast of artists.

By 1939, a distinctive English modern school had emerged whose roots can in large part be traced back to a common pool of ideas and practices from which generated the ideals of the Curwen Press. These include ideas of hands-on experience of the processes involved in making the work of art, whether as a unique object or as a serial production, with equal attention to the integrity of the materials used, and a sideways glance at the working conditions of the labour force involved. They were the ideals of the Arts and Crafts movement translated into twentieth-century terms without loss of continuity.

The idea of the artist as a useful member of society, who could realise the workings of the creative imagination and could be the primary source of the 'spirit of joy', persisted in Britain from the hopeful beginnings of the 1920s even up to the gathering clouds of war in 1939. Printing was seen as a useful and valuable area of artistic activity, with a long historical tradition behind it, in which distinctions between design and art were irrelevant. Several of the best designers of type and lettering, including Eric Gill and Reynolds Stone, were also figurative artists of a high order, while many others crossed the boundary or at least saw the other side clearly and sympathetically. At the Curwen Press, colour, which we take so easily for granted today, was not only given prominence, but was handled with vitality and sensitivity, rather than produced in the raucous or nauseous combinations that often passed for modernism.

At Curwen, and in like-minded centres of cultural activity, the idea of Englishness was developed without self-consciousness, chauvinism or sentimentality, but with the result that by 1939, when the question of whether England had a distinctive culture

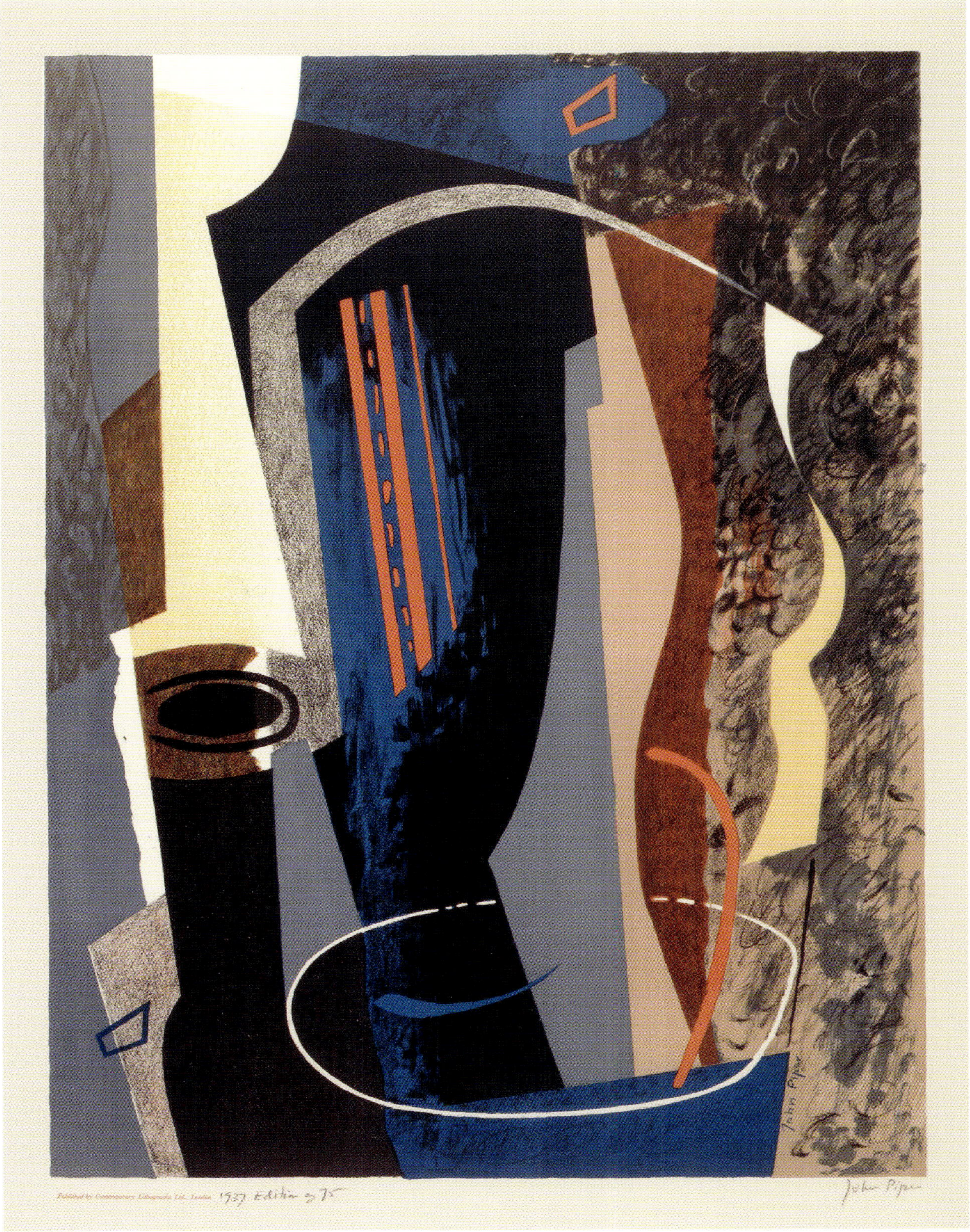
John Piper
Published by Contemporary Lithographs Ltd., London
1937 Edition of 75
John Piper

42
Edward Ardizzone,
Litho Poster Printing
and *Litho Artists*,
from the *Curwen Press Newsletter*, no.15, 1938

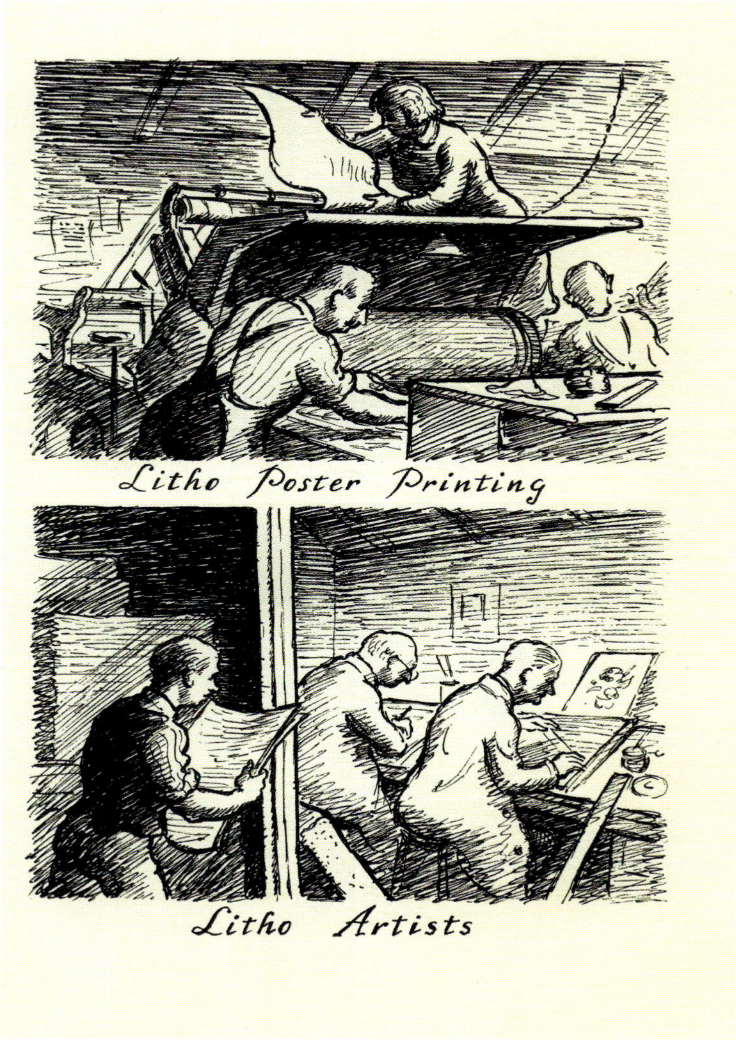

worth fighting for became a matter of life and death, the answer could be given in the affirmative.

The Second World War and after

During the Second World War, Curwen suffered from two hardships. The works at Plaistow received a direct hit from a bomb, damaging machinery and temporarily reducing factory floor space. Oliver Simon recorded that the fifteenth issue of *Signature*, the last of the original series of the magazine, was printed under the open sky. The bomb also destroyed the stock of lithographic plates that had been retained for possible future reprints. The metal belonged to the music company, but the images were the property of the Curwen Press. Had they survived, they would have become a fascinating archival source.

The second hardship was the difficulty of obtaining paper, although this was allocated to publishers rather than printers. Oliver Simon had developed a line in printing literary magazines such as *Life and Letters*, and Curwen became the printers for the most famous wartime magazine, *Horizon*, edited by Cyril Connolly, and first issued in January 1940, with Curwen taking over the printing in May that year. It seems that Oliver Simon was more than just the printer for the magazine, since he brought on board writers and especially artists. He shared Connolly's francophilia and Epicureanism, but also his broad sense of a cultural mission to extend and sustain civilising forces among the puritanical English.

Another of Curwen's contributions to the war effort was to print a magazine for the

43
Edward Ardizzone, *The Regulars at the Hero*, from Maurice Gorham, *The Local*, Cassel and Co., 1939

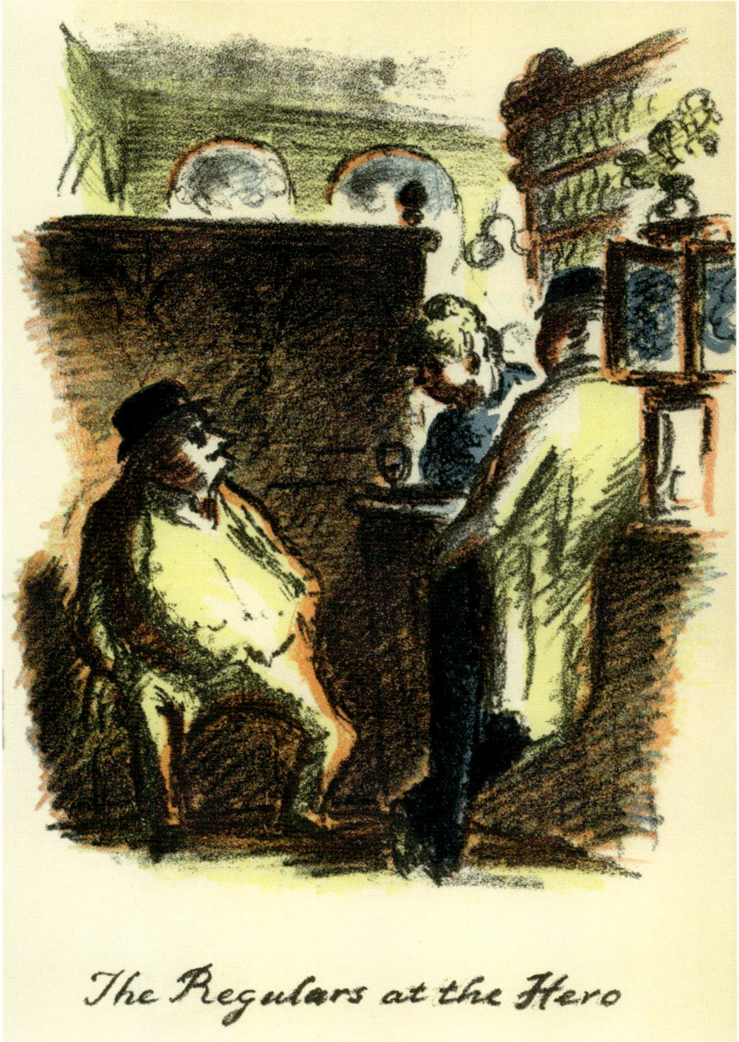

free French, *La France Libre*. As the Company AGM in 1943 recorded, 'the greater portion of our output is on Government Account, both English and Allied, and it is believed that within its limits, the firm is rendering useful service.'[21] Before the end of the war in 1945, a new building was planned for the site by the architect Geoffrey Jellicoe, but this absorbed most of the available capital, and in the rapid technological development of printing after the war, Curwen tended to lag behind in updating its equipment.

After the war, the Press entered a period in which reconstruction took priority over experiment (fig.44). Oliver Simon suffered from several severe bouts of illness, and although he was able to start a new series of *Signature*, running to eighteen numbers, he did not embark on new projects comparable to those before the war.

The new world of democratic culture to which *Horizon* looked forward did, in many respects, come into being, especially through the wartime Council for the Encouragement of Music and the Arts (CEMA) and its successor, the Arts Council. During the war, CEMA published artists' lithograph prints with some success, including several by Curwen artists such as Paul Nash, Barnett Freedman and Edward Ardizzone. For the Arts Council, the Curwen Press designed and printed many exhibition catalogues, contributing to the creation of a new 'official' style, still firmly classical in its centred compositions and frequent use of decorative borders, assembled out of individual type units by Bert Smith, a compositor at Curwen who excelled in this work. As Basil Harley ruefully remarked in a short history of the Press in 1970, 'Good printing was, of course, still in great demand, but all that had been put into making it universally acceptable by the Curwen Press in fact led to the increase of competition. There was no longer a monopoly of good print; craftsmanship counted far less than previously in view of the improvement in the capabilities of the plant.'[22]

The Limited Editions Club, for which Barnett Freedman and others produced illustrations before the war, continued as a major patron in the 1940s and 1950s and maintained the links between active lithographers and the Plaistow works. Freedman entered the last productive stretch of his career with glowing illustrations for Tolstoy's major novels, and for the works of the Brontës, showing a more adventurous approach to framing his illustrations on the printed page with asymmetrical borders of textured colour. On a reduced scale, the English equivalent of the Limited Editions Club, the Folio Society, founded in 1947, did the same, and built on the standards set by Curwen and the Nonesuch Press to make fine illustrated editions of literary and non-fiction classics available much more widely. Barnett Freedman's dream of a new generation of autolithographic artists feeding their work into the mainstream of book production had its moment, as evidenced by the Puffin Picture Books and Clarke Hutton's series of history books for Oxford University Press, but it proved to be a passing phase. London Transport, which had advocated autolithography in 1930s, found after the war that the in-house artists of the various presses they used did an excellent job and caused less difficulty than artists trying to draw the plates themselves. It was not a sudden ending, however, and commercial applications of autolithography, such as Ardizzone's pictorial menus for the Overtons group of restaurants, continued to be printed at Curwen until the final years of the Press.[23]

Oliver Simon's death in 1956 was a transition point, and Herbert, the more businesslike of the brothers, became the dominant figure for the next decade and a half. A second generation of Simons also began to play a role, with Oliver's son Timothy inheriting his father's mercurial talent and magnetic quality. His *Times* obituary described how 'a desk-drawer in his office was sure to contain some half-bottles of champagne, which would be brought out promptly in moments of either gloom or elation.'[24] Robert Simon, one of Herbert's three sons, loved machinery and its workings, as well as being a sculptor and graphic artist. All three Simons supported the idea of shifting the making of lithographs with visiting artists away from the main physical and financial core of the press into a distinct independent business, which became the Curwen Studio in 1958. This was almost inevitably to leave the main Curwen Press with less of a story to tell about the role of artists, although there were occasional excursions into more creative publishing. Henry Moore's set of lithographs in book form, *Heads, Figures and Ideas*, was published in 1958, and a special edition of Harold Pinter's play *The Homecoming* (fig.49), illustrated with photographic images by Harold Cohen,

44
Frances MacDonald,
The Composing Room at the Curwen Press, 1945

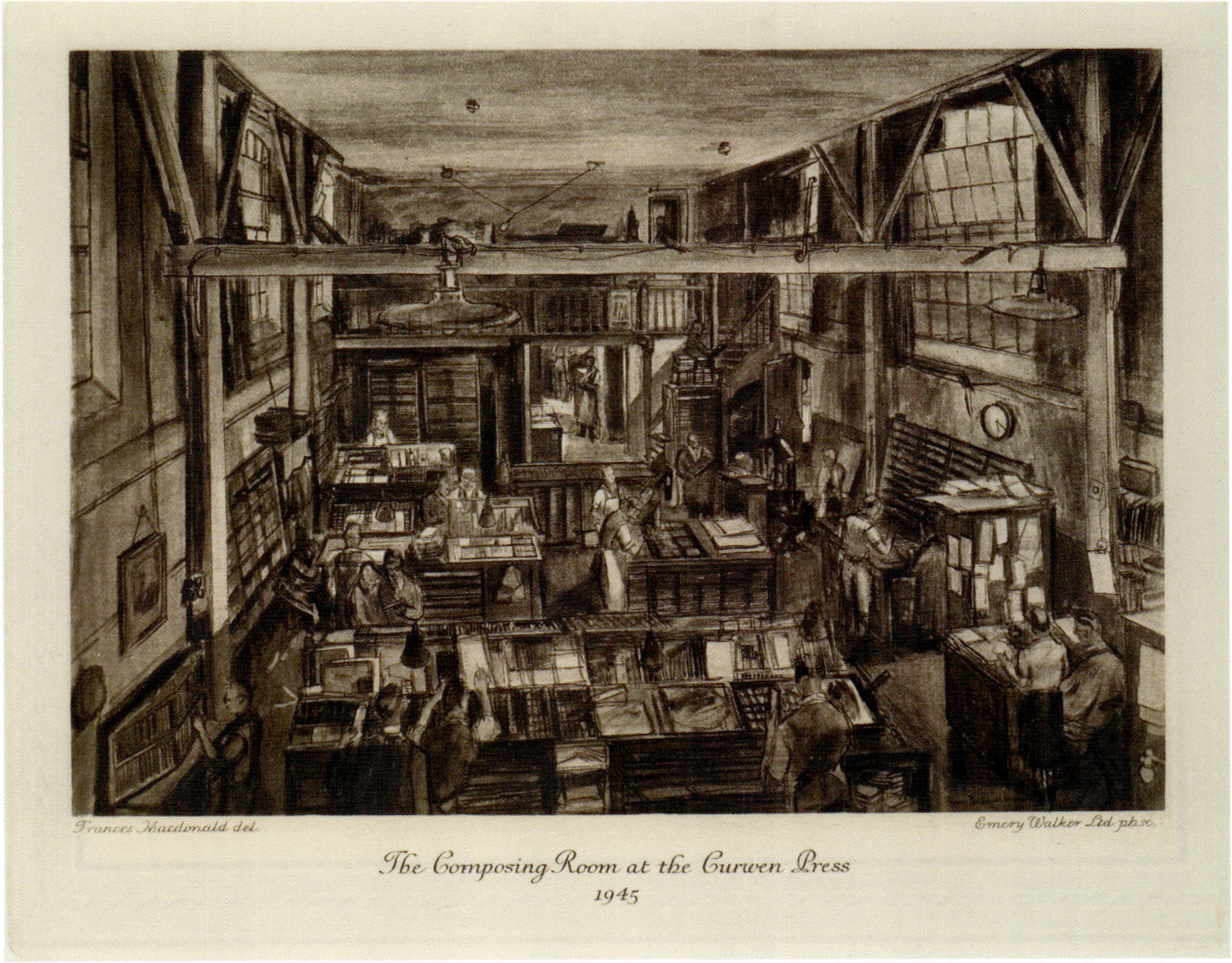

45
Monotype keyboard operators at the Curwen Press, 1950s

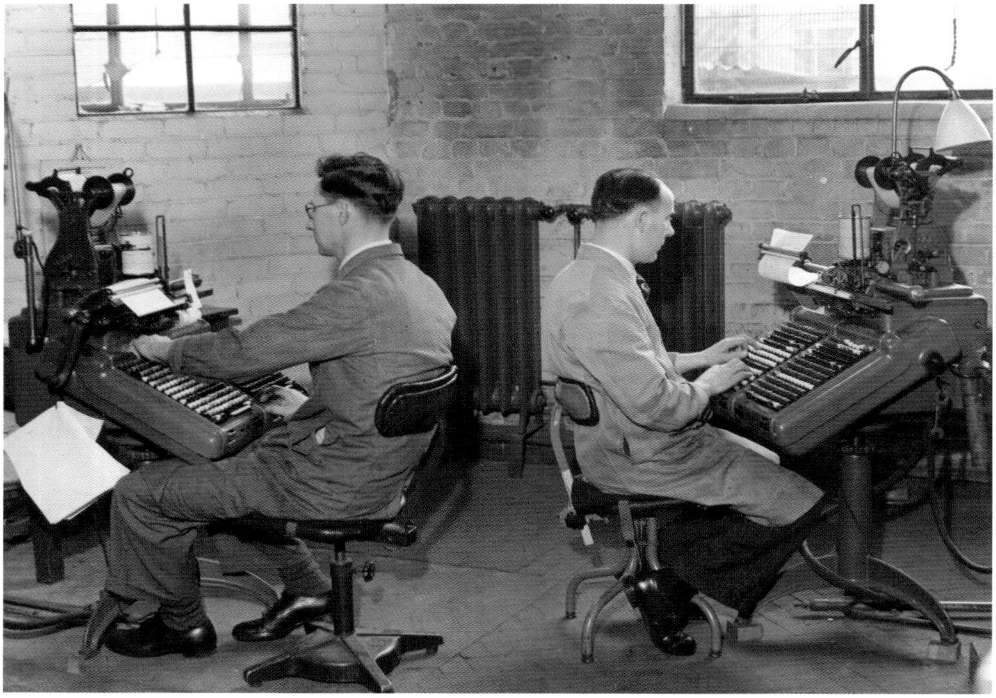

46
Handfeeding offset litho, 1950s

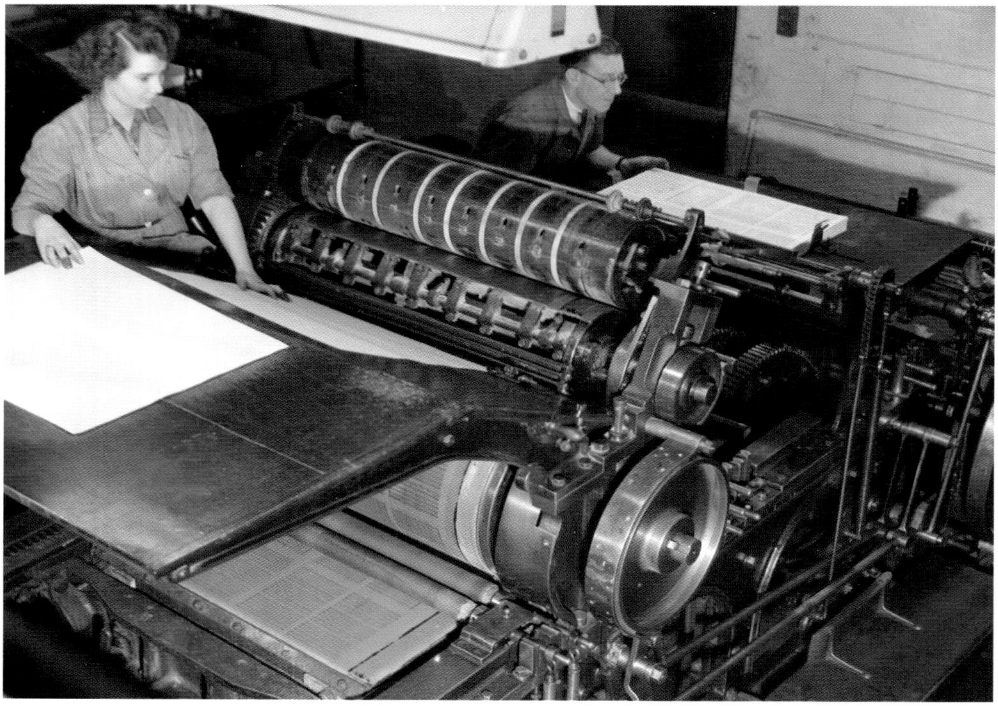

47
Making up and proofing pages, 1950s

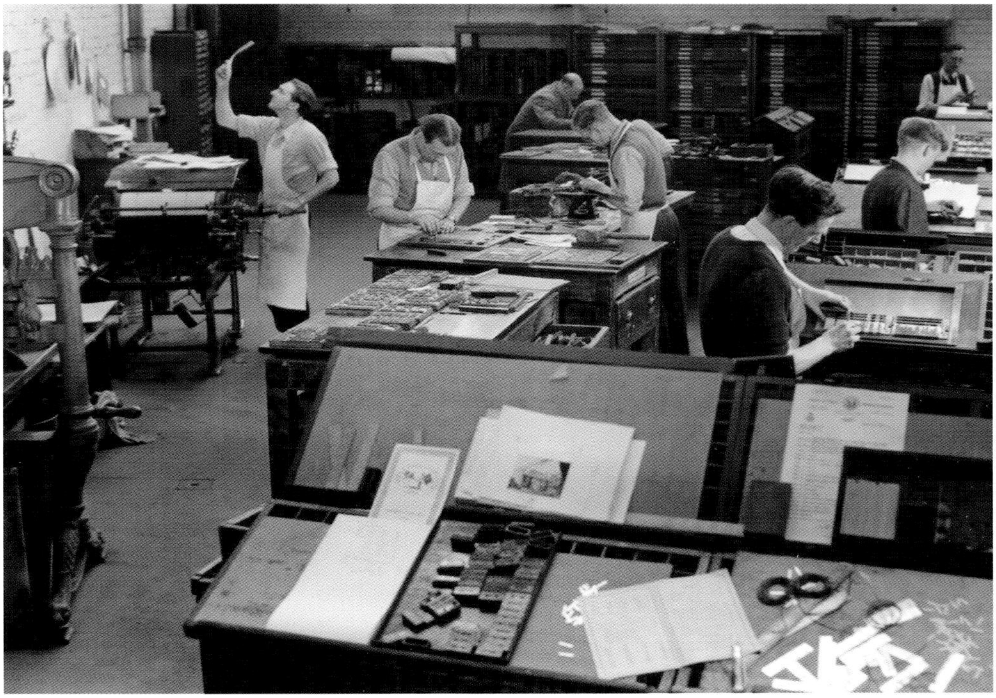

48
'Make ready' and lubrication for offset litho, 1950s

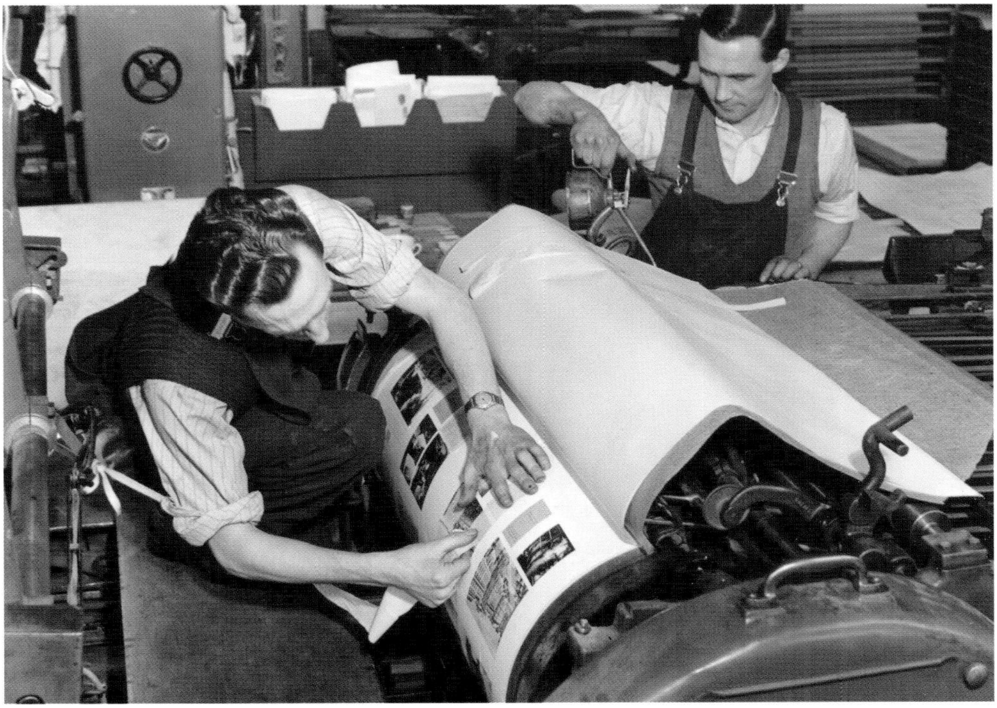

49
Harold Cohen, lithograph for Harold Pinter, *The Homecoming*, 1967

was published jointly in 1967 by Curwen and Harry Karnac, a small independent publisher specialising in psychology texts.

Work with the Limited Editions Club continued, with the plays of Euripides illustrated by Michael Ayrton and designed by Will Carter, a printer-publisher in his own right at the Rampant Lions Press (1967) and *The Spectator Papers*, decorated by Lynton Lamb and designed by John Miles, a representative of a new breed of graphic designer-typographers who was attached as a design consultant for the Curwen Press for a brief period. The everyday jobbing work of the press caught the wind of change. In 1963, Philip Gauld, one of the first designers in Britain to take up the new Dutch sanserif, Univers, created a new house style for Curwen that ran parallel with the more traditional look, but was no longer distinctive in a world where so many different influences were at work.

In 1960, £31,400 was spent on new plant, but there was also an unprecedented seven-week stoppage over a trade union dispute. By 1963, Curwen was still struggling to achieve good results with new colour printing techniques, and the AGM of the company heard that 'it has not been an easy path and development has been more costly than anticipated.'[25] Small family printing businesses were habitually undercapitalised, and by this time liable to be asset stripped or absorbed into larger groups, like Bob Gavron's St Ives.

Curwen was looking for a partnership, and the result was a merger between Curwen and M.R. Harley and Co. Ltd (trading as Harleyprint) in 1964, with Basil Harley as Managing Director under the chairmanship of Herbert Simon, who was sixty-six that year. Neither Robert nor Timothy Simon seems to have been entirely happy with their inherited roles in this stately but somewhat outmoded equivalent of a Cunard liner in the jet age. Timothy died aged forty-one having left Curwen for a career in general publishing soon after the Harley merger. Robert Simon took over the management of Curwen Prints Ltd (see p.122) and the associated gallery in Colville Place, off Charlotte Street, before retiring in 1978 to focus on his own work as an artist and designer. Herbert Simon also enjoyed having a hand in the Studio and Gallery, and ended his career in printing by writing a well-researched history of the Press, published in 1973 by George Allen and Unwin, where Harold Curwen's son-in-law, Rayner Unwin, was Managing Director.

Many print customers felt that Curwen had a reputation for high prices, and Robert Simon has commented that they were able to coast along with faithful clients who did not challenge the bills or seek other estimates. With the ascendancy of graphic designers, whose job included placing the work with printers on behalf of clients, this situation began to change. Basil Harley decided to focus on high-quality colour reproduction work, which matched his own interest in natural history and the works of art associated with it. Working with specialist publishers, the Press produced a mixture of original books in this field and facsimiles of historical classics. Calendars with wildlife themes were produced in large numbers as a promotion. While the exhibition *Artists at Curwen* at the Tate Gallery in 1977 was a valuable piece of

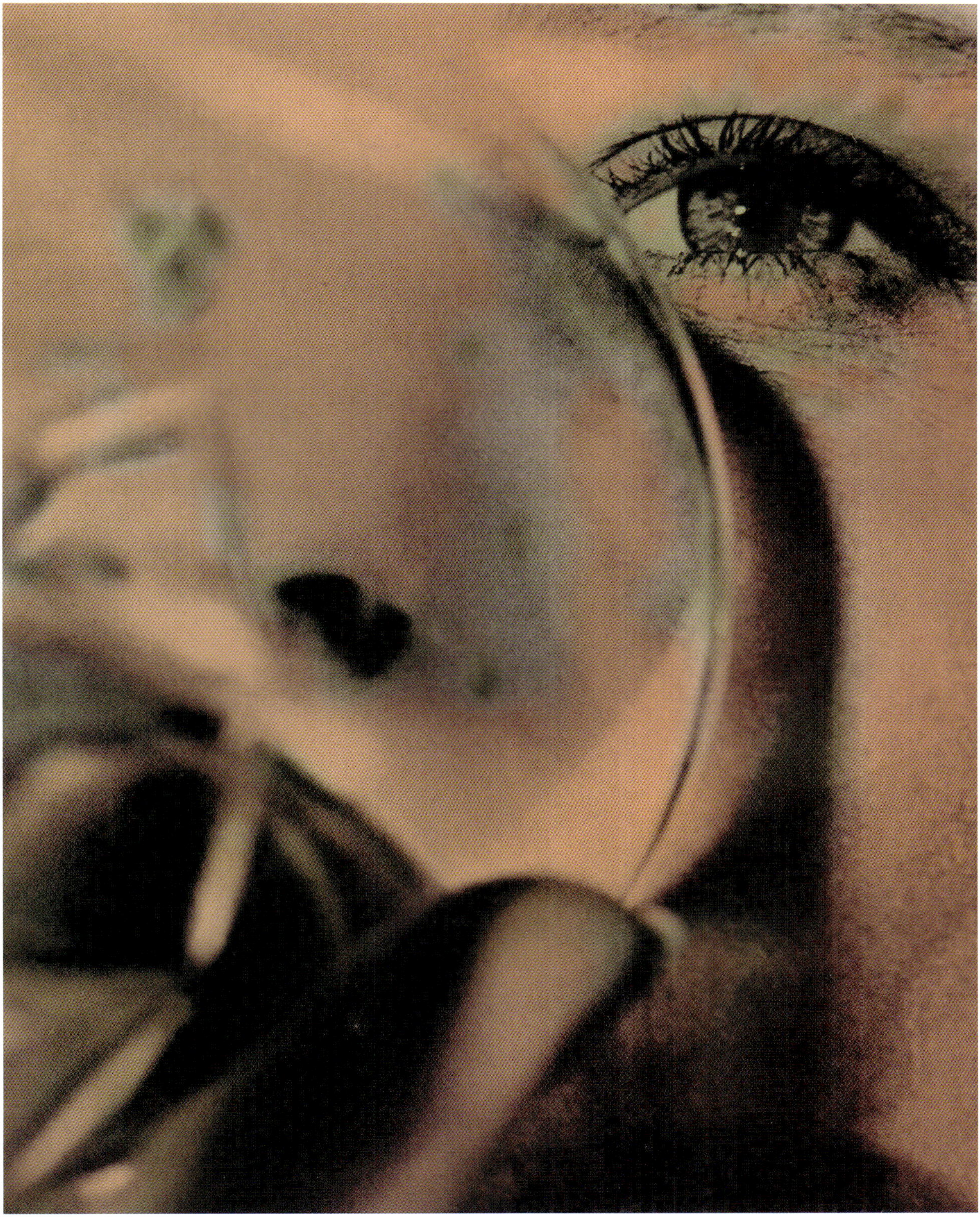

50
Title page, Gavin Stamp, *Temples of Power*, 1979

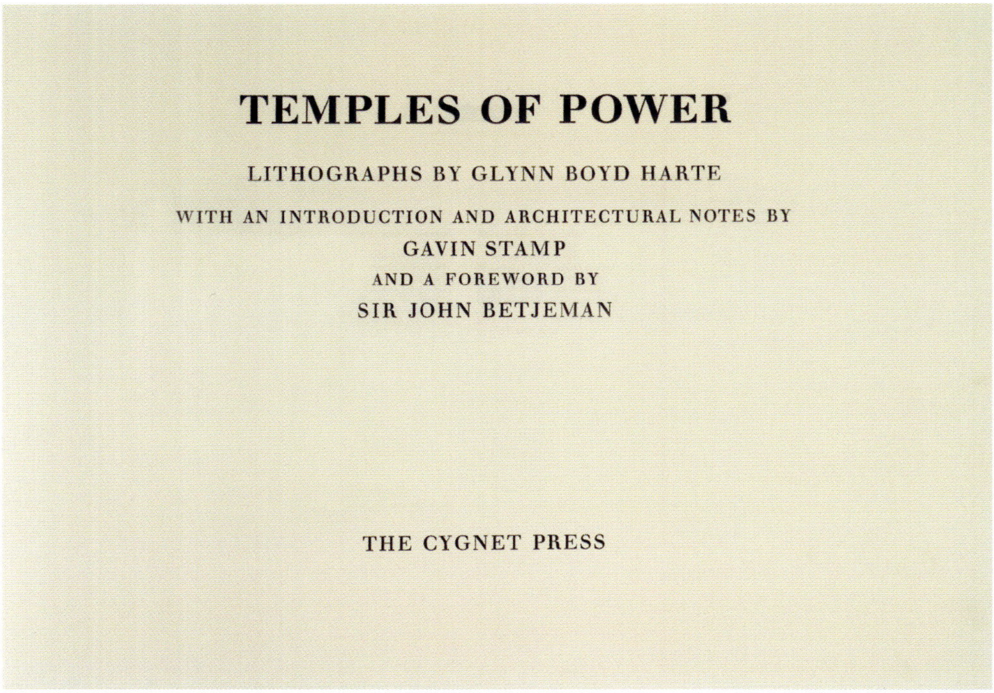

TEMPLES OF POWER

LITHOGRAPHS BY GLYNN BOYD HARTE

WITH AN INTRODUCTION AND ARCHITECTURAL NOTES BY
GAVIN STAMP
AND A FOREWORD BY
SIR JOHN BETJEMAN

THE CYGNET PRESS

publicity, it was clear that the most lively work had been carried on at the Studio rather than the main Press for nearly twenty years. The recruitment of Simon Rendall, a talented young printer and designer who also happened to be the grandson of the artist McKnight Kauffer who had worked with the Curwen Press fifty years before, brought a flavour of the 1920s back to Plaistow. Rendall was able to publish, under his imprint the Cygnet Press, one last book of pre-war magnificence, *Temples of Power* (fig.50–1), a catalogue of early electricity buildings in London, including the then-forgotten Bankside Power Station, later to become Tate Modern. The images were drawn and printed at the Curwen Studio and the text printed letterpress at Plaistow, and it was issued in the autumn of 1979.

After 1980, the flow of technological change turned into a deluge, as letterpress printing lost its competitive footing, and anti-union legislation under Margaret Thatcher meant that the workforce had to adapt to new technology that offered fewer jobs but lower production costs. Conflicts among the directors impeded attempts at reconstruction, and in 1983, the Curwen Press went into liquidation. Most of its valuable cultural property was rescued, including paper archives, which mainly went to Cambridge University, with the library of printed books going to the University of Alberta at Edmonton. Other visual treasures joined the fine collection of English printing and illustration at the Bryn Mawr College, Pennsylvania. Stock wood blocks by Ravilious and others went to collectors, and metal type and ornaments, some of them unique, found a home with the independent printer Ian Mortimer in Hackney. The buildings at Plaistow ceased printing 120 years after they had begun.

51
Glynn Boyd Harte,
lithograph for Gavin
Stamp, *Temples of Power*,
1979

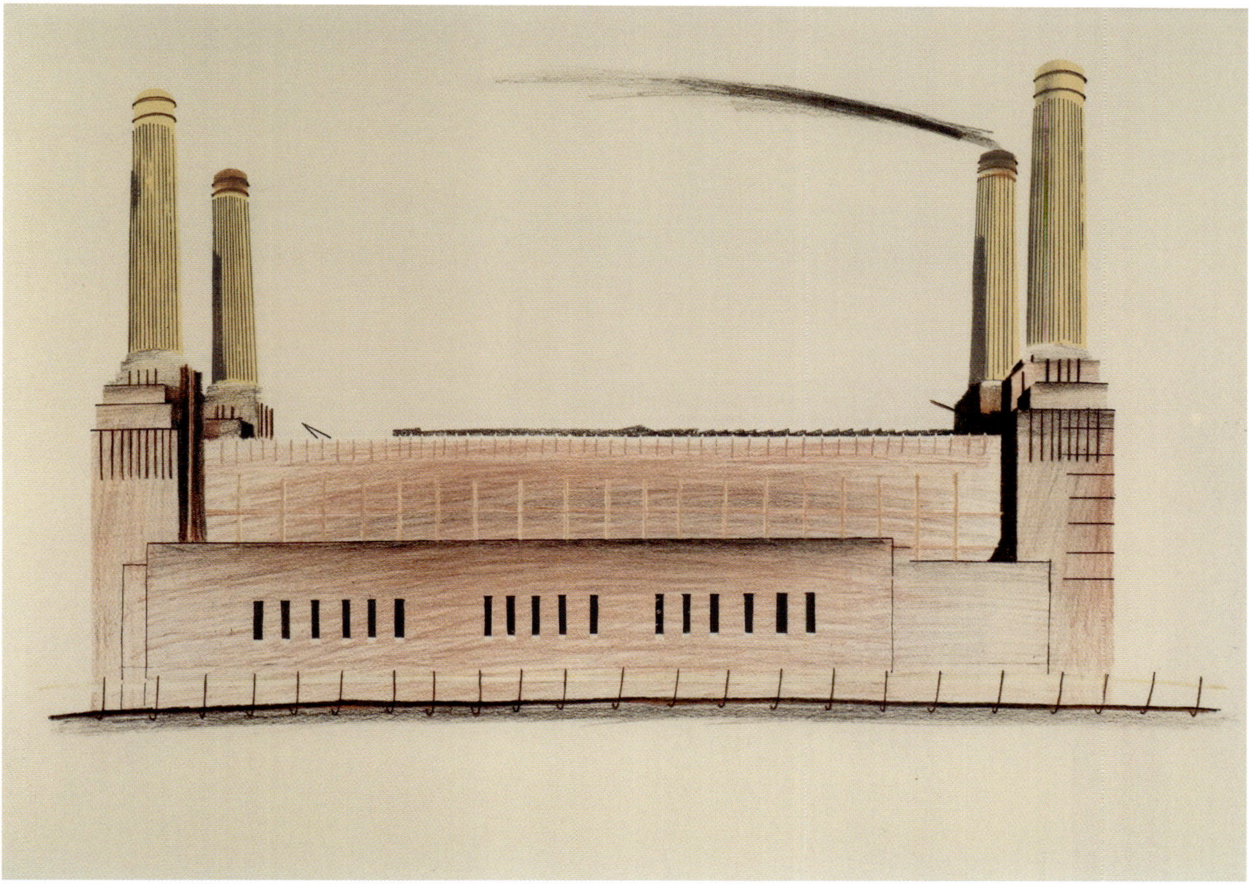

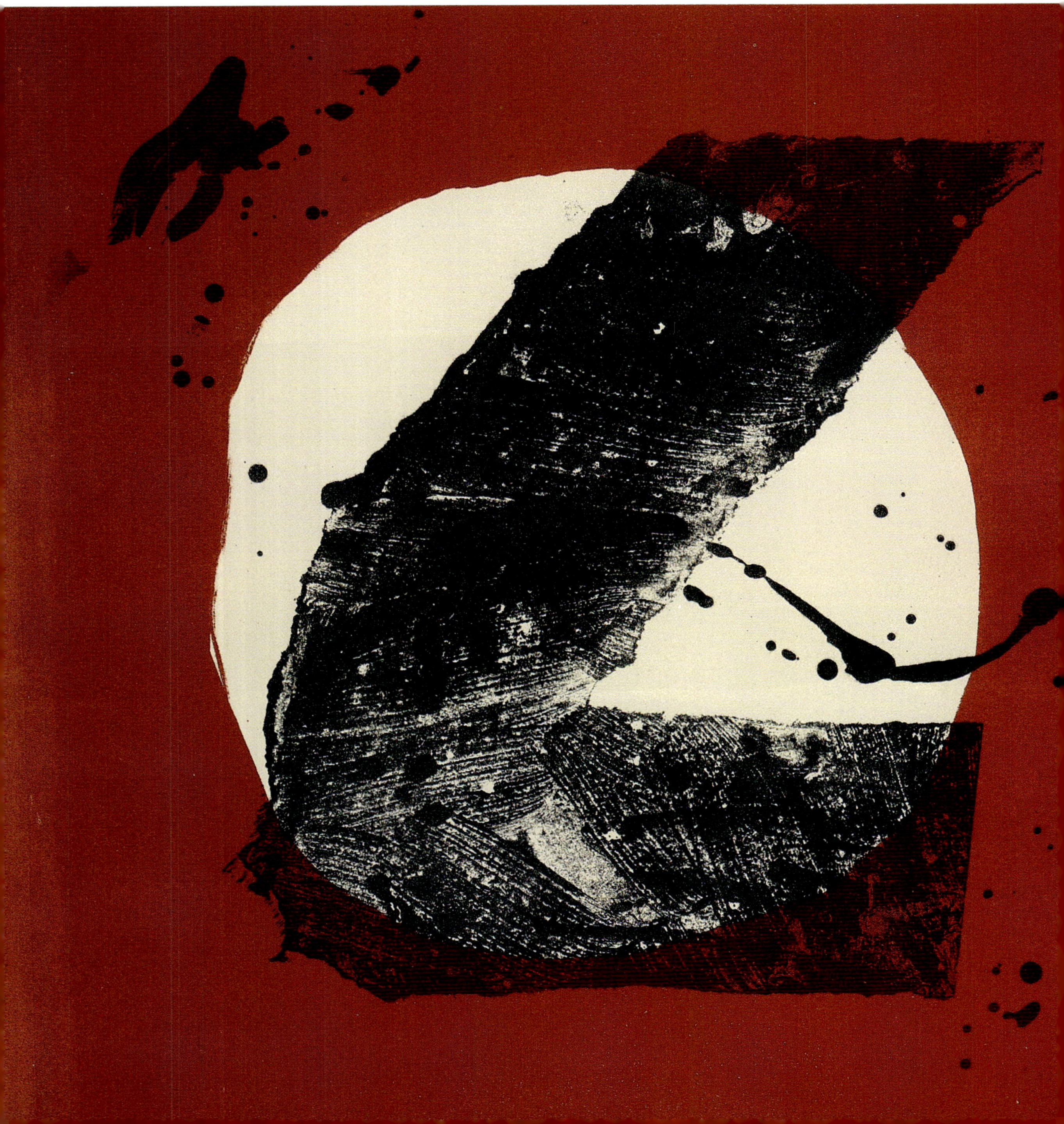

THE CURWEN STUDIO

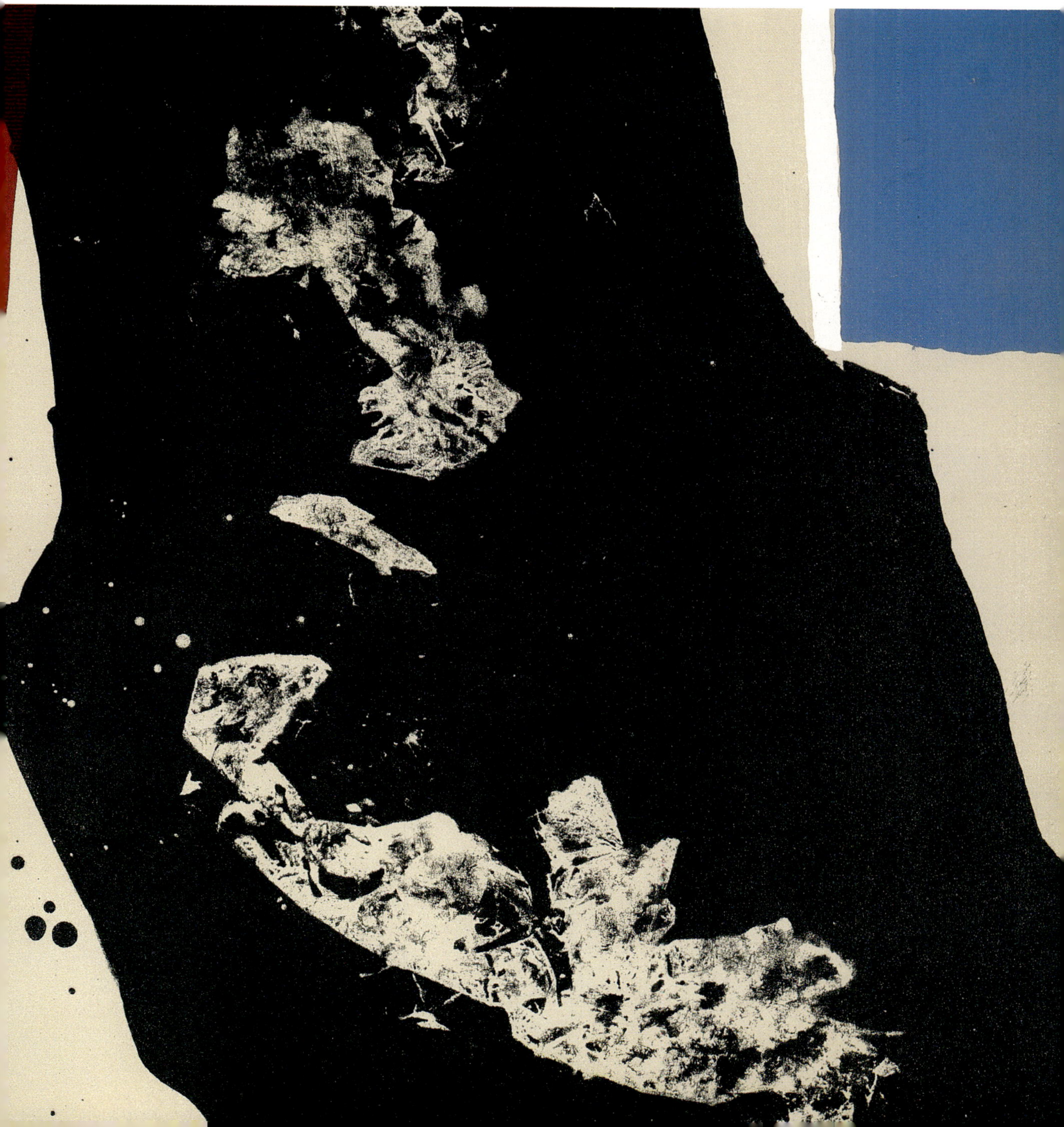

The stories of the Curwen Press and Studio are continuous, in a strictly business sense, and more broadly in terms of an ethos about printing and its potential to extend into the art world, but the decision to set up the Studio acknowledged a completely new form of printing activity that was emerging during the post-war years.

To understand the nature of the Curwen Studio and its operations requires knowledge of other activities, both nationally and internationally, within the same field, and further insight into the production and distribution of artists' prints. These are not necessarily issues of primary concern to the art historian confronted with the print itself, yet they are increasingly the kind of questions asked about the material artefacts of the more distant past, almost irrespective of whether they are properly called art.

The story of the Curwen Studio can be told in several ways, therefore. It can be seen in the context of individual artists, especially those who did substantial amounts of work in collaboration with the Studio, such as Henry Moore, John Piper and Ceri Richards. It can also be seen in the context of international and national printmaking activity in a period between the late 1950s and the mid-1970s, now widely acknowledged as a high point of avant-garde printmaking which has not since been equalled. In this sense, the 1977 Tate exhibition marked the twilight of the great names and their direct links back to the era of Oliver Simon, and also the end of a time in which lithography was likely to be the favourite medium for leading artists when deciding to make prints at all. The older technique of intaglio, as well as the more modern technique of silkscreen, were already of equal if not greater importance.

The foundation of the Curwen Studio

In essence, three people were needed in order to bring the Curwen Studio into being. From the company side, Timothy Simon is generally seen as the leading figure, although he had the active support of his cousin Robert Simon, and of Herbert Simon as a senior member of the Curwen Press Board. The timing of Oliver Simon's premature death from heart disease in 1956 seems to have mattered, not because he would have opposed the Studio idea, but rather because it heightened awareness that the links he had fostered between artists and Curwen were fragile. The later numbers of *Signature* up to 1954 do not provide direct clues about the possibilities in Oliver's mind, but they show him keeping up to date with the Parisian trends that fostered a climate favourable to bold experiments in lithography. There was, for example, an article on Nicolas de Stael in 1953, an artist whose bold use of colour, seen in an exhibition at the Whitechapel Gallery in 1956, had an immediate impact on English painters.[1] The three surviving Simons might not have made their move, however, had they not been encouraged by the print publisher Robert Erskine (fig.52) who gave them confidence that there would be a market for individual artists' prints in London. Erskine was also able to introduce them to their Studio director, Stanley Jones, and hindsight has shown what an inspired piece of headhunting this was, for it is unlikely that there was anyone as well fitted

52
Robert Erskine at St George's Gallery, *c.*1962

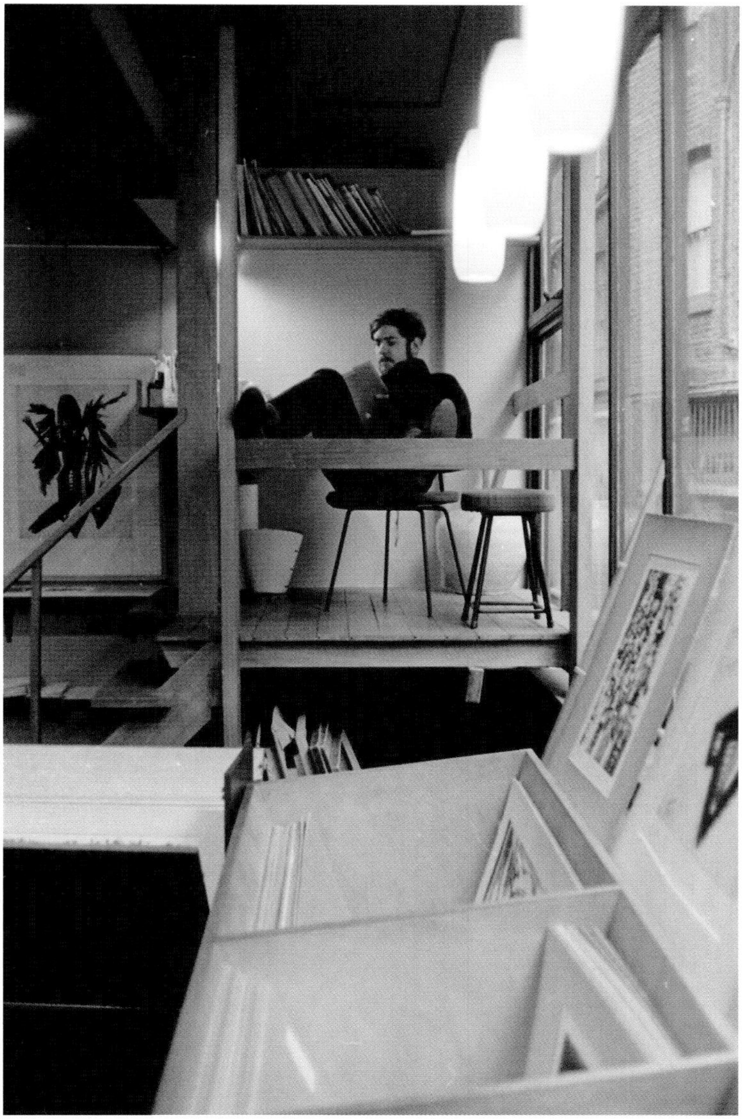

at that moment to take on the job.

The timing seems to have involved several coincidences, combined with a perception of longer-term trends and changes. While it had been possible to make the Contemporary Lithographs (see p.54) at the Curwen Press before the war, by the 1950s increasing commercial pressures and the additional burden of union regulation could not allow for the unpredictable delays involved in working with even the most reliable artists, let alone inducting new ones into the complexities of the process.

In 1968 the craftsman and educator David Pye famously made the distinction between the workmanship of risk, which covers many of the traditional crafts, and the workmanship of certainty, which applied to industrial standards, by whatever means they are achieved. It was possible to divide the production of artists' lithographs along these lines.[2] The preparation of lithographic plates or stones, and subsequent proofing, were stages requiring the active participation of the artist, and a flexibility of response on the part of technical assistants to allow for developments along the way. This was the workmanship of risk, which required openness to change, making it a valid artistic medium in the age of Abstract Expressionism.

Editioning, where each print must look exactly like another, was a different matter, and could be carried out by a workforce with different skills, equipment and space. In the litho shop at Curwen the commercial processes were still compatible with those of the Studio, and theirs was the workmanship of certainty, even though considerable skills of hand and eye were needed to achieve it.

Trade unions and management made their own distinctions along similar lines. The Studio was set up under a separate roof and did not employ union staff. The stones or plates prepared there could be transferred a short distance to the Curwen Press for editioning. One can imagine Ravilious or Freedman working happily at the Studio (had they lived long enough), as their contemporaries Bawden and Piper later did. Indeed, Ravilious's evident pleasure in making prints independently of book commissions anticipated the era when a market for such products would make this a commercially sensible move.

The artist's print

The change in the print market was crucial. It is a complex and fascinating story, seemingly driven more by inspirational individuals than by logical market forces. During the 1920s there was a buoyant market, especially in America, for modern English etchings, invariably conservative in artistic tone. Why this was the case is as hard to reconstruct as the reasons for the inflationary Dutch market in tulip bulbs in the seventeenth century. When the 1929 Wall Street Crash ushered in the Depression, etchers such as F.L. Griggs suffered financially while Graham Sutherland, whose early career was based on etching, turned to lithography for a combination of artistic and commercial reasons.

While the war years and after proved favourable for lithographed book illustrations, the artist's original print required more stable conditions to flourish. In Britain as in America the first decade after the war was surprisingly barren for printmakers, given the graphic tendencies of so many of the emerging artists of the time. The major exception was the English-born printmaker Stanley William Hayter (1901–1988) whose career was mainly played out in Paris and New York. Hayter was devoted to intaglio techniques, and almost single-handedly opened up their potential for modern artists. He favoured the direct method of engraving into the plate, historically used for reproductive copying rather than original work. Bawden's few essays in this technique, including a plate published in *Signature*, show how he too might have developed in Hayter's direction. In Paris before 1939, however, Hayter was part of the dynamic art world, and formed alliances with Surrealists. In 1927 he opened his Paris workshop, called Atelier 17 after the address of its first premises. He did his own work there, providing facilities for fellow artists and organised group exhibitions. Although printmaking had often been a convivial activity, nothing quite like this had been done before. Hayter's fame was extended during the war years in New York, where Atelier 17 continued, and again after 1945 in Paris to the end of his life. Hayter's book *New Ways of Gravure*, the first technical volume of its kind illustrated entirely by modern work, was originally published in the United States in 1948 and issued by Routledge in London the following year. In his conclusion, Hayter argued that while 'the mechanical complexity of some of the operations, and

53
Stanley William Hayter,
Myth of Creation, 1940

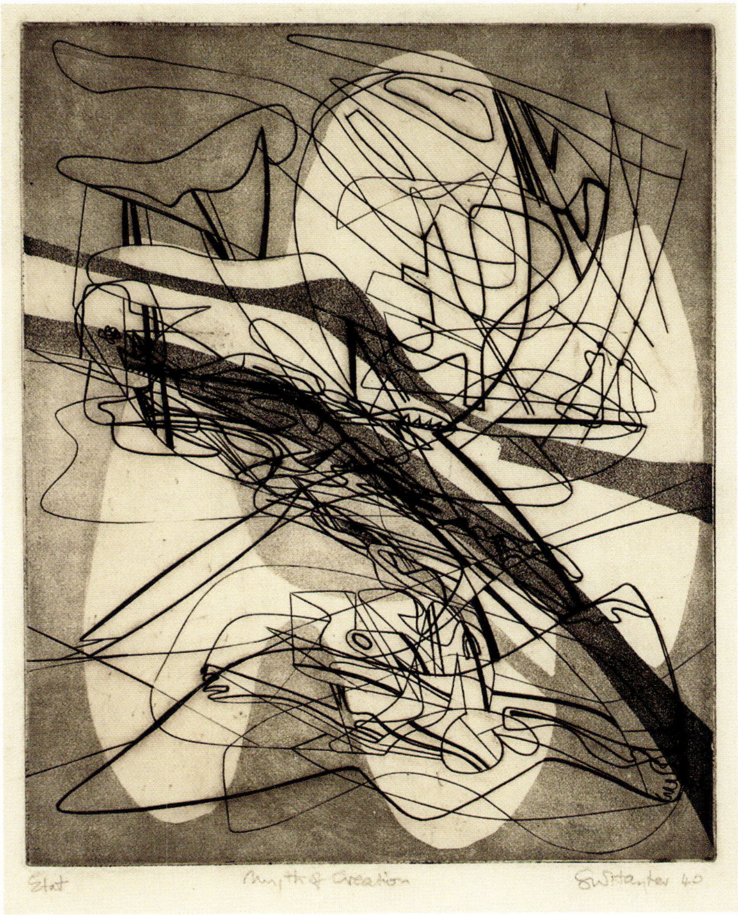

their reputed difficulty (generally exaggerated, in my opinion), might appear to hamper the development of expression, I consider that the very complexity of the means can be applied to provoke it. Thus the antithesis between inspiration (imagination-unconscious) and execution, in the view of our group, has no real existence.'[3] It was a view belonging to the age of Freud and Jung that had never before been so explicitly stated, even though all active printmakers would acknowledge its truth. Thus it was the very existence of something to push against that, in Hayter's view, 'led to the stimulation or activation of further and different areas of imagination which were previously dormant.'[4] In other words, printmaking in its new guise ought to be seen as especially suited to the current artistic climate, irrespective of commercial considerations.

Hayter's example was important for the modern printmaking movement in Britain and America. One of the Atelier 17 artists, John Buckland-Wright, produced an important textbook in 1953, *Etching and Engraving: Techniques and the Modern Trend*, which was reviewed in the final number of *Signature* by Brian Robb. He believed that 'one of the reasons for the slump in the print market, and the consequent unpopularity of the intaglio media with artists, probably lay in the narrow orthodoxy of some of its former practitioners, who formed a kind of closed shop, making etching and engraving a mystery which the simple painter might never penetrate unless introduced by an orthodox sponsor, and solemnly and properly initiated.'[5] The illustrations were more varied than those in Hayter's book, and potentially more sympathetic to an English artist uncertain how modern he wished to become. In a preface, John Piper wrote that a lot of students now wanted to study etching: 'They know that Picasso and Miro and other artists they admire have worked with Hayter … and they realise that etching and line engraving are not the stuffy crafts that people of the older generations tended to think them and make them: that they are not necessarily imitative or reproductive, or expressive only of the sentimental or the acceptedly pictorial. On the other hand, they can be vital and lively arts.'[6]

Picasso was a prolific printmaker. His *Vollard Suite* from the early 1930s is probably the best-known example of his work in intaglio, but he also began lithography with the Parisian master craftsman Fernand Mourlot. According to Picasso's dealer, Daniel-Henri Kahnweiler, when most of the newly liberated French were freezing in the winter of 1945, Mourlot received a fuel allowance for his studio, a factor that encouraged Picasso to spend time there.[7] His famous image of the dove, adopted as a symbol of peace by the Communist party, was drawn in washes on lithographic stone. That such a famous artist turned to lithography was important in itself, but Picasso was also prepared to push the medium further, experimenting with washes and with mixtures such as gouache and lighter-fuel to create mottled textures with a life of their own. He was one of many painters in France to discover lithography, and as Jean Adhémar wrote of the late 1940s: 'Lithography used to be a medium without vigour; now it was beautifully rich in colour and contrasting textures'. He quoted the painter Alfred Manessier, who recorded that he had been 'surprised by the power of expression one could obtain with it.'[8] While the tendency of intaglio to encourage neatness suited the aesthetic of the 1930s, the post-war mood was suited to lithography, where messy work could be revelatory, and colour was much easier to develop.

Stanley Jones

The French expertise in lithography was developed in the nineteenth century and its easy relationship with the art world was facilitated by a more relaxed culture of labour relations in printing generally, so that the demarcation of art and industry did not affect the Parisian studios such as Mourlot. This model could not be reproduced exactly in 1950s London, but it was none the less a reminder of the level of technical expertise needed to launch the Curwen Studio. The difficulty was to fill the gap between knowing too little, which was the probable fate of the individual artist trying to make lithographs in a home studio or an art school, and knowing too much, which could describe the rather inflexible practices of the trade that resisted artistic experiment.

Well beyond the range of other printmaking media, lithography requires knowledge and experience of chemical reactions, without which the drawing on the plate or stone can be left in an unstable condition, unable to withstand the impact of extended printing. This was the experience of the artist Ceri Richards when he became head of the lithographic studio at the Slade School in 1954. While the Slade had a flourishing early history of intaglio printmaking, it was historically less significant in lithography than the LCC Central School under the control of Ernest Devenish and the artist Clarke Hutton, or the revived Royal College of Art, where the studio was run by the artist Edwin La Dell with Ernest Devenish's brother, George. The Bath Academy of Art at Corsham Court, one of the most progressive and exciting art schools in Britain after the war, was under the direction of Clifford Ellis, whose own public work, in collaboration with his wife, Rosemary, consisted mainly of posters and book jackets. He therefore understood printmaking, and Corsham employed Henry Cliffe as a lithographic teacher. Other schools offered lithography, and it was possible to find technicians who had acquired some knowledge in the trade, but the emphasis was more on commercial work and illustration than fine art. This was the art school world which Stanley Jones entered, initially at Wigan Art School in his home town in Lancashire.

Stanley was born in 1933. His father was an engine driver, and other members of the family worked in a variety of skilled trades, including an uncle who was a bookbinder based in a printing firm. His first print was made on a brass plate with his mother's mangle while he was fourteen, and he made his own discoveries among art books at Wigan Public Library. He applied to the Slade at the age of sixteen and was provisionally accepted, but was advised to wait until he had passed the School Certificate. Unfortunately, an obstructive County Education Officer not only refused to fund his studies at the Slade, but also cut off the possibility of studying in Liverpool or Manchester. During four years at Wigan Art School, however, Stanley was first able to try stone lithography and liked the process, although most of his effort was focused on painting and drawing. He was able to move to London for a post-graduate diploma at the Slade in 1954, and while lithography was not widely promoted as an option, he was able to take it up again as a relief from the rather relentless life drawing and observational painting encouraged under William Coldstream's leadership. John Piper was, however, one of the visiting staff representing a different tendency, and discussed with Stanley his own experiences with lithography, which included some work with Mourlot.[9]

The link between Stanley Jones and two artists, John Piper and Ceri Richards, was established, significant because both played a leading role in the first years of the Curwen Studio. After breaking away from a job in advertising and starting to teach during the war, Ceri Richards took his place among the small group of London artists alert and responsive to events in Paris. His work nearly always reveals its influences transparently, but the visible presence of Picasso, Matisse or Max Ernst does not diminish its interest or value. Compared to the painter-lithographers of the 1930s, Richards used the medium experimentally, working on prints in developing series, and, like Picasso, trying out techniques simply to find out what effects they produced. As Stanley Jones has written, 'Often the accidents of processing would intrigue Ceri, and such discoveries would form the basis for other prints … To capture an idea in terms of print was for Ceri a journey without end.'[10] The prints were like butterflies, beautiful but short-lived, for after one or two prints, the image on the stone or plate began to break up. Jones virtually became his studio assistant at the Slade, trying to help out by finding the source of the problems.

Clearly, for a publisher wishing to commission an edition, the apparently experimental and unpredictable nature of lithography presented real difficulties, but ones for which the solutions lay in the superior experience of the Paris lithographic workshops. This idea was promoted by Robert Erskine, who opened the first print gallery in London specialising in modern limited editions. Erskine, who later commissioned a major print series from Ceri Richards, made the suggestion that, after finishing at the Slade, Jones might go to Paris to learn from the masters. Jones himself was inspired by hearing Hayter lecturing and showing a film about colour etching at the Slade and talking to him afterwards. So it was that Coldstream and the college registrar, Ian Tregarthen-Jenkin, managed to find small sums of scholarship money to send Jones to Paris in 1956 with an agreement from Hayter that he would help. Hayter gave Jones a letter of introduction to Gérard Patris (fig.54) who ran an establishment similar to Mourlot's very close to the post-war Atelier 17 in the rue Daguerre, Montparnasse. It was a fortunate time to be in Paris, with many of the great artists still active in the locality. Jones became friendly with Giacometti, and delivered proofs to Braque, who might hang them on the studio wall for a whole year before deciding what to do with them next. The former Futurist Gino Severini lived and worked up six flights of narrow stairs, with lighting operated on a sequence of time switches. Jones and Patris would deliver litho stones in the evening, using Patris's pre-war open-top car, and struggle up the stairs with them trying to reach the next switch before being plunged back into darkness.

The work in the Atelier Patris was the opposite of a unionised workshop with clocking in and out. Different studio assistants came and went, although Dado Meodrag Djuric, a refugee Surrealist from Yugoslavia living illegally in Paris, was a constant figure. Food was bought in the rue Daguerre street market to keep the printmakers going through late night sessions or for lunches in the courtyard in fine weather, where litho stones were ground down ready to receive fresh drawing. The studio was open seven days a week in order to keep up with the competition. Editions of up to 200 in sometimes as many as nine colours were inked and printed by hand, using laborious star-wheel presses.

In addition to technical knowledge of subjects such as the proper use of nitric acid, gum and other chemicals, Jones learnt about the printer's role as an intermediary between artist and publisher, whose concerns about speed and cost might interfere with the creative process. No other English artist undertook a training of this type, and one day Robert Erskine arrived at the Atelier to speak to Stanley about

54
The Atelier Patris,
Montparnasse, 1957.
Gérard Patris, Sugaii,
Nono Reinhold
and Stanley Jones

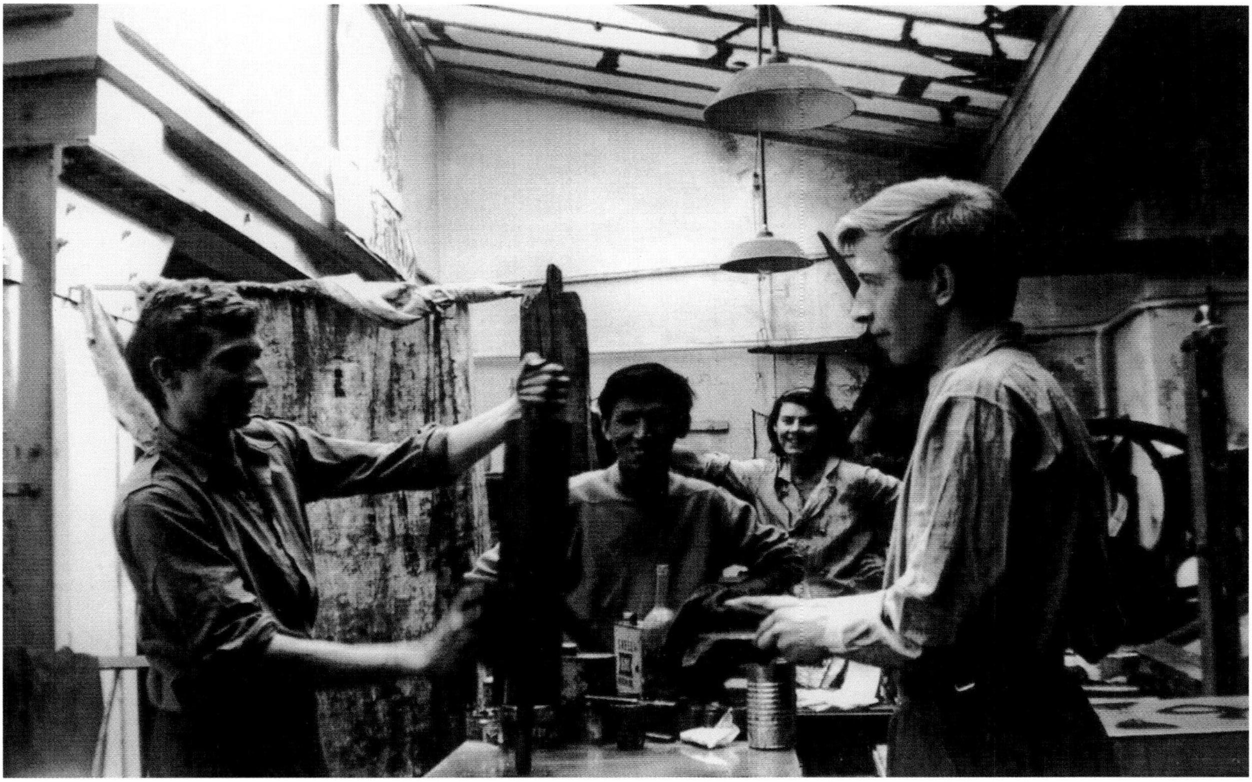

coming back to London to run the Curwen Studio, which Erskine had developed as an idea with Timothy Simon. After brief hesitation, Stanley agreed to come on a trial basis for two years, although he regretted leaving such an agreeable if hard-working life in Paris.

Printmaking and the market in the 1950s

If the timing of the Curwen Studio's foundation had its own logic in the story of the Simon family and the Curwen Press, it also owed much to the belated emergence of a market for artists' prints in London. The years from 1957 to 1958 were significant in many other ways. This was the time of John Osborne's play *Look Back in Anger* and the launch of a new realistic and impolite trend in the theatre. As post-war austerity began to give way to consumerism, changes occurred at all social levels, encouraging the Prime Minister, Harold Macmillan, to announce in 1958 that 'most of our people have never had it so good.' Before the war, virtually the only public art exhibitions were at the Royal Academy, and the display of Picasso's *Guernica* and associated etchings at the Whitechapel Gallery in 1939 was more a political than an artistic event. During the war, CEMA began to organise exhibitions, and, as Bryan Robertson recalled, 'it was discovered from overwhelming evidence that a very large proportion of the extremely mixed public attending these modest exhibitions in small hamlets, country towns and villages had never seen an original work of art in their lives before the creation of CEMA. A new public had been found for art, uneducated but interested and often enthusiastic.'[11]

There was a feeling that if modern art were to become democratic, then prints might be the best way to achieve it, but despite the persistent presence of colour reproductions of paintings, there were a few people who believed strongly in the concept of the original print. Brenda Rawnsley's School Prints series in 1947 tried to kick-start a market with long runs of unsigned prints, many of which were pre-war in flavour, and not readily distinguishable from the style and content of the 1937 and 1939 Contemporary Lithographs produced by the Curwen Press. When Rawnsley and two supporters hired an aeroplane in 1947 and flew to Paris with packets of Plastocowell, a relatively new transparent plastic medium for lithography, in order to call on Matisse, Leger, Dufy and Braque with a view to making an international series of School Prints, they were well received by the artists, and achieved the coup of ambushing Picasso on the beach and persuading him to contribute, 'pour les enfants du monde'. The following year, Henry Moore contributed a print to the series. The intended market of schools turned out to be a limited one, and this wonderful, crazy venture was, in the short term, totally uneconomical.[12]

The fashion for all things French persisted. An exhibition at the Victoria and Albert Museum in 1948 to celebrate the 150th anniversary of Alois Senefelder's invention of lithography showed the nascent revival in France. Frances Byng-Stamper and her sister Caroline Lucas, two remarkable women in Lewes, East Sussex 'much addicted to France and vintage claret', started publishing prints during the war. Dissatisfied with printers in London and, after the war, Paris, they bought their own press and operated it themselves. Up to 1956, the Miller's Press produced work by Vanessa Bell and Duncan Grant, who lived locally, and by John Piper and Ceri Richards, as well as a larger body of prints by Robert Colquhoun and Robert MacBryde. The images were mostly drawn on transfer paper.[13] Among London galleries, the only one to show an active interest in commissioning modern prints was the Redfern. Some artists had lithographs printed in Edinburgh by Harley Brothers (a company unconnected with Harleyprint that later merged with Curwen Press).[14] The company had remained in 'the stone age' so far as lithography was concerned, and alongside its main business of printing labels for spirits bottles, the managing director, Johnston Douglas, offered an editioning service to artists. Many major artists, and some emerging young talents, had work printed by Harleys, including John Piper, Michael Ayrton and Terry Frost from England, and the Scottish artists Elizabeth Blackadder, William MacTaggart, Robin Philipson and Anne Redpath. The Harley project overlapped with the early years of the Curwen Studio, but resembled more closely the pre-war studio facilities of the Curwen Press since there was no resident artist-printmaker. The whole company closed in the early 1960s.

The line of the story that led to the foundation of the Curwen Studio did not stem from either the Miller or the Harley enterprises, however dynamic. In 1949, Bryan Robertson, later famous as the Director of the Whitechapel Gallery, was appointed to run the Heffer Gallery in Cambridge, an adjunct of the well known bookshop. Among his activities, he showed contemporary prints, mostly lithographs, published by the Guilde de la Gravure, based in Zurich, which were bought by undergraduates and other university people among whom Robertson became a well-known figure. The artists included Clavé, Manessier, Singier and Campigli. One of Robertson's customers was a student, the Hon. Robert Erskine, who recalled: 'They all sold at a flat rate of three guineas, which seemed a fair enough price to pay to help a chap feel thoroughly in touch with the international swim and to annoy the hearty fellows from the Rugger Club.'[15]

Erskine, a bearded and unconventional member of an ancient Scottish family, was soon in Paris visiting the Atelier Lacourière in Montmartre, where artists and others came and went 'to admire the view, to work on a plate, or to drink the excellent Muscadet which Mme. Lacourière kept in her Income-tax files. It was for me the navel of the world, and with the pungent odour of printing-ink hovering in the atmosphere, the foundation of St George's Gallery Prints became inevitable.'[16] This was opened at 7 Cork Street in 1954 in the back room of an art bookshop with the same name.

Erskine's enthusiasm was unbounded. He did not only want to exhibit, but to publish, and saw an urgent need for a facility in Britain that could match both the flair and the professionalism of the Paris ateliers. 'The first problem was to do with production and presentation. Lithos arrived in the gallery crooked on their paper, punched through with ugly registration-slots, and seldom matching the colours of the accepted proof. Etchings all too often presented an anaemic pallor where the artist had hoped for a rich velvety black ... The faltering argument accounting for these horrid blemishes was that the mount would cover them up, or that people wouldn't notice: but I could only think of the stacks of superbly-printed editions on their crisp deckle-edged paper all neatly interleaved with tissue in the store at Lacourière's.'[17]

The simple answer might have been to send artists to Paris to make prints, and this was done in the early years of his gallery, but British customs imposed a limit of seventy-five for any edition that was considered as art for tax purposes. Above that level, purchase tax was payable. In addition, prints shipped from France had to remain in a bonded warehouse until the artist had visited in order to sign them. These were not conditions compatible with the hard-pressed lives of most working artists. Although Erskine sometimes used Harley Brothers in Edinburgh, the process was too remote from London.

Erskine tried various means to convince the public that prints were authentic works, not merely reproductions. He exhibited prints by Picasso, Hayter and by classic Japanese woodblock artists, and commissioned a suite of eight etchings from Anthony Gross on the theme of Le Boulvé, the French property that Gross visited every summer. Erskine promoted the idea that original prints were an affordable kind of art for fresh-minded people in the straitened economic circumstances of the time. Resale prices of prints exhibited at St George's Gallery rose steeply through the decade, and showed that as an investment prints were financially sound.

Erskine's mission included a thirty-minute film, 'Artist's Proof', made in 1956 with the Shell Film Unit, showing six artists at work on different processes. The writer G.S. Whittet commented that 'Erskine with his dynamic gospelling ... merits the awakening of lethargic British art museums to their responsibilities for a native art that can be collected within their means.'[18] He was able to attract a wide range of artists, known and unknown, to make prints because most of the existing dealers could not be bothered to handle work with such relatively low profit margins. His principal showcase was a regular mixed show called *The Graven Image* staged at the Whitechapel with Bryan Robertson in 1959, and in 1961 at the galleries of the Royal Watercolour Society in the West End. In 1962, Trust House Hotels offered £1,000 in prizes for printmakers, one of which was won by Stanley Jones himself. The Curwen Studio was created in this artistic climate, where an enthusiasm for prints comparable to Paris or Zurich was burgeoning. Erskine's involvement in the print world lasted less than ten years, but Pat Gilmour summarised his invaluable legacy: 'Erskine's contribution lay not so much in what he published – although he put out some excellent prints – but in doing the spade-work in public relations for the idea of editioned originals rather than reproductions. He had a genuine and attractive desire to produce good art cheaply for the general public, writing in an article in *Arts Review*: "... And I mean the Mums and Dads in Pinner and Wigan".'[19] Stanley Jones has described him as 'symbolic of the kind of aristocrat who has aesthetic taste and interest, a patron of schemes and people.'[20]

Erskine may have been less aware that something very similar was starting in the USA, where, as in Britain, there was a very quick development in lithography from almost a standing start, when artist's technical needs, stimulated by work coming from Paris, began to pull apart from the services available locally through the printing trade. The history of artists' lithographic work was similar to that in Britain, although less connected to art schools. In place of Curwen and other commercial presses of the 1930s that looked favourably on artists, printmaking, including lithography, was officially sponsored as part of the Works Progress Administration (WPA) in the New Deal, with the result that there was more of an output of political artists' prints than ever occurred in Britain. The war dispersed most of this effort, although Hayter's Atelier 17, lodged in the New School of Social Science in New York, provided first-hand experience of a collaborative workshop that was lacking in Britain before Curwen.

In the immediate post-war years in America, as June Wayne, the founder of Tamarind Lithography Workshop, recalled, lithography 'was kept alive by artists who printed their own stones and who as "printmakers" were consigned to an aesthetic limbo by critics, curators, and even by fellow artists who knew little of the medium and cared less.'[21] Suddenly, the situation began to change. Two significant workshops were founded in a span of five years differing widely in their motives and modes of operation, but both focused on lithography and, for no self-evident reason, both founded by women, for which the only English precedent was 'The Ladies of Miller's'. Tatyana Grosman, a Russian-born émigré, was at least as eccentric as them. She started her Universal Limited Art Editions in 1959 as a way of making a living after her husband had a heart attack. It operated from her rural home at West Islip, Long Island, where the length of an edition run was generally determined by the time of sunset on the day of printing, and generous meals were enjoyed in the workshop, which took over the house. Her list of artists was astonishing, starting early on with Larry Rivers, Jasper Johns, Robert Rauschenberg, Robert Motherwell and Sam Francis. In 1970, Pat Gilmour quoted the French magazine *L'Oeuil* on Grosman's work with Jasper Johns: 'Lithography had not been so well served since Odilon Redon'. 'The stone age has certainly had a revival', she added.[22]

In 1960, June Wayne, an artist with several years experience of lithography in the USA and in Paris, opened Tamarind in Los Angeles as a non-profit venture 'To Restore the Art of the Lithograph in the United States'. It was supported by the Ford Foundation, and operated non-commerically, in Wayne's words, as 'other-directed.' There were thus major workshops on each coast in the 1960s, with some mutual suspicion and resentment. Both workshops operated with master-printers on the French model (initially Bob

Blackburn at ULAE and Garo Antreasian at Tamarind), who were not themselves the owners of the enterprise. This mirrored Stanley Jones's role at the Curwen Studio, although the latter's business structure, initially as part of a larger company, and then as an independent limited company, was different.

What is especially revealing about the American parallels, however, is their relationship to developing trends in the avant-garde, especially the emergence in the post-war period of New York and, to a lesser extent London, as major artistic centres independent of Paris. Around 1958, the dominant mode was Abstract Expressionism, with its focus on the authentic mark of the artist, on the use of colour and on the autonomy of the process and materials. For these purposes, lithography, as Picasso had begun to demonstrate, was superior to other printmaking techniques in terms of freedom of personal expression. In this respect, printmaking and artistic developments evolved in parallel in an unprecedented way, and the medium of lithography, for a short period, became central to artistic concerns. There was a joke that while in the early 1950s you could meet painters on the train from Long Island to New York on their way to visit their analyst, by the end of the decade they would be going to have a session with their lithographic printer.

Lithography was seen as a form of therapy in itself. An article on 'American Artist-Printmakers' in 1959 commented on the relationship between the return to craft-based printmaking and the wider world of DIY and home craftsmanship: 'At a time when the camera seems to have achieved perfection in photo-mechanical reproduction, with photo-engravers turning out magnificent plates for gigantic presses to churn out, with absolute precision, thousands of colour reproductions in mere minutes, there is also a powerful revival of the slow autographic methods, the lithograph, the wood cut, the etching and engraving – and the more recent silkscreen.'[23] As Erskine himself wrote in 1959, 'most artists who make both prints and paintings use their two media against one another almost therapeutically: for the current idiom in visual art has subordinated craft to philosophy to such an extent that it offers little satisfaction to a person who needs something to bite on, some obstacles to overcome in the course of working, which the struggle with the processes of printmaking supplies.'[24]

St Ives

Robert Erskine, fearing perhaps that Stanley Jones, having been brought from Paris to run an enterprise that did not yet exist, might slip back there, proposed to the Simons that the Curwen Studio should make a start immediately, even though its intended premises in Plaistow would take six months to get ready. He arranged for a press to be transported to St Ives and set up in the middle of what was, at the time, Britain's most famous artistic colony. The Cornish fishing town was first occupied by Edwardian artists such as Stanhope Forbes, and from the 1920s was a centre for artist-craftsmen including Bernard Leach and the Creseyde silk-printing workshops managed

55
Peter Lanyon,
The Returned Seaman,
1973, posthumous
lithographic version
of 1949 relief print
for Curwen's
Penwith Portfolio

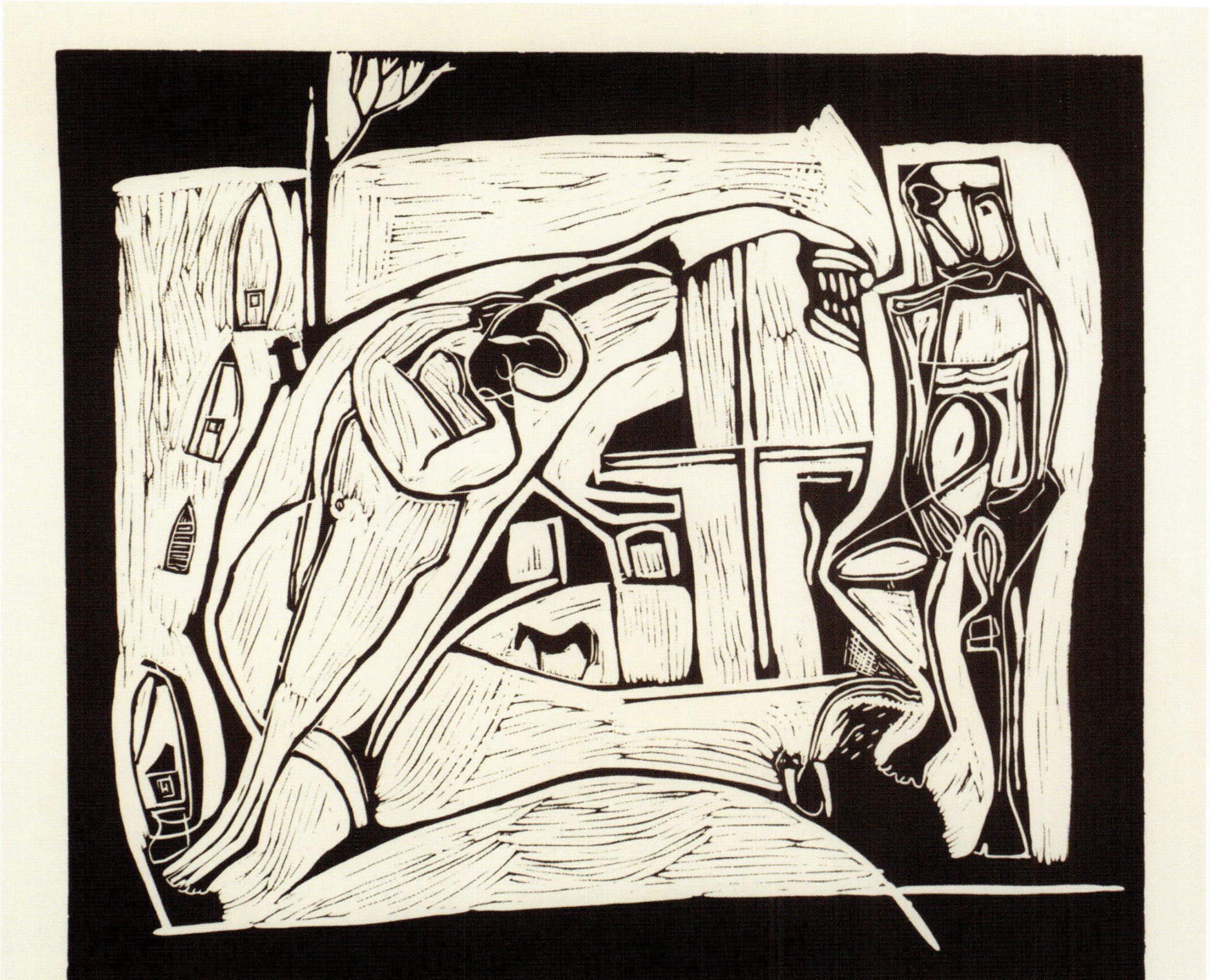

56
Patrick Heron, *Red and Yellow Image*, 1958

57
Sandra Blow, *Abstract Landscape*, 1958

by Tom Heron. The town drew Ben Nicholson and Barbara Hepworth, with their children, at the beginning of the war, when they began their residency as guests of the critic Adrian Stokes and his artist wife, Margaret Mellis. Hepworth had a friendship with Herbert Simon going back to the 1930s, and this may have helped to win his support for the operation.[25]

Nicholson and Hepworth worked to stimulate the Penwith Society of Arts as more artists of a younger generation gathered in the congenial environment, including some with local connections, such as Peter Lanyon (fig.55) and Patrick Heron (fig.56), who had grown up there, along with Terry Frost, who originally came as a sculpture assistant to Hepworth. In the early 1950s, there was no equivalent grouping of major progressive talent even in London, where the 'Kitchen Sink School' of realist painters was dominant.

Erskine arranged to rent premises in Fore Street from local artists Bruce Taylor, a sculptor, and his wife Jenny. Early in 1958, equipment, including a Winstone press, was conveyed on a couple of lorries. There was a tang of salt when the direct printing press was fitted with an electric motor and drive belt by a firm of boat engineers based in Newlyn. Erskine came down with his 'Artist's Proof' film to host an opening evening, gathering most of the St Ives artists into the Taylors' sitting room, several of whom had ceased to be on speaking terms for a number of years previously. Peter Lanyon, for example, came to resent the presence of non-native artists in Cornwall and would 'cut' Barbara Hepworth, who had helped him in the past,

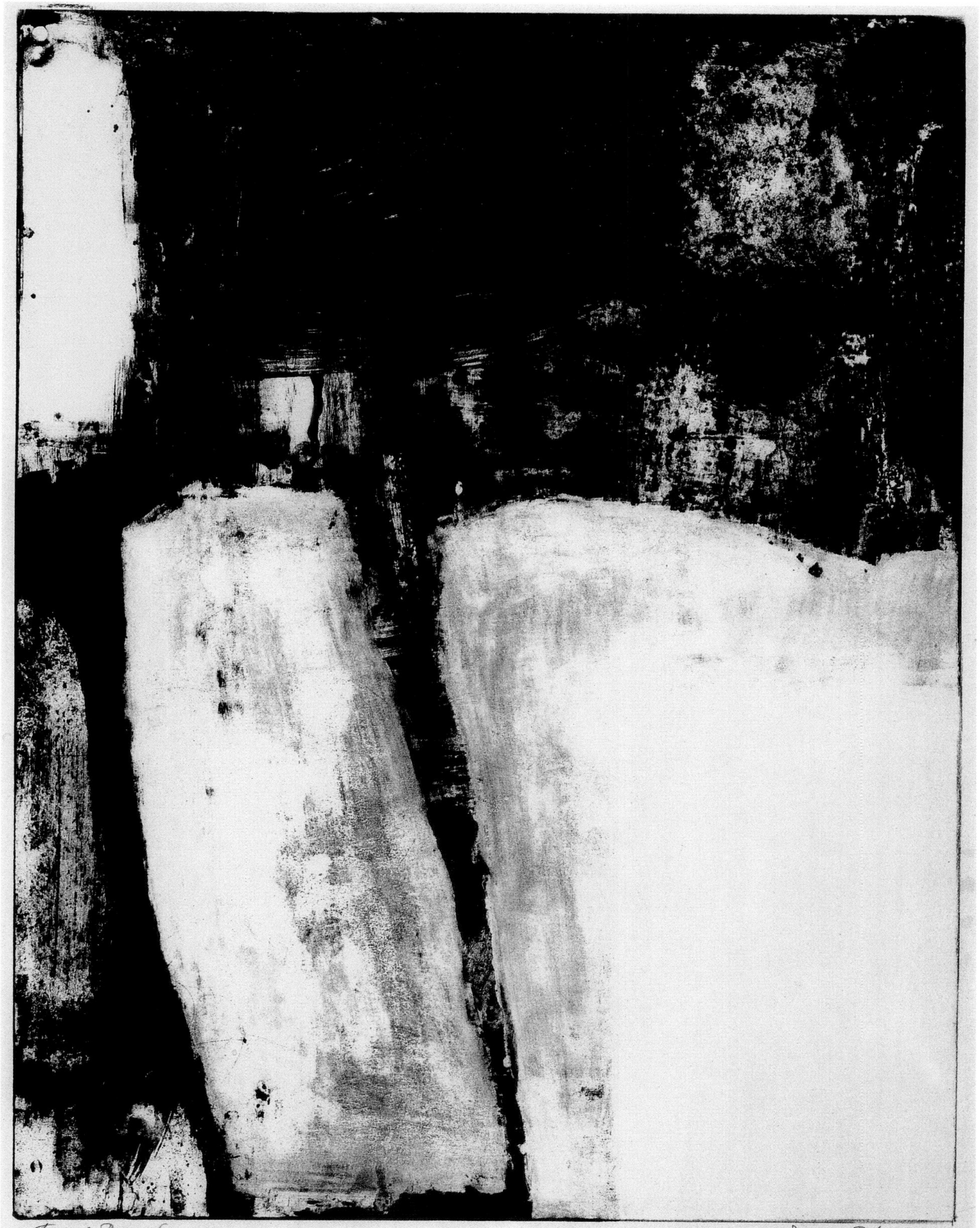
Trial Proof

58
Entrance to the Curwen Studio at St Mary's Road, Plaistow, 1959. Peter Baer, Stanley Jones and David Zaig

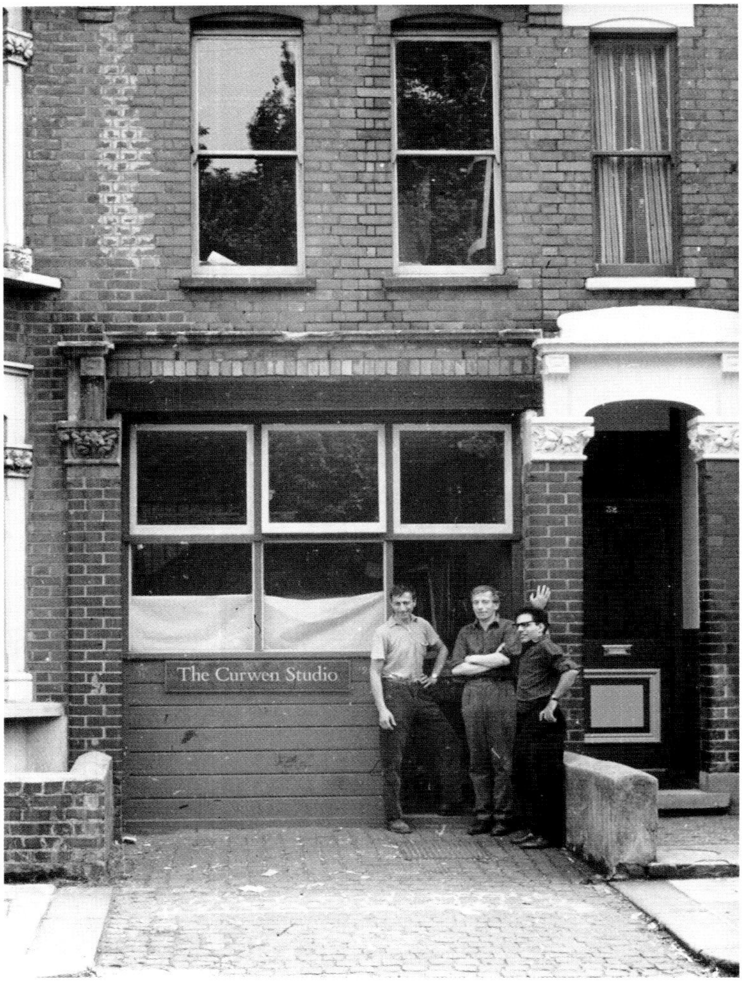

in the street. Stanley Jones, so recently immersed in a more liberal atmosphere in Paris, learned 'to be very diplomatic and careful', a skill necessary at all times in a printing studio, and one he has demonstrated for a lifetime.

The studio in St Ives lasted, as intended, only so long as it took to prepare a new building in Plaistow. It was, in Jones's view, a lesson in how not to manage a studio, since there was no proper administration and artists could not always be depended on to turn up. Erskine paid Jones's salary 'when he remembered'. However, a range of artists created prints, some for Erskine as publisher, some independently. They included Patrick Heron, Bryan Winter, John Wells, Alex McKenzie, Terry Frost, Peter Lanyon and Sandra Blow (fig.57). Some went on to work in the Curwen Studio during the time it was based in London, or even, in Heron's case, after its move to Cambridge in 1989. Hepworth's connection with Herbert Simon and her pleasure at working with Stanley Jones led her to undertake several further major lithographic editions with him. Prints were taken to proof stage at St Ives, and editions were printed at Plaistow, following Jones's return in November 1958 (fig.59).

St Mary's Road, Plaistow

St Ives and Plaistow were both working environments, but they had little else in common. St Mary's Road ran down the side of the main works site of the Curwen Press, and the new building was a converted stable, only a few steps away from the parent organisation, but crucially under a different roof and relatively out of sight

59
Stanley Jones, *Porthmeor*,
1959

60
Ceri Richards,
Le Poisson d'Or from
The Hammerklavier Suite with Variations, 1959

(fig.58). Having been fully engaged at St Ives, Stanley Jones only saw the conversion when it was complete, but appreciated the scale of the press room and the separate well-lit space for artists to work in. The working arrangement was that images would be prepared for printing in the Studio up to proof stage, and then the plates would be transferred to the litho shop of the Press for editioning on faster-running machines, although at this stage the printing was always direct, rather than offset, with the consequence that a thicker film of ink could be maintained. Jones recruited assistants who, like himself, were artists rather than trade printers, many of whom came from the Slade or Camberwell. Peter Baer was one who stayed longer than most.

The Curwen Studio operated in Plaistow between late 1958 and 1964, when it moved into central London and acquired a marketing arm in the form of the Curwen Gallery.

It was the policy of the Curwen Studio to make its facilities available to any artist who requested them. It did not have sufficient financial security to allow a more selective approach. Since the overheads of premises and staff time were relatively high, any print undertaken represented a considerable financial outlay on the part of a publisher or artist, so normally they would be sure of their market before proceeding.

It is not unreasonable to focus on the more famous artists that have made prints at Curwen down the years, especially when printmaking was a significant aspect of their work as a whole. There were, however, few artist-printmakers who worked exclusively in lithography, and probably none whose print *oeuvre* can be adequately described solely in terms of their work at Curwen. This limitation (if such it be) suggests that, short of a complete logging of all Studio activity, revealing through this would be, it is more informative to examine the Studio's most significant achievements in the context of its less well-known output. The mixture of work is part of the story, and this changed and developed through the years.

Anti-academicians: Artists at Curwen 1958–65

In 1961, a Swedish critic, Olle Lundgren, described a group of post-war English artists as 'anti-academicians', whose work, 'while showing some influence from American Abstract Expressionism, is marked by a thoroughly English lyricism, positively "anti-American" in its lack of vehemence.'[26] The label is appropriate for many of the artists who worked at the Curwen Studio in its first ten years (although for some, such as Henry Moore, the association lasted well into the 1970s). These were artists with strong affinities to the School of Paris, and, as Lundgren wrote, less immediately connected to New York, although no absolute distinctions can be made. Lithography, with its tactile and physical qualities, served the British and Americans equally well, but without the technical professionalism and administrative flexibility of the Curwen Studio it is unlikely that lithography could have played such a role in this moment of renaissance in the London art world.

Ceri Richards was among the artists who

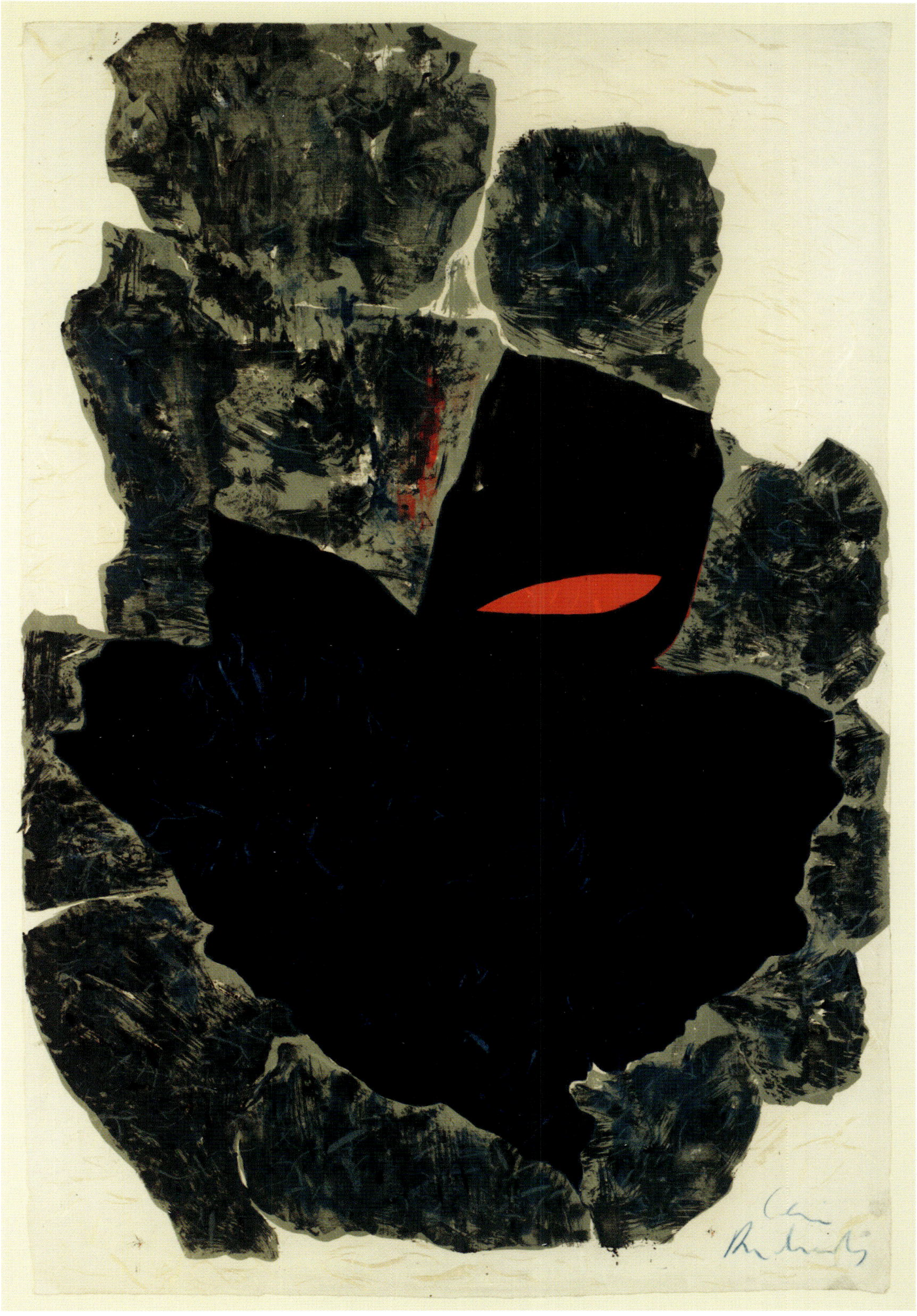

61
Ceri Richards, *La Cathédrale Engloutie* from *The Hammerklavier Suite with Variations*, 1959

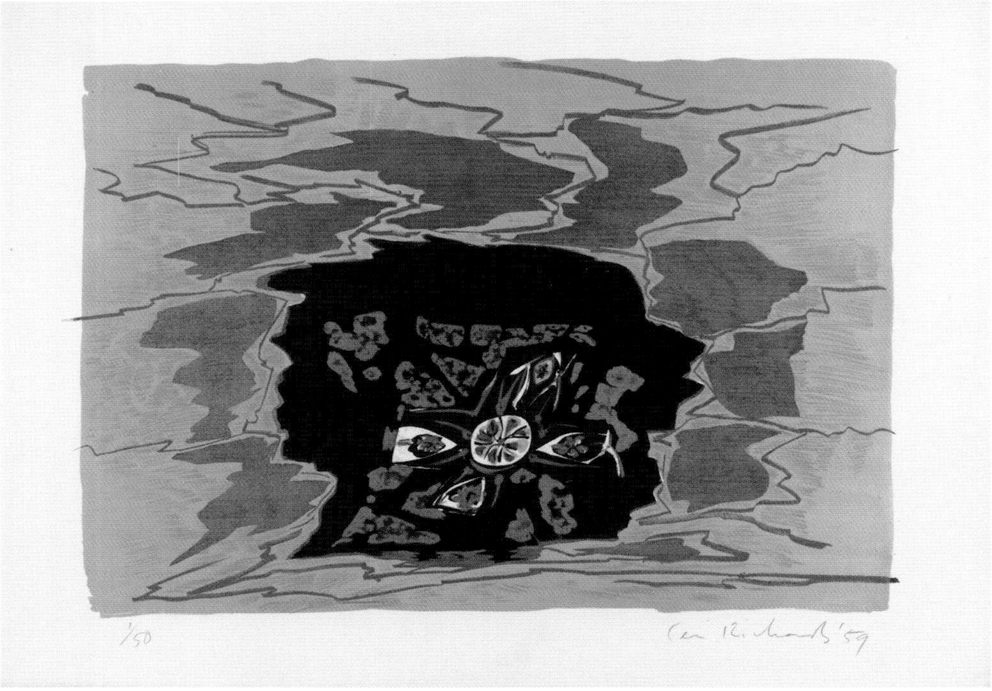

came to the Studio in the first year, finding new artistic possibilities through drawing and brushwork, and through the attention to inking and printing, all made possible by Stanley Jones's increased knowledge and experience since they had worked together at the Slade. This is particularly noticeable when one looks in sequence at Richards's prints before and after the setting up of the Studio. *The Hammerklavier Suite with Variations*, 1959, was a publishing commission from Robert Erskine, who followed Ambrose Vollard and other French publishers in commissioning 'suites' of prints from a single artist, for which Richards's musical theme was apposite. The depth of colour in these images shows up the relative poverty of his earlier efforts. In addition, the paper became a consideration in itself. Richards chose a Japanese paper with prominent strands of straw on the surface of the sheet, tinted a pale yellow and reflecting the light. The reflective quality still worked with a film of ink on top, so that a shimmer came into broad areas of deep brown and blue in *Le Poisson d'Or* (fig.60), one of the prints inspired by the piano music of Claude Debussy, giving the suggestion of flashing fish under water. The work with litho ink shows that thumbprints were among the methods of application. This print has gained notoriety because pieces of straw frequently came away during the printing process, and had to be stuck back by hand, evidence, if no other were needed, that serious experimental printmaking was no longer possible in a world of timesheets and tight budgets.

Three of the set were on the theme of *La Cathédrale Engloutie*, which Richards had been exploring in paintings over many years. It is the title of one of Debussy's *Preludes*, evoking the lost town of Dunwich in Suffolk, whose bells may supposedly be heard from beneath the waves on still days. The images are far from literal. The third in the series (fig.61) suggests looking down

62
Ceri Richards, *And Death Shall Have No Dominion* from *Twelve Lithographs for Six Poems by Dylan Thomas*, 1965

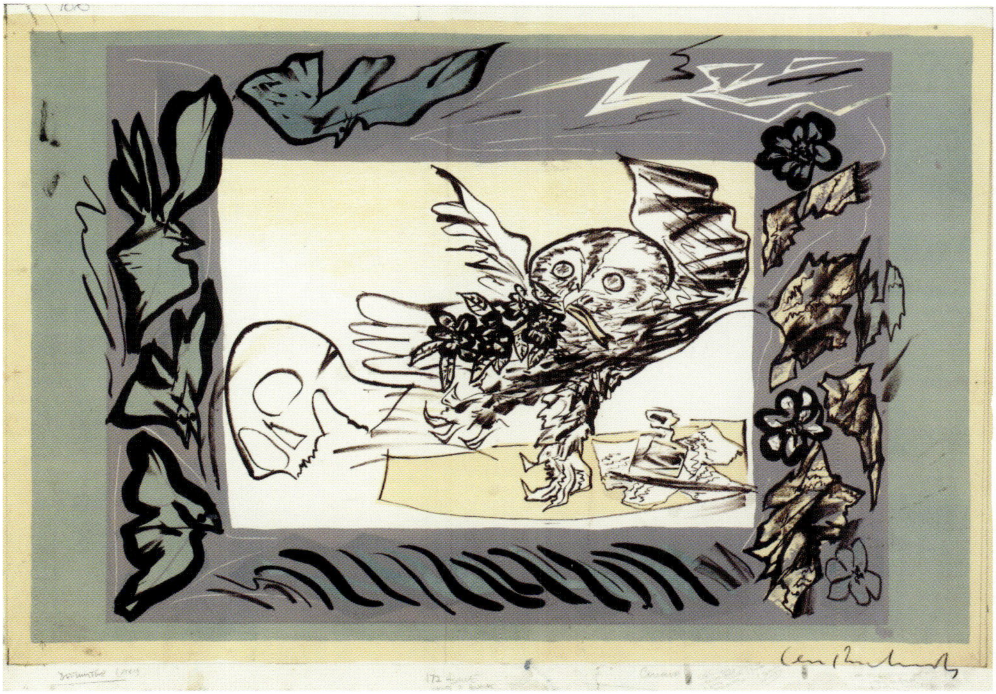

from the surface of water, with a rippling effect indicated in the overlaid tones of grey in the background. The Italian poet Roberto Sanesi, who compiled the catalogue of Richards's graphic work, saw this group of prints as 'the first finalised realisations of his visual researches into the various possible associations, both within the legend itself and its correspondences with the prevailing tendency of the Welsh sensibility towards mystical metamorphosis – all of which are blended with his own personal understanding as a painter of the perennial flux of procreation, death and resurrection.'[27] These prints make rich use of colour overlays, not the tight-fitting registration in pursuit of an illustrational effect as practised by Ravilious or Freedman, but a more painterly and experimental approach in tune with the post-war spirit. Each colour would be individually mixed, and during the proofing process it could be adjusted to achieve the desired cumulative effect. The careful research into suitable inks and how to use them was a further factor that gave the Curwen Studio an advantage over commercial printers. Stanley Jones recalled how Richards liked to keep changing his mind about his prints during the proofing stages, coming in with new ideas for colours and drawing out the process leading up to the final image.

The title print of the Richards's *Hammerklavier Suite*, a bold, Braque-like rendition of a piano and its keyboard, also on Japanese straw paper, won first prize in the International Print Exhibition at Llubjana in 1959, giving the Studio a trophy in its first year of existence. Six years later Richards made another set of prints, for Marlborough Gallery, newly established as the premier dealer in the more established of the modern British artists. This was based on the poems of Dylan Thomas (fig.62) who, like Richards, was born in Swansea. He died in 1954 at the age of forty. For Mel Gooding, these prints demonstrate

63
Robert Colquhoun,
Two Horsemen, 1960

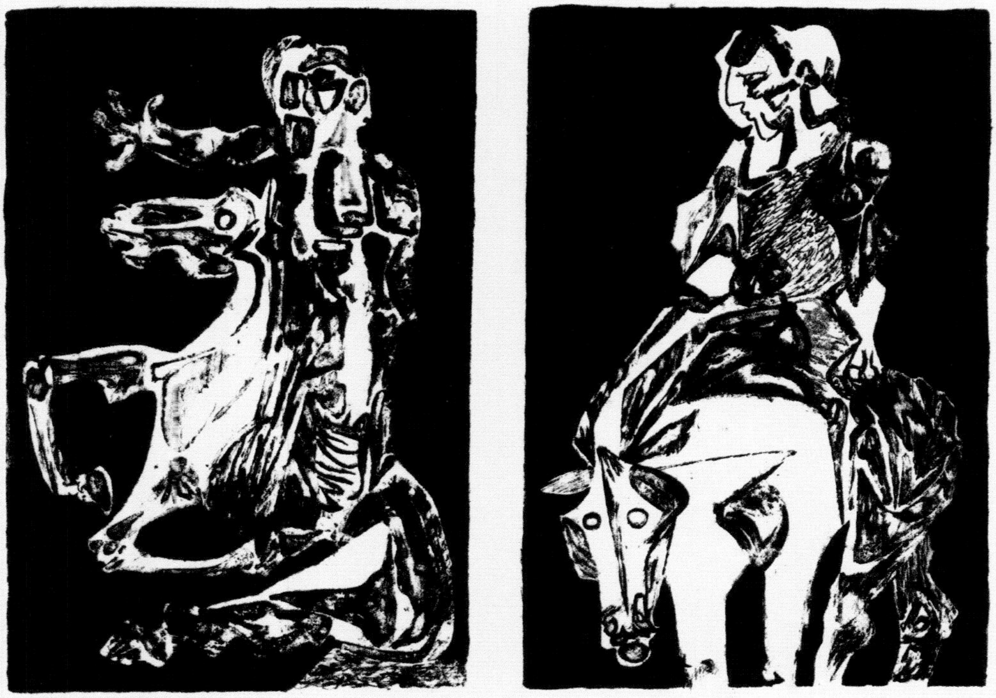

64
William Scott, *Barra*,
1962

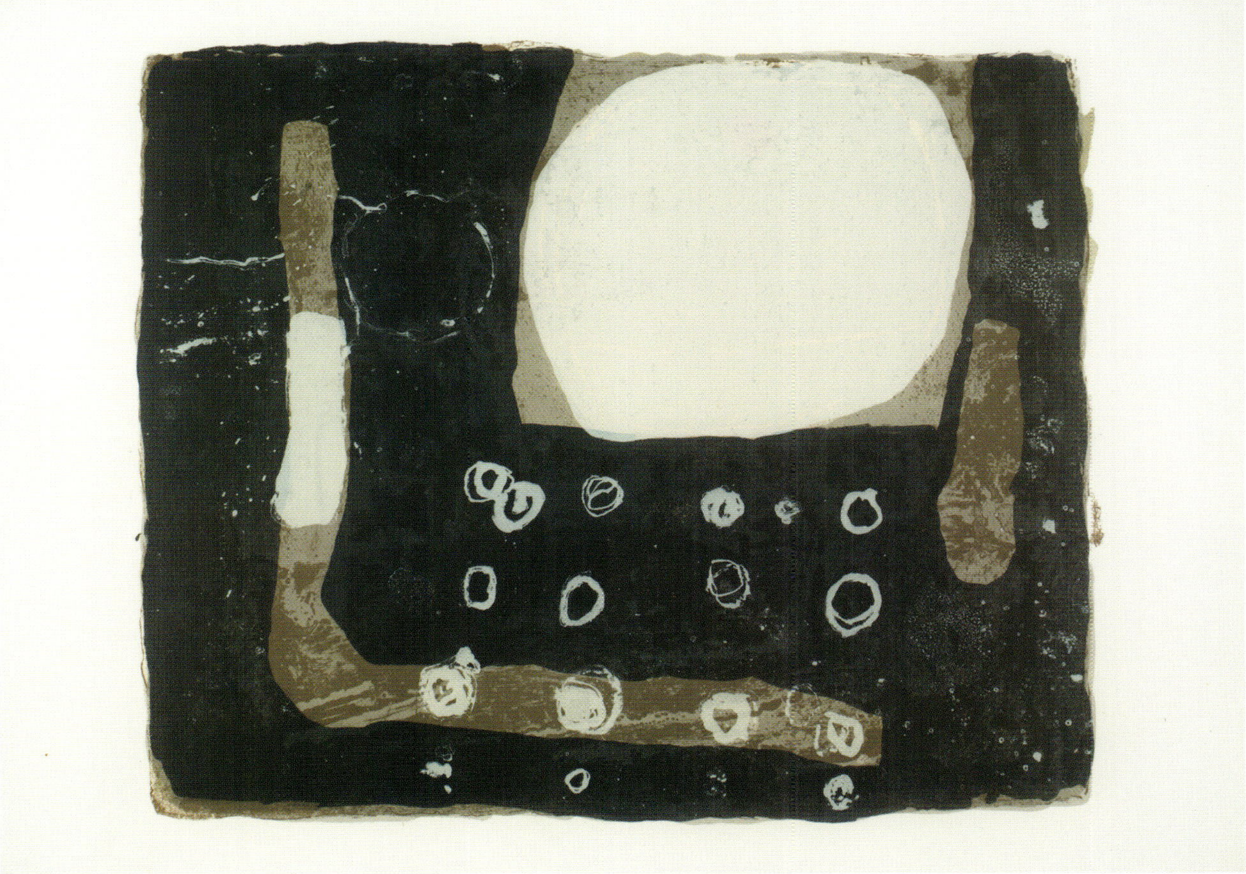

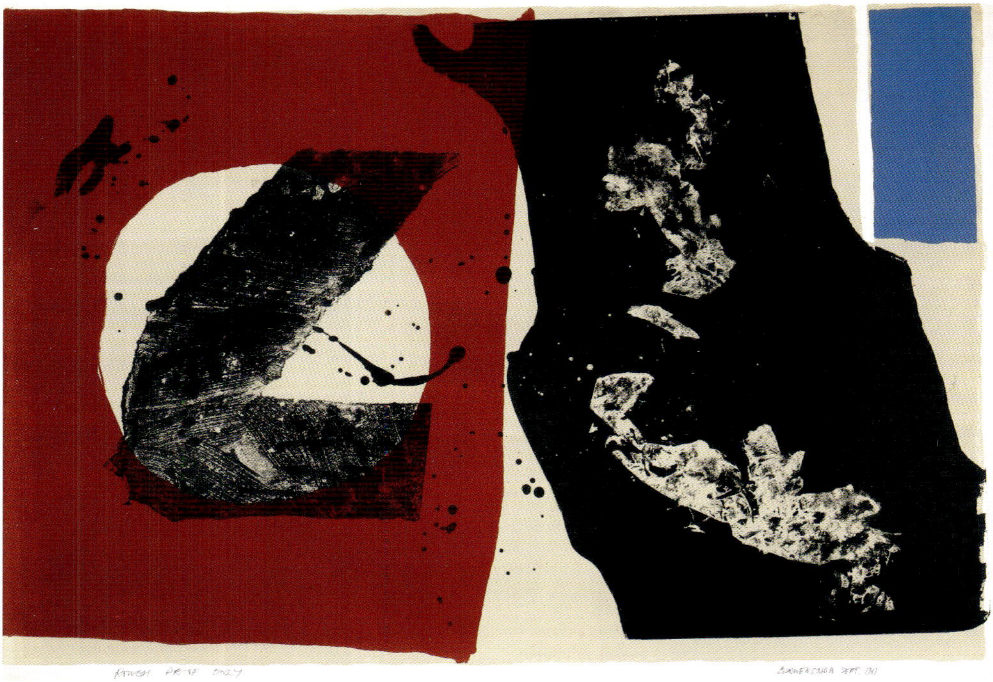

65
Alan Davie, *Sleep my Angel*, 1961–2

66
Prunella Clough, *Wall and Scrap*, 1962

that Richards 'had come to see lithography as a medium in which he could express his deepest imaginative insights.'[28] While reminiscent in some respects of the neo-romanticism of the 1940s, these works, like the poems on which they are based, transcend the histrionic limitations of much work that falls in that category and reach a more universal level of meaning.

'The two Roberts' (Robert Colquhoun and Robert MacBryde), an inseparable couple of artists since their first encounter at Glasgow School of Art in 1933, were associated with neo-romanticism, having studied in Paris before the war before being lifted out of poverty and despair in wartime Scotland by Peter Watson, the backer of *Horizon* magazine, and introduced to artists such as Graham Sutherland, John Craxton and the young Lucian Freud. Colquhoun experimented with monoprinting in the 1940s, a rare use of the medium at such an early date. Both artists made prints for the Miller's Press, and were embraced by the sisters in Lewes, who gave them accommodation and enjoyed drinking with them. When Robert Erskine commissioned them he made the mistake of paying in advance, so that Stanley had to go and find them in a Soho pub, and lost a day's work. They settled to work, in 1960 making two prints each in one or two colours, when many of their supporters believed they were no longer capable of doing good work. Colquhoun's *Two Horsemen* (fig.63), one of two prints, divides the horizontal sheet into a pair of images, each black-and-white outline echoing the shape of the other. MacBryde made three prints during this time. After Colquhoun's death in 1962, MacBryde only lived a further four years.

William Scott (fig.64), one of the artists included in the original coining of 'anti-academicians', worked at the Studio from 1960 onwards, creating a series of prints commissioned by Robert Erskine named after Scottish islands. They were not in any sense representational, and his typical large

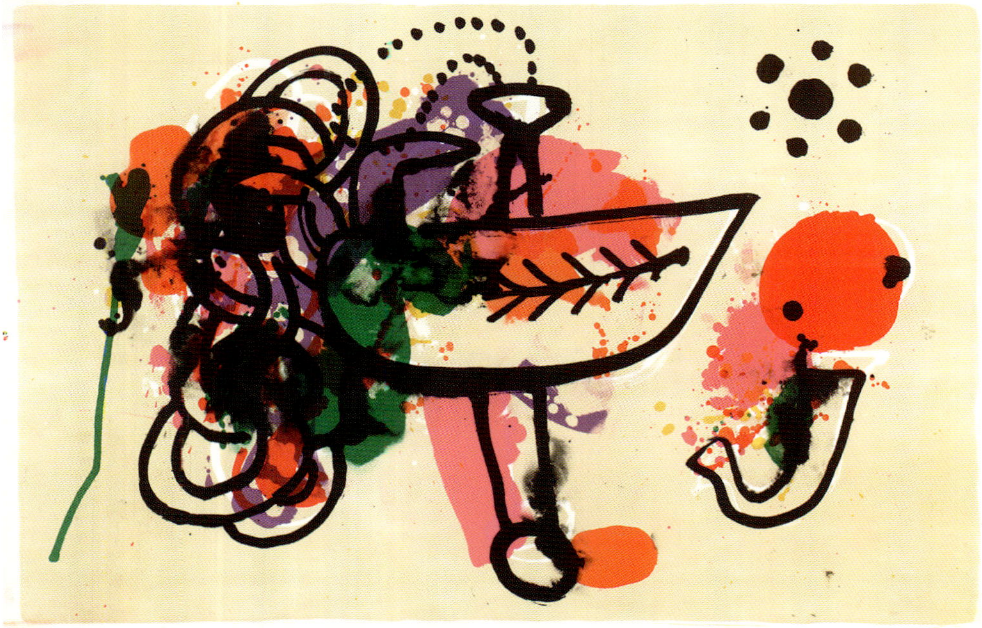

shapes lent themselves to careful colour mixing and solid direct printing from stone. As Stanley Jones wrote in 1988: 'Attractions such as the richness of colour, over-printing, textural variety and linear possibilities provided him with constant challenges. At the proofing stage, he was able to make variations on his ideas by altering colours and their order of printing.'[29]

Alan Davie's approach to painting drew deeper than most on the subconscious, and he carried this into his printmaking, starting with a series of monotypes made in Paris in 1948. The flexibility and spontaneity of the monotype process is normally hard to translate into lithography, which relies on a degree of planning even if made to appear accidental, but Davie came close to doing so. By 1960, the characteristic elements of his painting were in place, including large gestural stokes of paint defining major elements, complemented by an obbligato of minor events, the whole consciously shamanistic in its symbolism, as in the Tate's *Entrance to a Red Temple*, 1960. These images were well adapted for printmaking, yet Davie's first print at Curwen, *Sleep my Angel*, 1961–2 (fig.65), is not such a signature work, effective though its bold contrasts in three colours are. The three separate versions of *Celtic Dreamboat*, 1965 (figs.67–9), a more typical work, were achieved by Davie making a series of stones that were each proofed in a range of colours before moving on to the next part of the image. As Pat Gilmour commented, the old litho craftsmen would have found this hair-raising.[30]

This was a period when several Scottish artists, Davie among them, developed a typically exuberant and free manner of working. A younger representative was Elizabeth Blackadder. She made three lithographs with Harley Brothers, who were conveniently located for her studio in Edinburgh. When Robert Erskine saw these prints he commissioned Blackadder to make more at Curwen on the theme of

67
Alan Davie,
Celtic Dreamboat,
1965

68
Alan Davie,
Celtic Dreamboat,
1965

69
Alan Davie,
Celtic Dreamboat,
1965

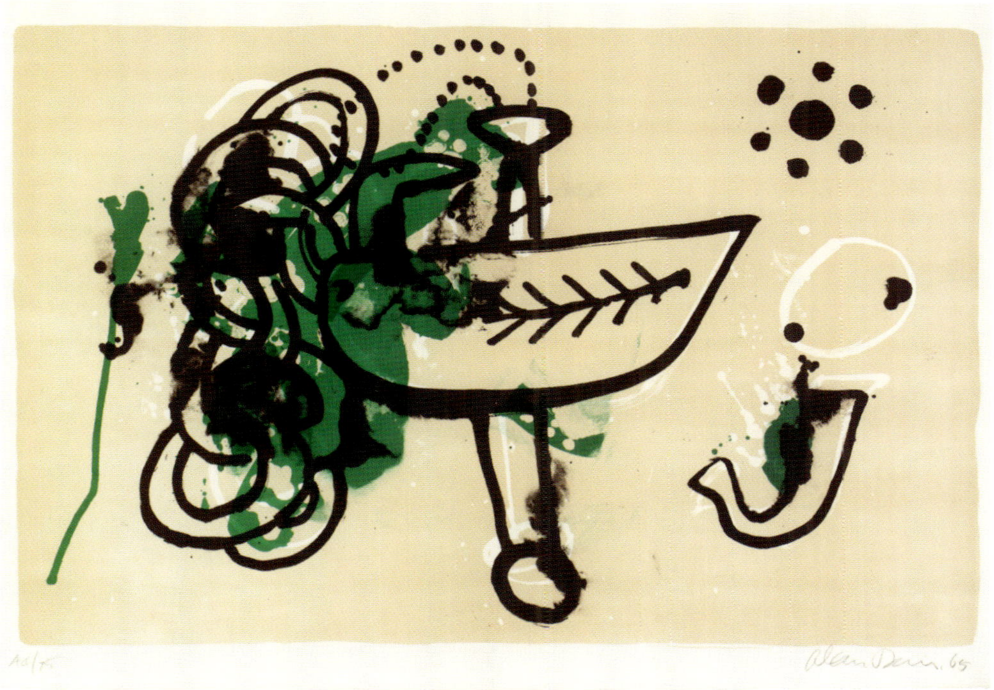

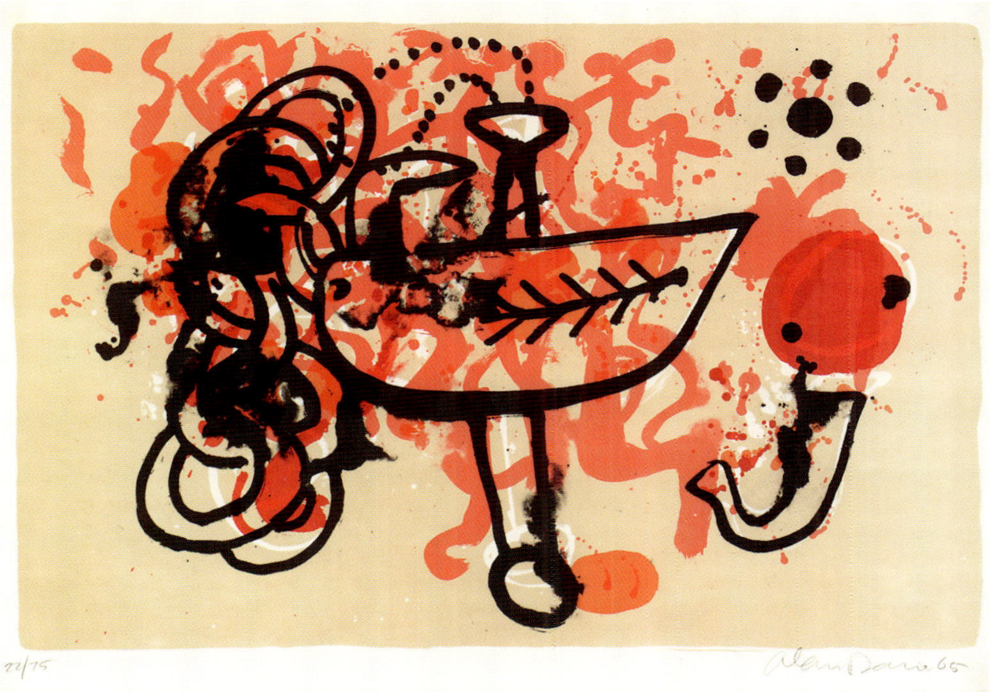

70
Elizabeth Blackadder,
Dark Hill, Fifeshire, 1960

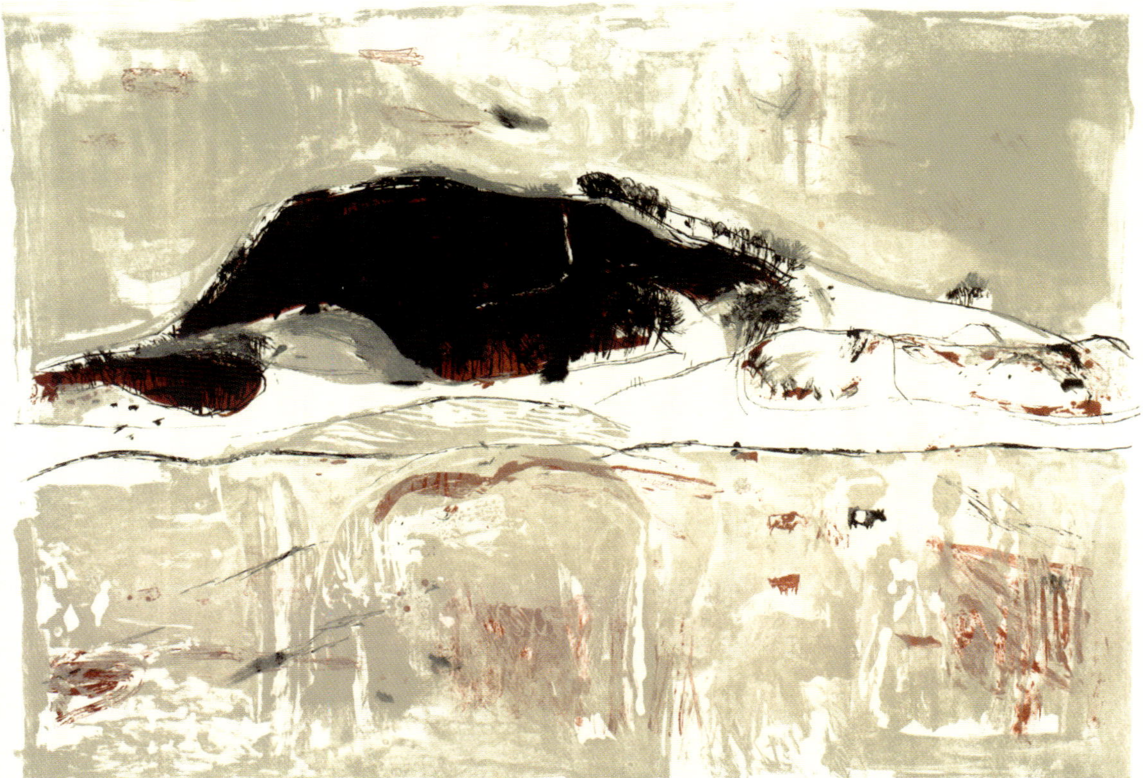

71
Elizabeth Blackadder,
Staithes, 1962

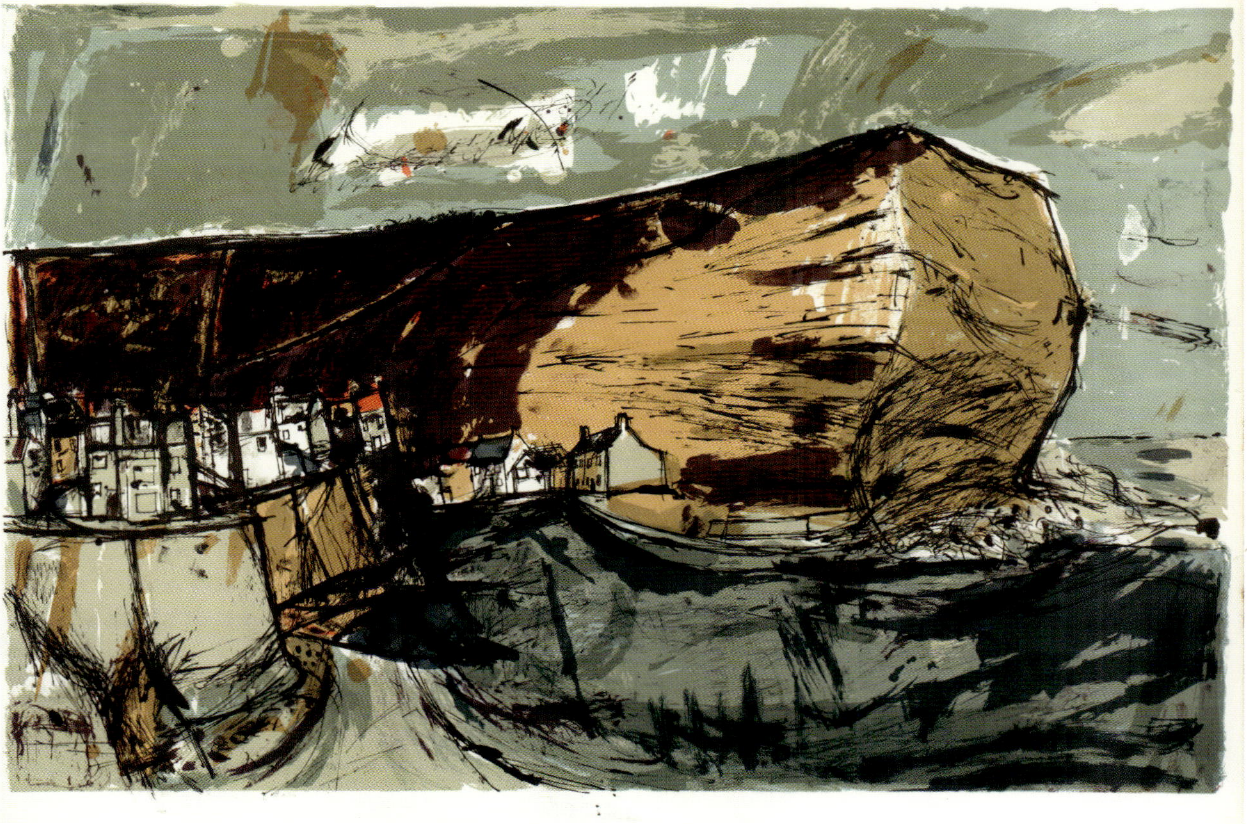

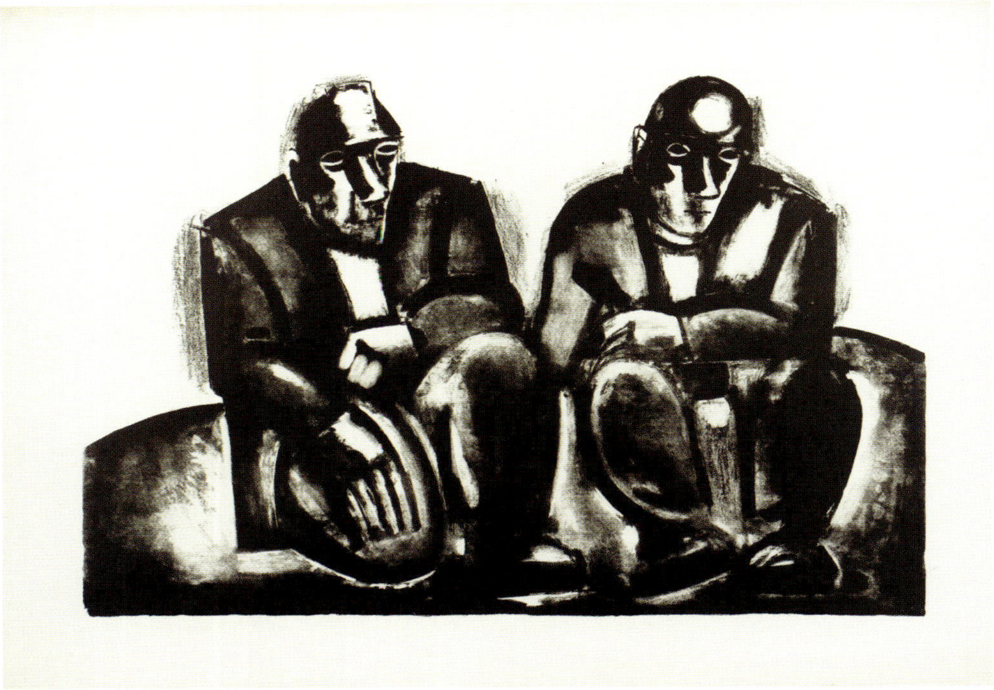

72
Josef Herman,
Two Miners, 1961

the Fife landscape. At this time the Post Office was reviving its pre-war tradition of patronage by commissioning topographical prints to hang in the austere post office interiors, with the message 'Please use the correct address'. Blackadder's *Staithes* (fig.71), proofed at Curwen before being transferred for long-run production, was among these – a late echo of the 1930s ideal of autolithography for the masses before the limited edition print and the commercial poster parted company forever. Stanley Jones commented on her work: 'There was a freshness and directness in the approach of some of the Scottish artists then – Alan Davie was the prime example, also William Scott – and Elizabeth took that approach too. The colour separations were not aligned tightly to the key drawing, and she became progressively more painterly. If you look at the use of semi-opaque colour in *Dark Hill, Fifeshire*, for example, you see how she made it hold everything together, like a piece of painting or gouache work.'[31]

One artist whom Jones remembers with special affection was the Polish-born Josef Herman (figs.72–3), whose reputation was built on his atmospheric drawings of Welsh miners, captured in prints such as *Two Miners*, 1961. The print was commissioned by St George's Gallery and recalls the vision he had of miners returning from work against a copper-coloured sky in the village of Ystradgynlais in Breconshire. Herman worked at Curwen steadily through the early 1960s and returned for a further spell in the mid-1970s until his death in 2000.

John Piper

In December 1958, Herbert Simon wrote to John Piper: 'We have just set up a lithographic studio for expert proofing of hand drawn work. It is an engaging institution and I hope you will visit one day.'[32] Piper's close links with Curwen in the pre-war years had set him up as an artist well known to the public not only on account of his architectural subject-matter,

73
Josef Herman,
Man Leaning on a Pick Axe, 1967

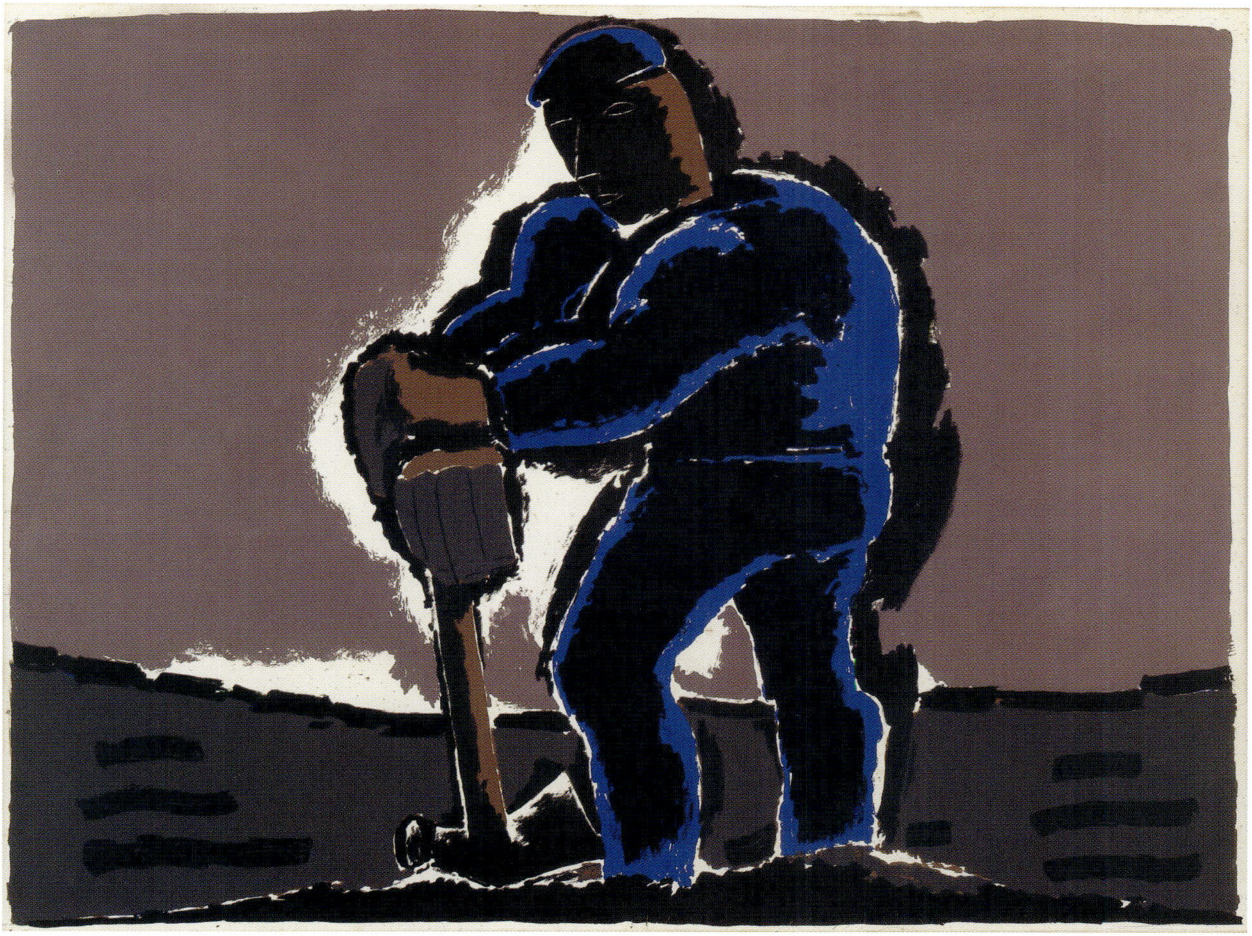

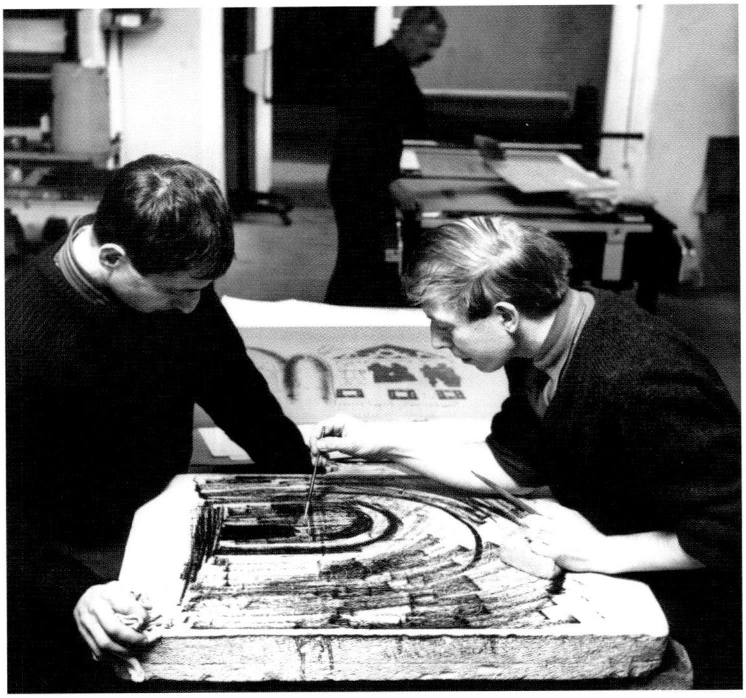

74
Peter Baer and Stanley Jones working on John Piper's *Malmesbury, Wiltshire: The South Porch*, from *A Retrospect of Churches*, 1964

75
John Piper, *San Marco, Venice*, 1961

but in terms of his almost Arts-and-Crafts belief in the value of commissioned work, whether for mosaics and murals in buildings, stained glass, or the more commonplace field of book jackets and illustration. His interest in print processes went back to his time at the Royal College (1927–30) when he studied lithography with the stained-glass tutor Francis Spear. As Anthony West related, 'Spear taught Piper and his other students that the only purpose of teaching them the conventional lithographic technique was to enable them to bash it as soon as they had mastered it.'[33] Such a background was a cause of frustration in 'the undiscoverable world of commercial printing', as Piper described it in 1949, 'with the promise of its litho and gravure trial-proofs and block-makers' pulls, and the dreary disappointment of the uncontrollable run.'[34] Piper reckoned that only three printers in England were capable of printing artists' work properly (Curwen, Cowell's and Baynard, one assumes). When commissioned by Robert Erskine in 1953, his work was printed by Mourlot in Paris, but he was made to undergo the required penance of signing the edition in a bonded warehouse once it had crossed the channel.

In Stanley Jones he found, as so many other artists have done, the ideal collaborator, and their work together was among the most adventurous from a technical point of view of any done there. The sense of an adventurous exploration of process can be seen building up through his first four or five prints at Curwen Studio, reaching an early peak in Piper's 1961 print *San Marco, Venice* (fig.75). It relies on unusually bold texture, largely produced by free spattered work in gouache over a layer of wash drawing, originally done on very thin transfer paper. This was a technique developed by Picasso that Piper wanted to emulate. The effect is that the gouache acts as a resist, and by stopping out the lithographic ink beneath it, will leave white areas on the print. A straw-coloured yellow

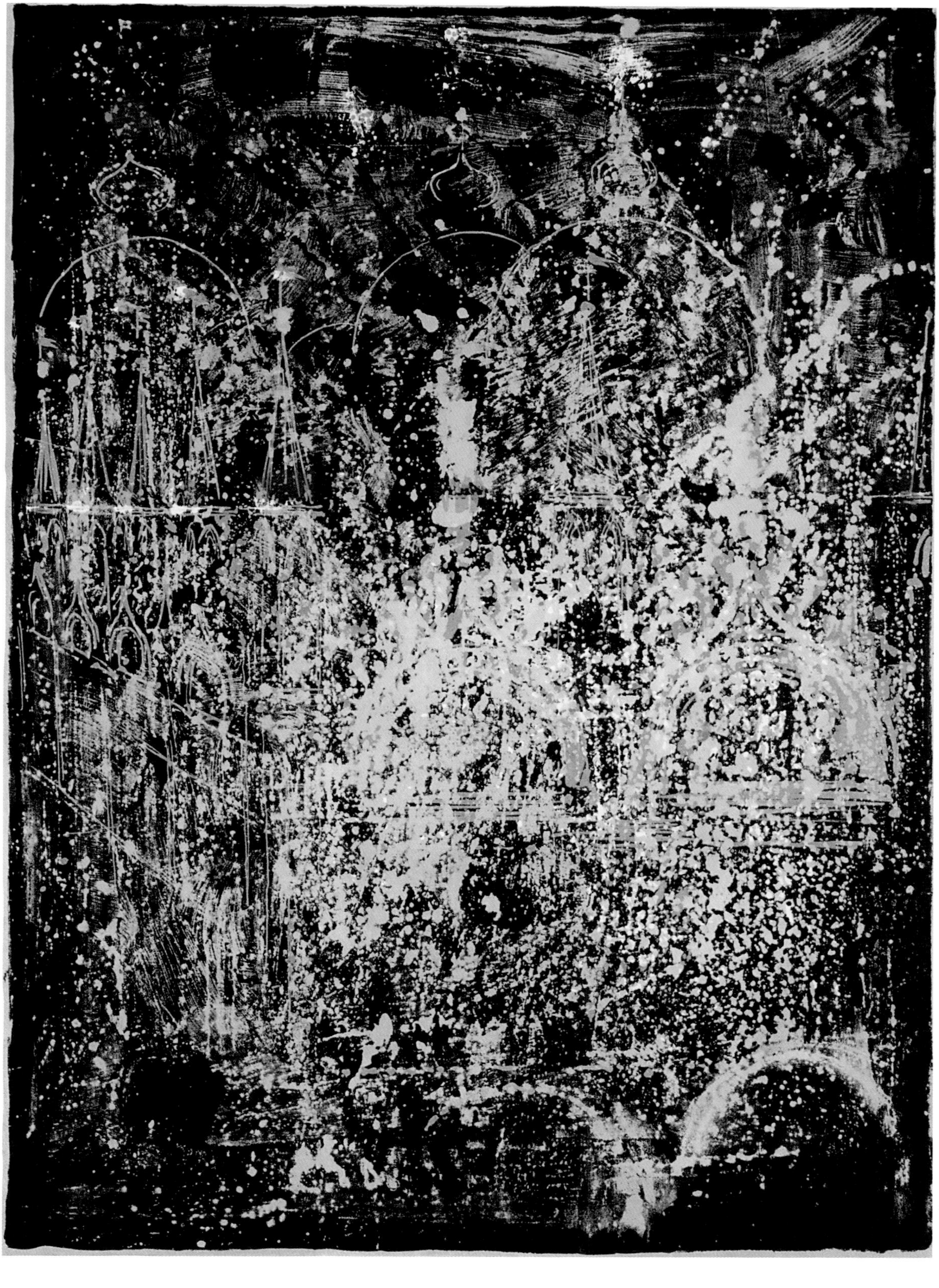

was printed as a base colour, with the black plate, including the traces of the gouache highlights, printed on top, the latter recreating the outlines of the building, especially its wave-like crestings of white marble. It is something unusual in Piper's work, borrowing the visual language of Jackson Pollock to convey the sensibility of John Ruskin about the relationship of stone and water.

In the autumn of 1963, Piper began work on a portfolio, *A Retrospect of Churches*, commissioned by Marlborough Fine Art, and comprising twenty-four lithographs, with a text by his friend the poet and architectural writer John Betjeman (fig.74). The work was begun at Plaistow, and was still in progress when the Curwen Studio moved to the West End of London in 1964. The prints are large, and in some cases use bright colours, although most are sparing in the number of colours used together, and none attempts to reproduce the qualities of a painting. In many respects they represent a series of trials of different technical qualities of the medium, as well as different ways of depicting buildings. Piper, then aged sixty, recapitulated past moments in his own work, and seems to have reflected on some aspects of the contemporary art scene. The juxtaposition of flat colour shapes with black line is especially suggestive of his stained glass work, which had developed rapidly since the late 1950s, culminating in Coventry Cathedral in 1962. Of the church prints, however, none is more innovative than *Llangoffan, Pembrokeshire: The Baptist Chapel* (fig.76), a typical Piper subject.

The 1964 print was one of the first in England or America to combine a photographic image with other more strictly 'autographic' methods, in this case frottage in addition to more conventional drawing. While Piper had himself been an eager photographer since boyhood, and had frequently published photographs to illustrate his own writings and those of others, he had not integrated them into 'fine art' works before. The inclusion of the photograph challenged the conventions about what might or might not constitute an 'original print'. While photographic reproduction was beginning to take over the printing industry, the world of limited editions had neither the interest nor the technical ability to employ it, until a chance visit by a salesman, Les Lawson, to the new Studio premises in Midford Place. He introduced a new process of photo-polymer plates, made of aluminium, also known as the diazo or continuous tone process. This allowed for work prepared on transparent film to be transferred onto plate with UV light. It offered a more faithful way of retaining the artist's personal touch in a variety of media than any previously available method. Piper's print showed the potential for combining photography with other image-generating techniques.
As Jones had recorded, '*Llangoffan Chapel* began as a collage idea, deriving its background texture from taking a rubbing from paper of the underside of a lithographic stone. Subsequently, drawing was added to the main photo-collage, and the completed idea, with textures, was re-photographed and set down onto deep-etch lithographic plate.'[35]

The result was closer in spirit to the

76
John Piper, *Llangoffan, Pembrokeshire: The Baptist Chapel*, from *A Retrospect of Churches*, 1964

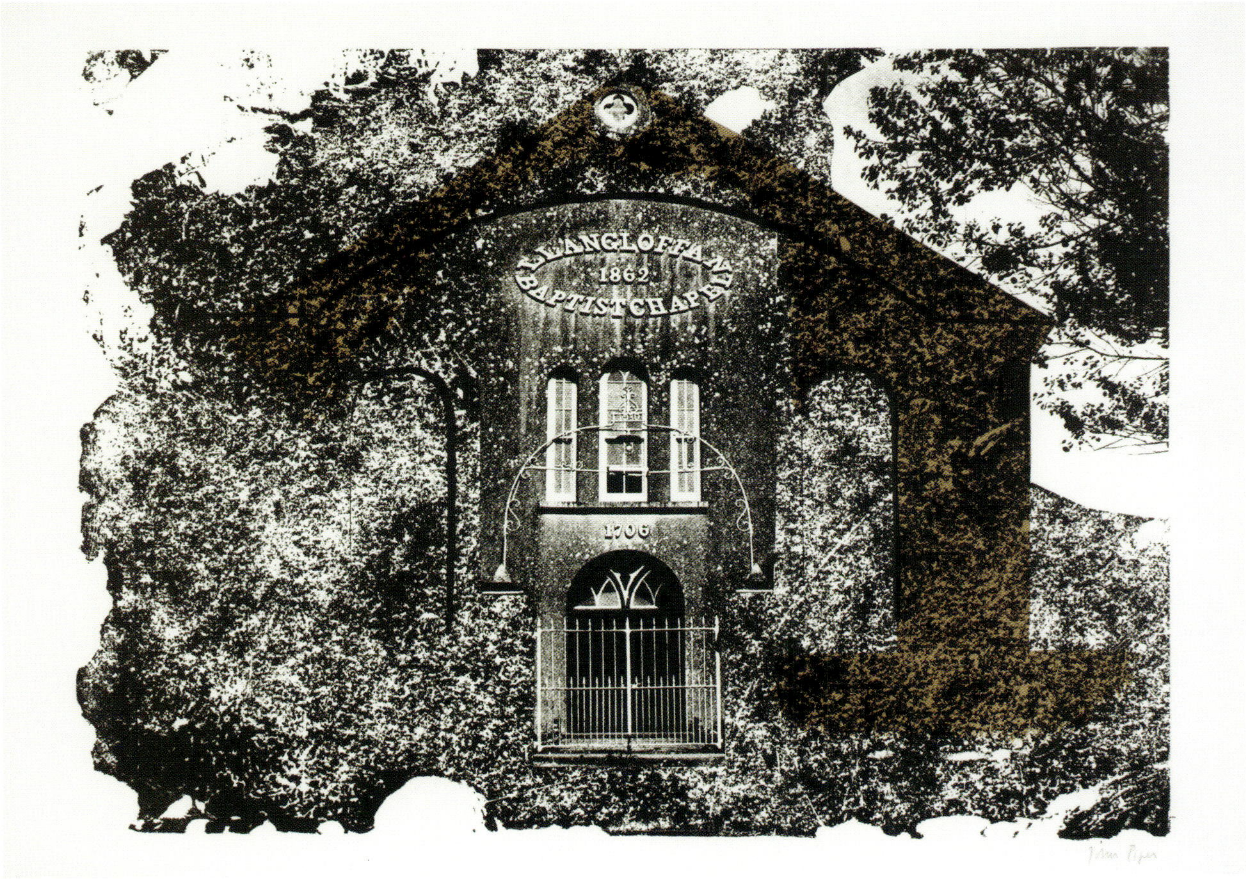

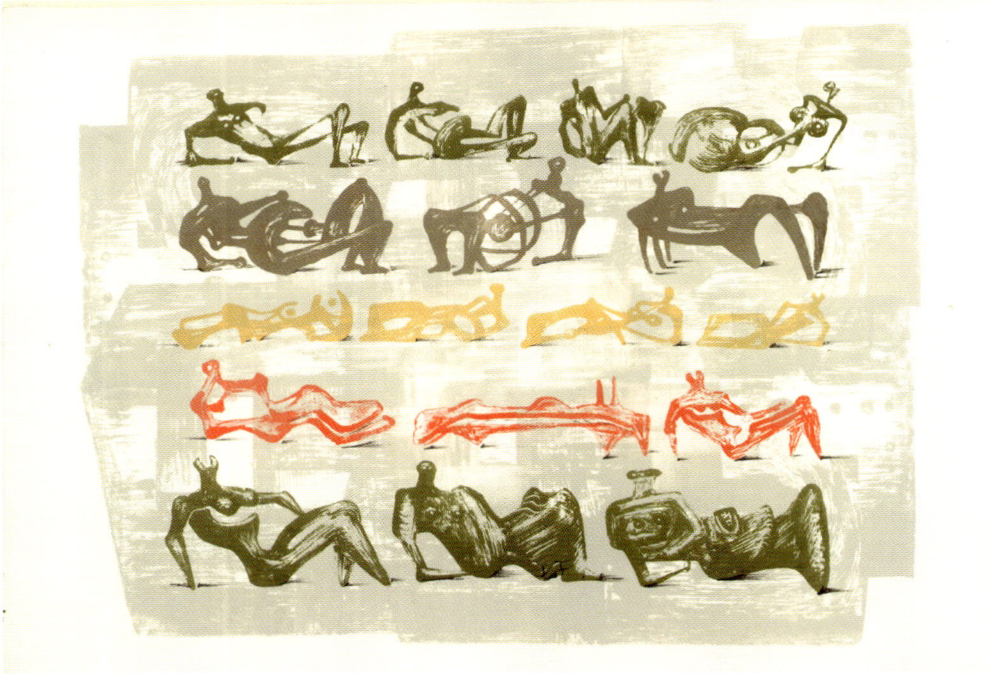

77
Henry Moore,
Seventeen Reclining Figures with Architectural Background, 1963

artists' prints, including many of Piper's own, that were being made using silkscreen from around 1960 onwards. The relative absence of tactile qualities from the medium and the ease with which images could be generated from different materials were attractive techniques for artists at the time of the nascent Pop art movement at the beginning of the 1960s, some aspects of which had been anticipated by Piper with his interest in 'bashing' both the media and conventions of printmaking, and using found imagery.

By contrast, the more conservative American litho studios initially refused to take on Les Lawson's innovation, so that Curwen remained for some time the only studio in the world to offer this technique.

Henry Moore

In presenting a large body of his prints to the British Council in 1984, Moore wrote: 'My graphic work has often been an introduction to many people who have gone on to look at sculpture'. While eagerly collected, his prints are none the less overshadowed in the public perception by other aspects of the artist's work. Many of Moore's themes for prints came from existing drawings and sketchbooks, but by recreating them as limited editions he was able to develop them visually and make them more widely available. He worked with a number of print media (although mainly in etching and lithography) and with several lithographic printers. In England he experimented with Plastocowell in the 1950s, and went on to provide images for printing by Desjobert and Mourlot in Paris later in the decade.

Moore liked to work on his own turf, at Perry Green in Hertfordshire, where he moved during the war. In 1971, after working with printers based in London and elsewhere, he installed an etching press there, and probably produced more etchings than lithographs overall. However, he was prolific in both areas after it became clear

78
Henry Moore, *Five Reclining Figures*, 1963

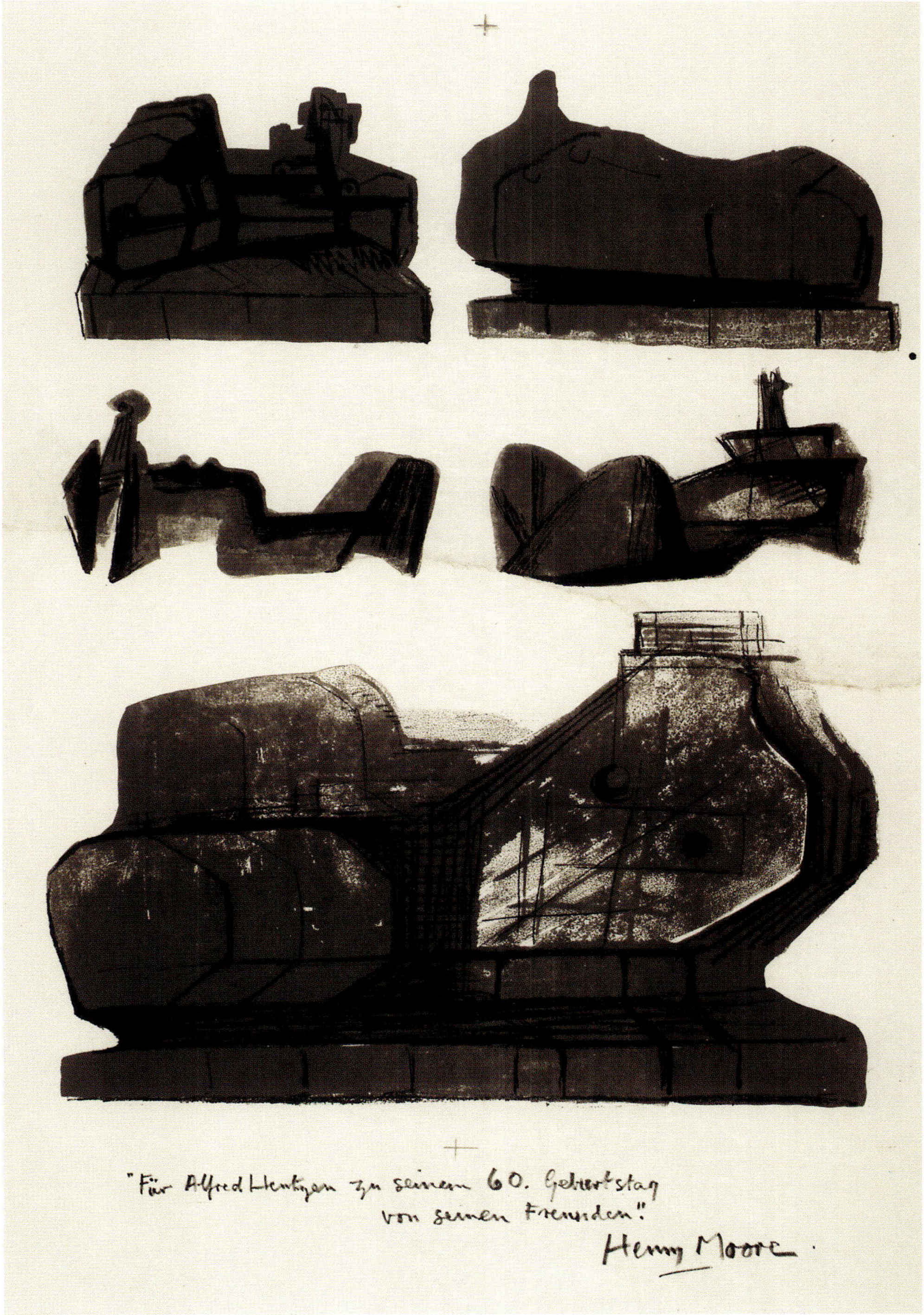

79
Henry Moore,
Reclining Figure with Sea Background,
1973

that there was a market for his graphic work. He produced work in the first year of the Curwen Studio (*Six Reclining Figures*, 1958), and worked with Robert Simon on *Heads, Figures and Ideas*, a book commission for George Rainbird Ltd, in the same year. Moore was unconvinced about the prospects for selling individual graphics, so in 1963 Timothy Simon offered to publish a print for him. This was *Seventeen Reclining Figures with Architectural Background* (fig.77), which quickly sold out and gave him confidence to continue. In the harsh winter of 1962–3, sculpture work in unheated buildings was problematic, and Moore had an intensive bout of printmaking, of which this was one of the products. He continued to alternate graphics and sculpture, making the most of a broken ankle that temporarily prohibited him from sculpting. A wartime Nissen hut known as the Gildmore Graphics Studio became part of his growing property at Much Hadham, and this was used as a space for the display of proofs, preparation of new work and storage of plates, which Moore, unlike most artists, decided to archive.

Here Stanley Jones made regular visits, often accompanied by one of his assistants, to bring new proofs and to discuss corrections prior to editioning, a process that could take anything between a couple of weeks or five years.

For the earlier Curwen prints, Moore used transfer paper to prepare his images, which usually did not depend on a tight registration. But he was apt to use the wrong materials for drawing which made the work useless for its intended purpose, and he was therefore especially keen on the photo-polymer plates, which allowed him to work with whatever came to hand. He welcomed the process for this reason, but also found that he could achieve more sensitive effects with it. Pat Gilmour explained in a catalogue essay of 1975 how the exposure of the plate made a difference to the quality of the image. In the new Curwen premises at Midford Place, Stanley Jones set up a dark room for the purpose, and added this to his skills as a master printer. 'Light softens the diazo coating so it can be washed from the aluminium, leaving only the ink-attracting printing surface. The longer a transparency is exposed (one might liken this control to the pressure exerted on a transfer paper going through the press) the more diazo coating will wash away. Thus long exposure means that only the very darkest areas of Moore's positive will be captured, short exposure means the lightest working can be retained, and of course an infinity of gradations is also possible.'[36] As Jones himself noted, 'This has given the artist an accuracy of texture control whilst also giving him greater freedom of approach to the complexities of colour printing', the latter achieved because of the transparency of the film as compared to the opaque transfer paper.[37] Apart from the drawings, the lithographs were the only other substantial medium in which Moore used colour at all, and they demonstrate his liking, at times, for strong colours and effects. He also enjoyed the give-and-take of a medium that could be permitted to develop a life of its own (figs.77–9).

Apart from an interval of two years,

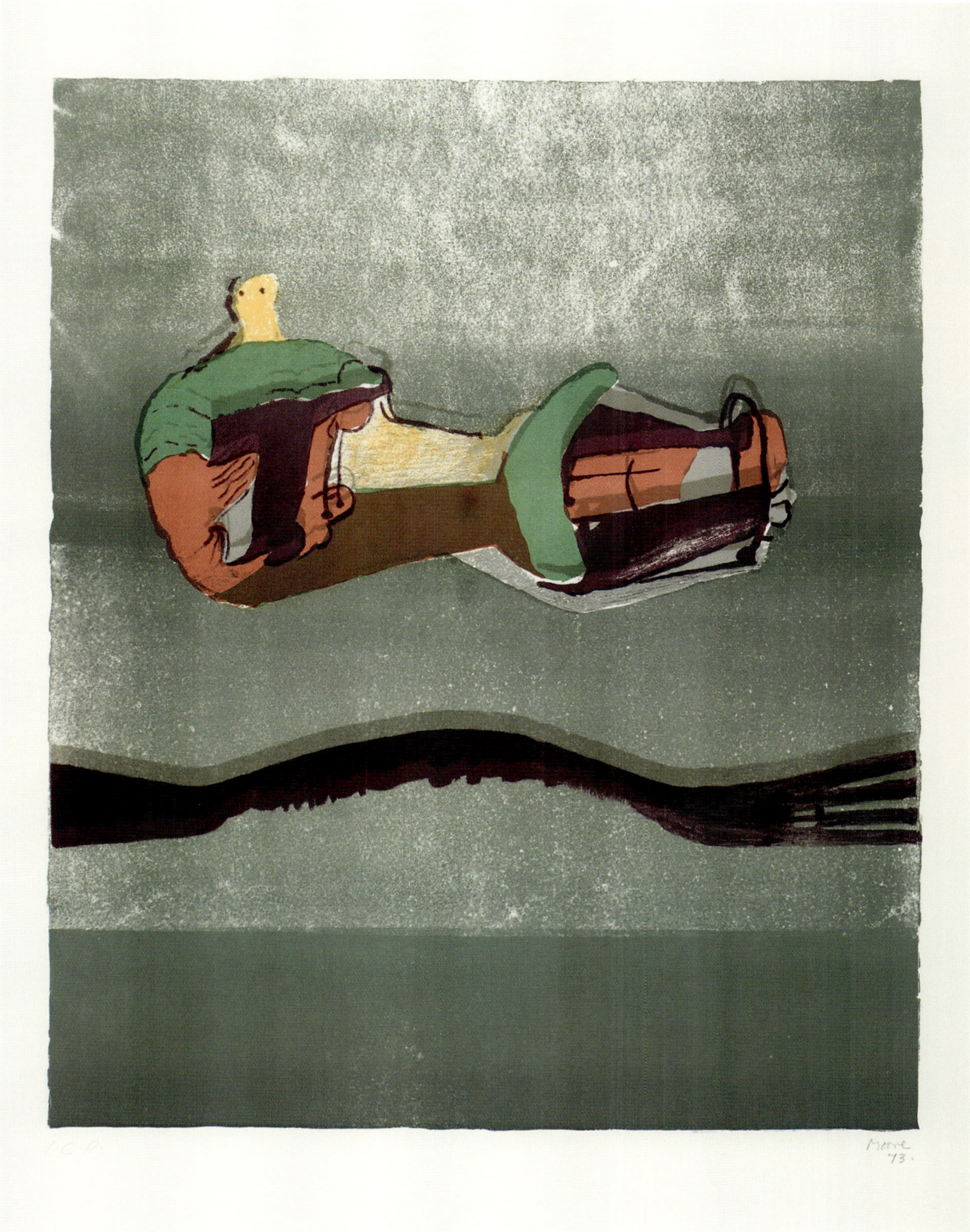
Moore
73.

80
Barbara Hepworth,
Porthmeor, 1969

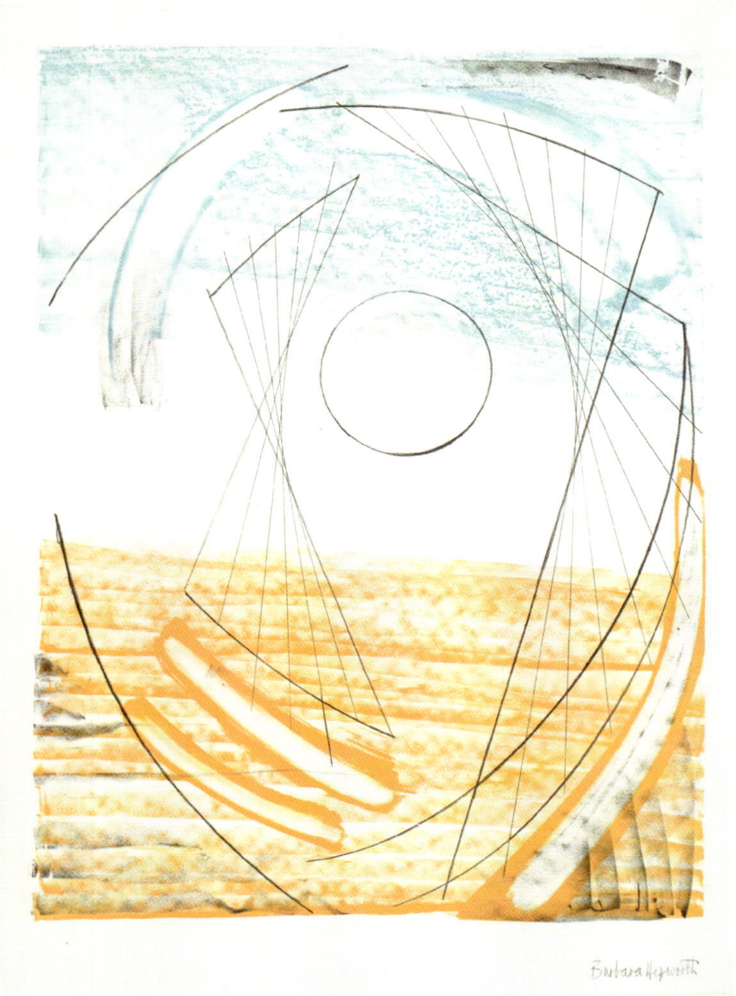

during which Moore entered an agreement through the Marlborough Gallery to print exclusively in Switzerland, his later lithographic work was all done by these means, and he enjoyed the collaborative element. On his occasional visits to the Midford Place studio, he liked to duck under the big press and remove 'wasters', using them as sheets on which he could make new drawings of his own, on top of an existing overlay of images. He became his own publisher for print editions, and from the Curwen Studio's viewpoint it was a very valuable arrangement since for many years there was a fairly reliable flow of work, unmatched by even the most constant of their other artists. Moore for his part recorded that 'Stanley is one of the nicest people I know. He is so amenable, so receptive to any suggestion of experiment.'[38] No wonder the relationship lasted so long.

Barbara Hepworth
Unlike Moore, Barbara Hepworth left only a small body of work in print form.[39] Stanley's initial contact with her during his six months at St Ives was not renewed until Herbert Simon approached her again in 1966, suggesting that she would enjoy working on stone. Initially, Stanley spent two weeks with her in St Ives in 1968, and the following year, Curwen Prints published the suite *12 Lithographs by Barbara Hepworth*, each on a sheet 23 × 32 inches, and composed as a series of variants on ideas familiar from her sculpture. It is typical of her lithographs that areas of pure form are suspended in a field of textured surface, the former resembling her highly polished work in marble or bronze, the

81
Barbara Hepworth,
Cool Moon, from
Aegean Suite, 1971

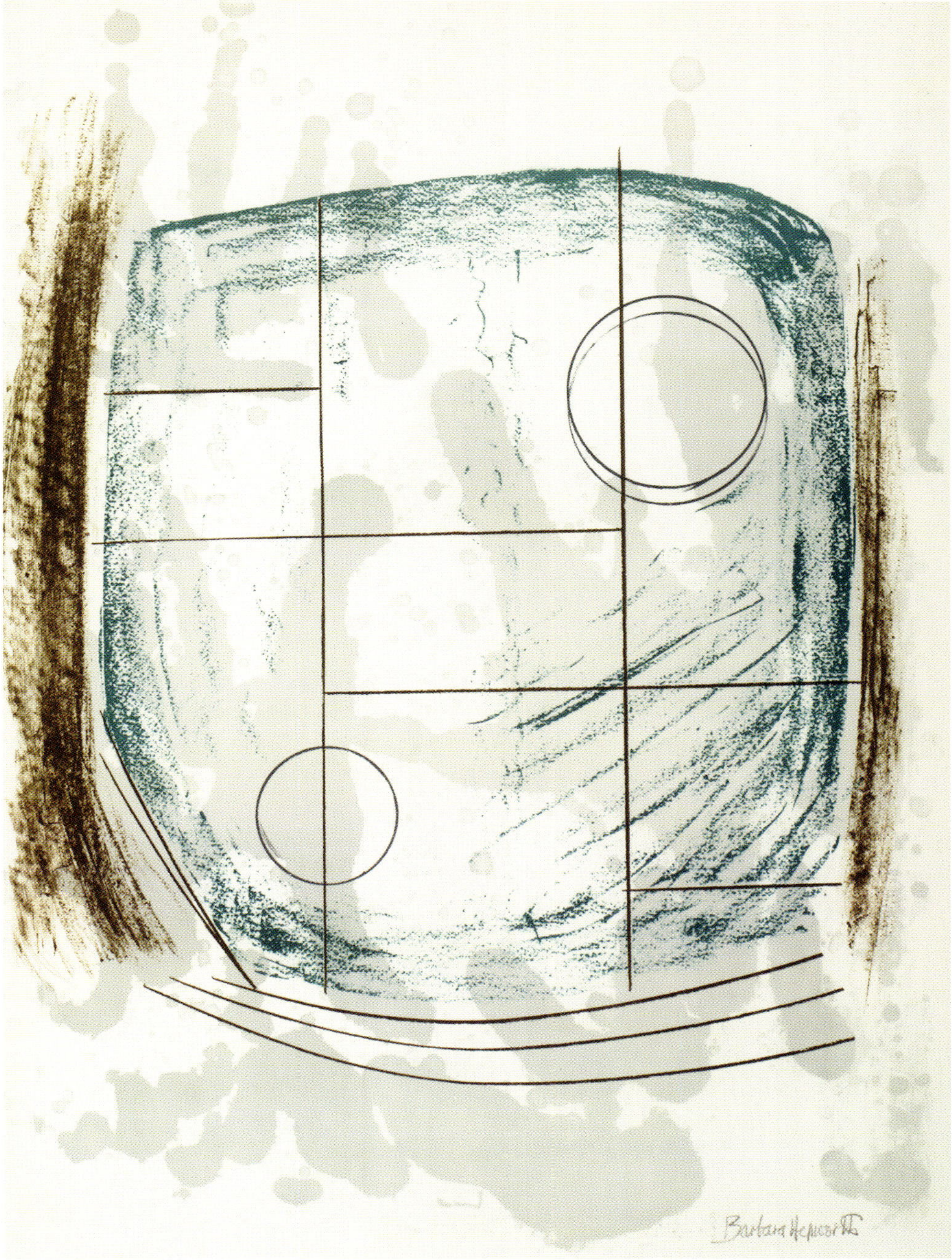

82
Elisabeth Frink,
Spinning Man I, 1965

latter her patinated bronzes. In some cases, the prints construct grids, more in the manner of Ben Nicholson or Mondrian, or Hepworth's own sculpture, *Crucifixion*, 1966, which is a constructed rather than modelled form. Some of the titles of the prints, again matching those of certain sculptures, evoke locations, either in Cornwall or classical Greece. In two cases (*Mycaenae and Sea Forms*), the print is embossed so that it literally enters the third dimension. The plates were made by a combination of direct drawing onto zinc, and the use of painted washes on grained film. Proofs were sent from London to St Ives for correction (fig.80).

The series was commercially successful, the publishing policy of Curwen being that prints forming a series should always be available as individual items, in order not to deter potential customers. Hepworth invited Stanley to spend a summer holiday in St Ives with his young family so that he could guide her work over a longer period, and the outcome was the *Aegean Suite* (fig.81) in 1970-1, consisting of nine images, essentially a development of the same techniques and subject matter as the earlier prints. Few other artist-printer relationships in the Studio's history so clearly demonstrate that without the impulse of a publisher and the availability of appropriate and sympathetic facilitators, these works would simply not have existed. In between the two suites, the screenprinters Chris and Rose Prater at Kelpra Studio made another set of prints with Hepworth, commissioned by her dealer, Marlborough. Chris Prater recalled how Hepworth's subtle tonality was in fact much better adapted to lithography than screenprinting, for which a large number of workings were needed.[40]

Elisabeth Frink and others

Elisabeth Frink was a sculptor of a younger generation who did not follow the abstract trend of the late 1950s led by artists such as Anthony Caro. She was a productive printmaker in each of the three main media, beginning with lithography when Timothy Simon commissioned a series of prints in 1964 when the Studio was still in Plaistow. Stanley Jones has commented on the affinity felt by many sculptors for the printmaking process, probably because they are used to collaboration with bronze foundries and other skilled technical workshops. Unlike Moore, Frink chose to develop imagery in her prints that, while recognisably akin to her sculpture, was a separate stem of creativity. She enjoyed the feel of stone in her early printmaking, scraping the stone with a blade for some of the *Spinning Man* series of 1965 (fig.82), based on the French 'birdman' Valentin who jumped from planes, only opening his parachute at the last minute, and who eventually fell to his death. Her second series, *Images*, 1967, drawn on zinc and film, used a second colour more boldly, finding two-dimensional shapes in the outlines of animals and birds, often conveying the sense of motion through multiple outlines and apparently 'slipped' register of colour overlays.

Frink's further sequences of lithographs, beginning in 1970, developed the potential of floating washes of litho ink, as Stanley Jones explained in 1998: 'She had changed

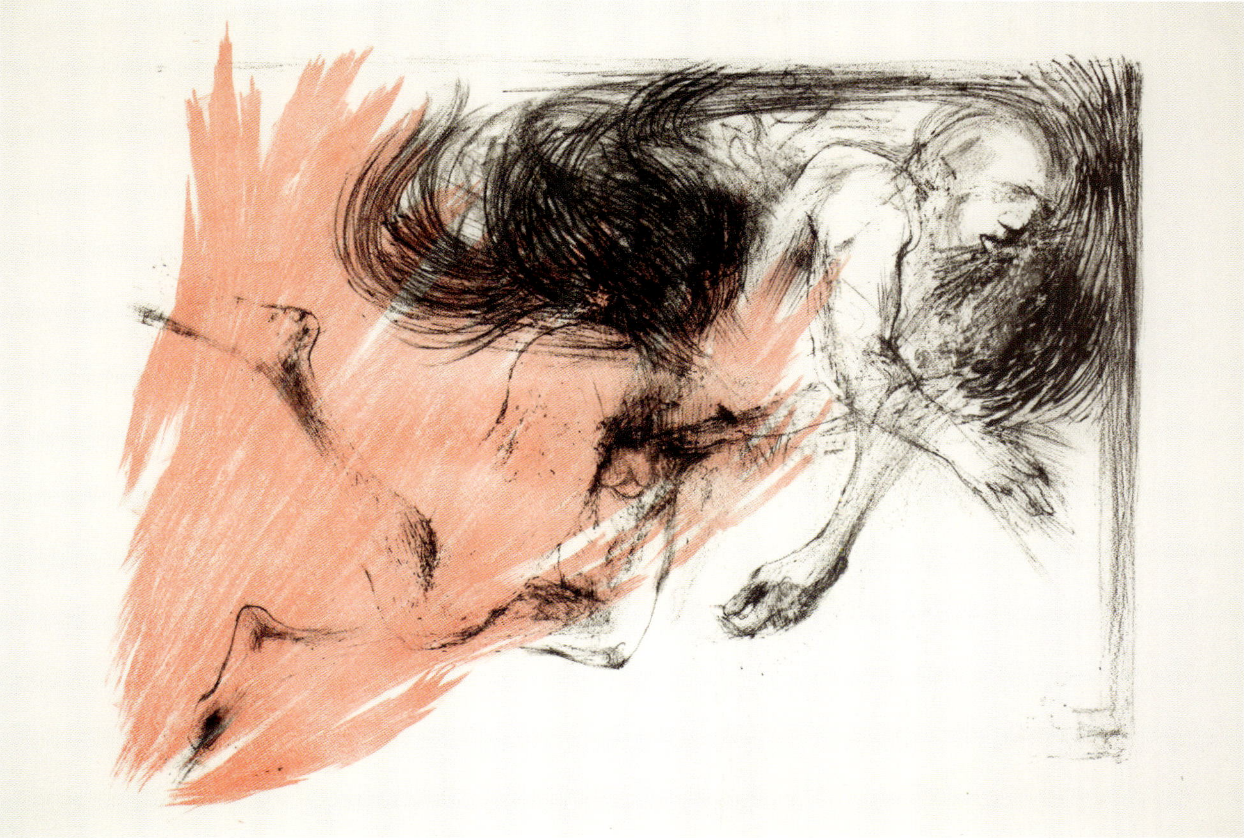

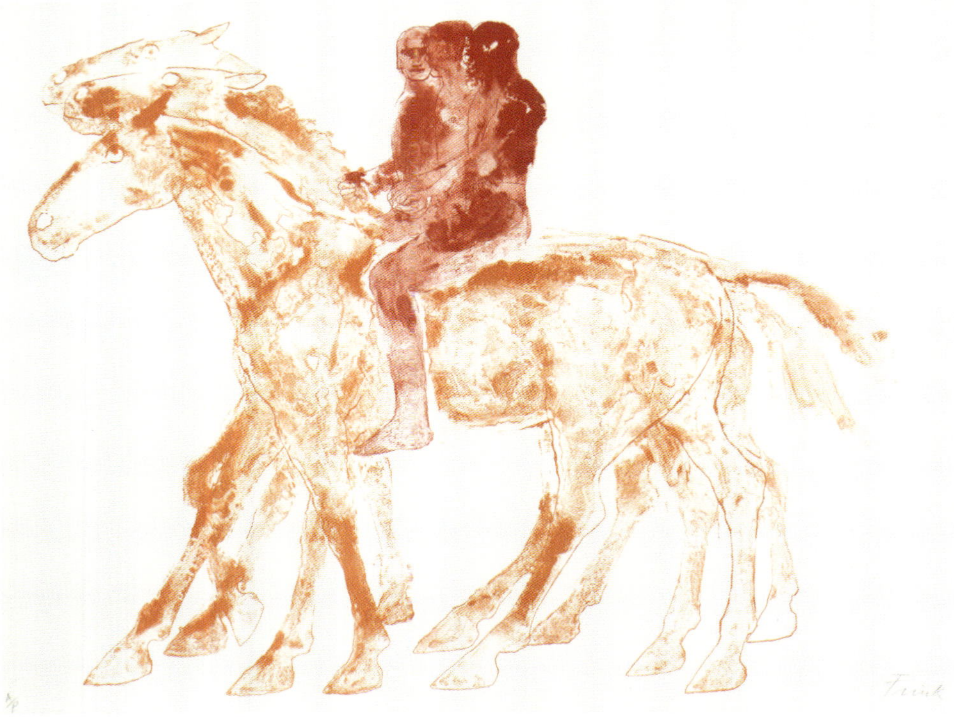

83
Elisabeth Frink,
The Three Riders,
1972–4

her style of drawing and wanted to create a molten look to her images – like the patina of bronze. So I needed to develop a lithographic technique to parallel the casting technique of her bronzes.
To interpret this in lithography required a new approach. I showed her how to use diluted washes of colour in the portrayal of the horse and the rider. This time she didn't use transfer paper but grained zinc plate. Onto this she would draw, always very fluidly, very generally, in charcoal, the outline of the animal. Into the centre of this I would pour distilled water – it spread out due to the granularity of the plate. Then I poured lithographic ink which is very black, greasy and sticky, into the pool of distilled water. She could then use a brush and play around with this – pushing ink into particular areas of emphasis.' [41] Extending this method, Frink was shown a technique used by Picasso and Braque, in which distilled water is poured over the existing drawing to create a mottled texture with a tidemark edge, 'which we always called *peau de crapaud* [toad's skin].' In later prints, she drew on transparent film for the diazo or photo-polymer process (figs.83-4).

By the mid-1960s, the Curwen Studio had become well established through its work with some of the leading names in the English anti-academy. Surprisingly, Graham Sutherland, despite his pre-war associations with the Curwen Press, worked only sporadically in the Studio. This was doubtless because he lived mostly in France, and used French printers, while, by the time the Studio came into existence, his strong personal link with Oliver Simon was severed by the latter's death. He produced a small black-and-white portrait image of Helena Rubenstein, echoing his oil portrait of her from 1959, which Sutherland revisited in the Tate. In 1971 he made a fine, imagined portrait of Alois Senefelder as a poster for the exhibition *Homage to Senefelder* at the Victoria and Albert Museum, based on the Felix Man collection of lithographs

84
Elisabeth Frink,
Eagle Owl, 1972–3

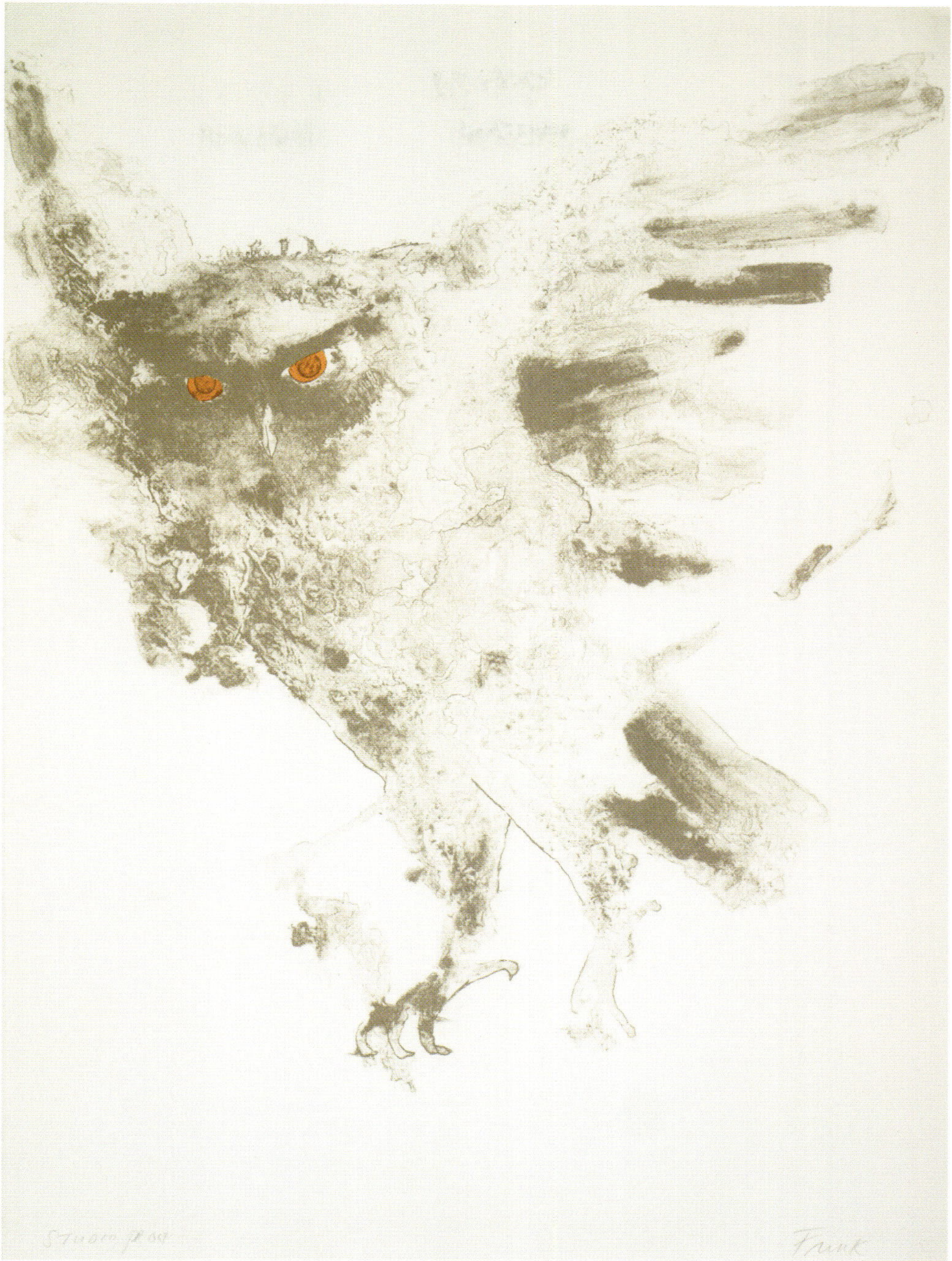

85
Graham Sutherland,
Hommage to Senefelder,
preparatory zinc plate,
1971

86
Graham Sutherland,
Hommage to Senefelder,
exhibition poster, 1971

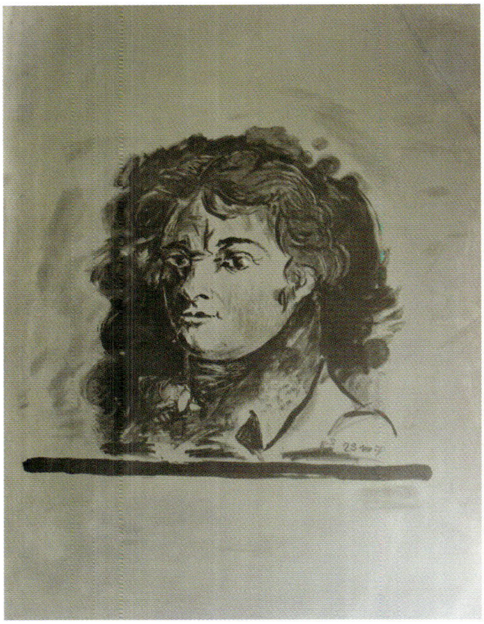

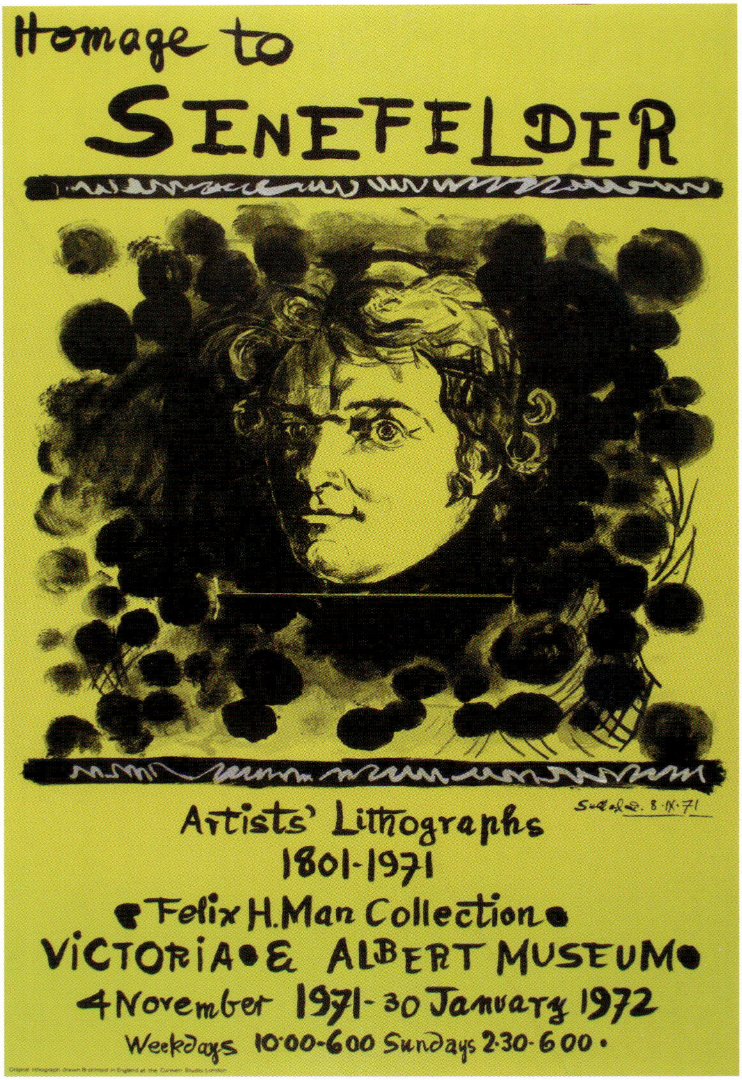

87
Robert Adams,
Screen I, 1962–3

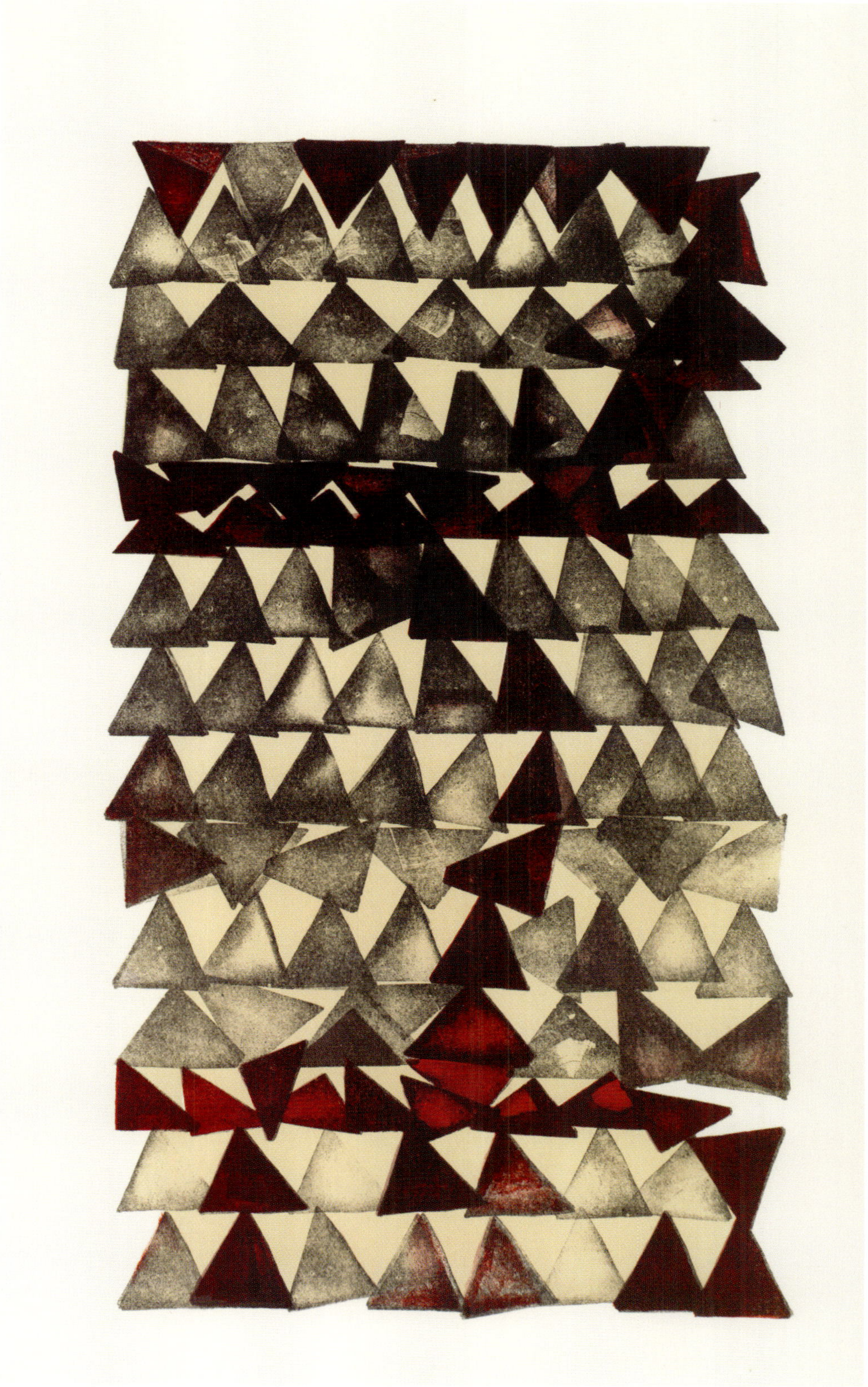

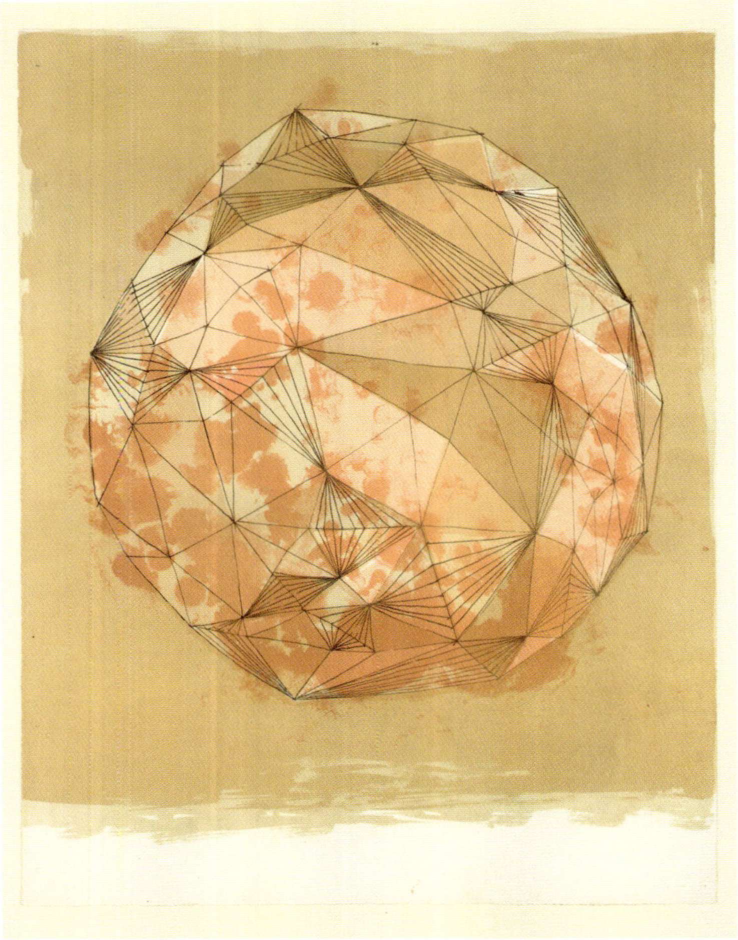

88
Lynn Chadwick,
Moon in Alabama,
1963

(figs.85–6). The preparatory plate for this print is one of a handful that have been retained at Curwen Studio as a trophy.

Among the less widely known artists of the period who made a body of prints at Curwen during the early years, Robert Adams, a leading abstract sculptor of the constructivist tendency, made a set of three prints, *Screen*, in 1962–3 (fig.87), using what Pat Gilmour called 'an errant piece of rubberised blanketing, dipped in lithographic drawing medium and repeatedly stamped onto the printing plate.'[42] This was the kind of exercise then being carried out in the 'Basic Design' foundation years of several British art schools. Lynn Chadwick (fig.88) and Reg Butler (fig.89) were commissioned by Felix Man and the associated gallery and publishing business of Wolfgang Ketterer in Munich for the Europaeische Graphik I portfolio in 1963, and, in Chadwick's case, the publisher Gerald Cramer of Geneva, the cataloguer of Moore's graphics. Chadwick's *Moon in Alabama* series of 1963, variations on a faceted sphere, is a sculptor's image, yet developed with a consciousness of the potential of printmaking for changing colour ways. The *Moon* series, 1965–6, for Marlborough Graphics uses only floating areas of flat colour and is less recognisably by Chadwick, but a series of *Figures*, 1969, again for Marlborough, uses some of his signature forms of faceted bodies.

Moving to London: New structures

In 1964 Curwen Press and Harleyprint merged, and a workspace in a basement off Tottenham Court Road, formerly used by

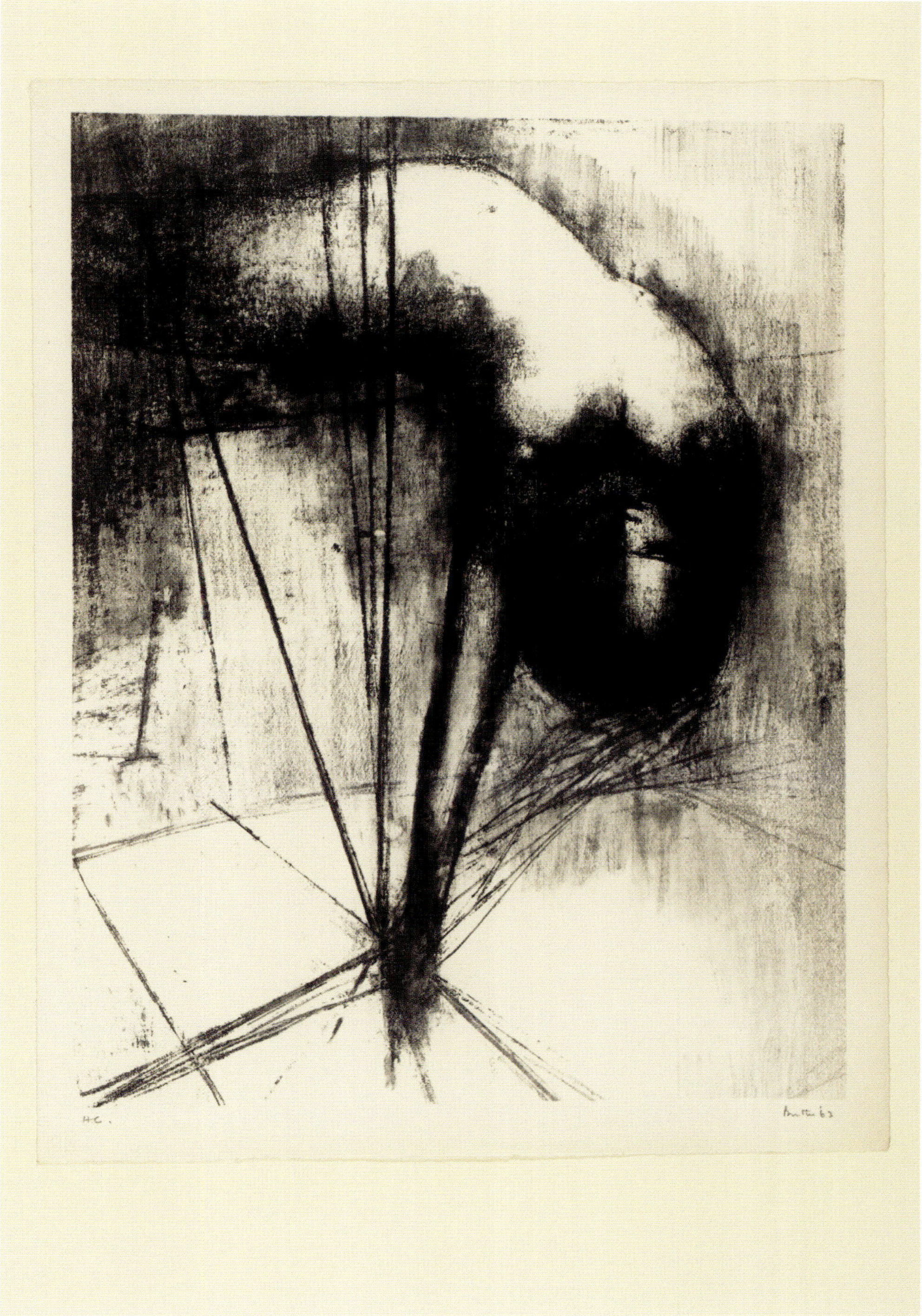

89
Reg Butler, *Figure in Space*, 1962–3

90
Trevor Bell,
Five Stages, 1961

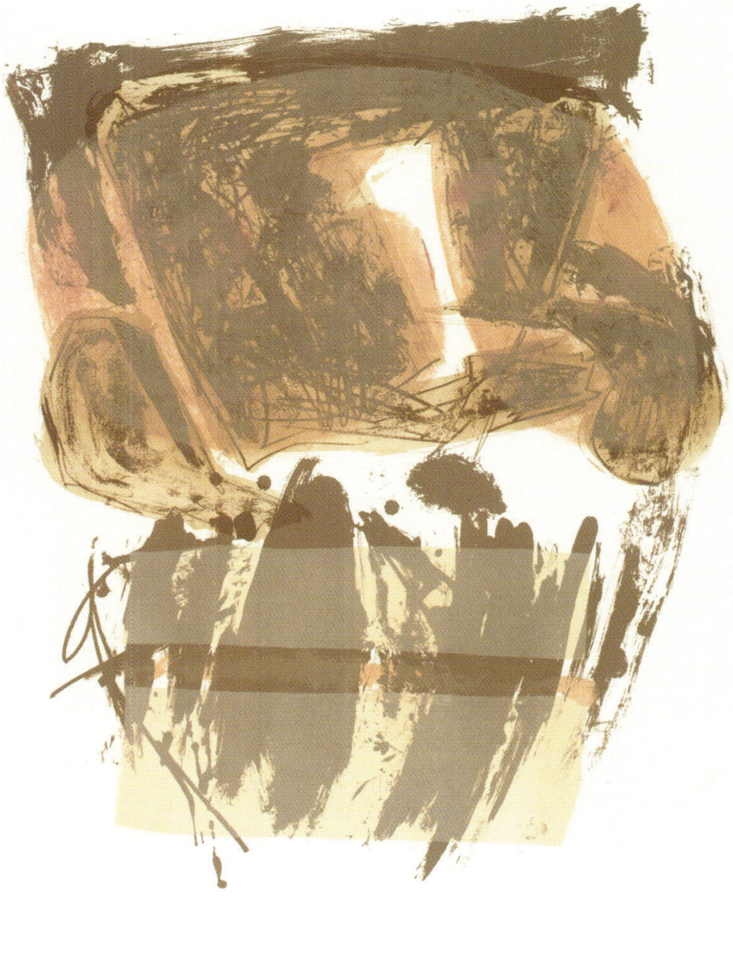

Harleyprint, became available for use by the Studio. Given the buoyant state of the print trade in the early 1960s and the confidence that the directors, including Basil Harley, had in the market, it was natural to think of expanding the operation and giving it a higher profile by positioning it near the Slade School, in the Fitzrovia area of London, with its historic and continuing connections with art and design.

The transition brought other consequences. It was decided to give the Studio its own editioning press, a Ratcliff 'Reliable' offset machine from the 1920s, thus more or less breaking the link to production with the parent company. It was a picturesque machine, already obsolescent, requiring two operators, one to feed in paper, the other to check the running and stand at the receiving end (figs.42, 46). It ran with a satisfying repetitive rhythm of clunks. There was also a flatbed proofing press, and a direct press originating from the Curwen music printing division.

The company was keen to move two of its printing staff, who were approaching retirement, to work in the new Studio at Midford Place, and it was accepted that, as a result, it would become for the first time a unionised workplace. In the early twenty-first century, it is hard to convey the significance of this. The machine operator belonged to the National Graphical Association; the feeder to the NATSOPA, the union pilloried by *Private Eye* as 'Notsober'. While many stayed at the Curwen Studio for years and gave loyal service, their recruitment was in the hands of the local union branch, and each had to be

91
Kenneth Armitage,
Seated Group, 1960

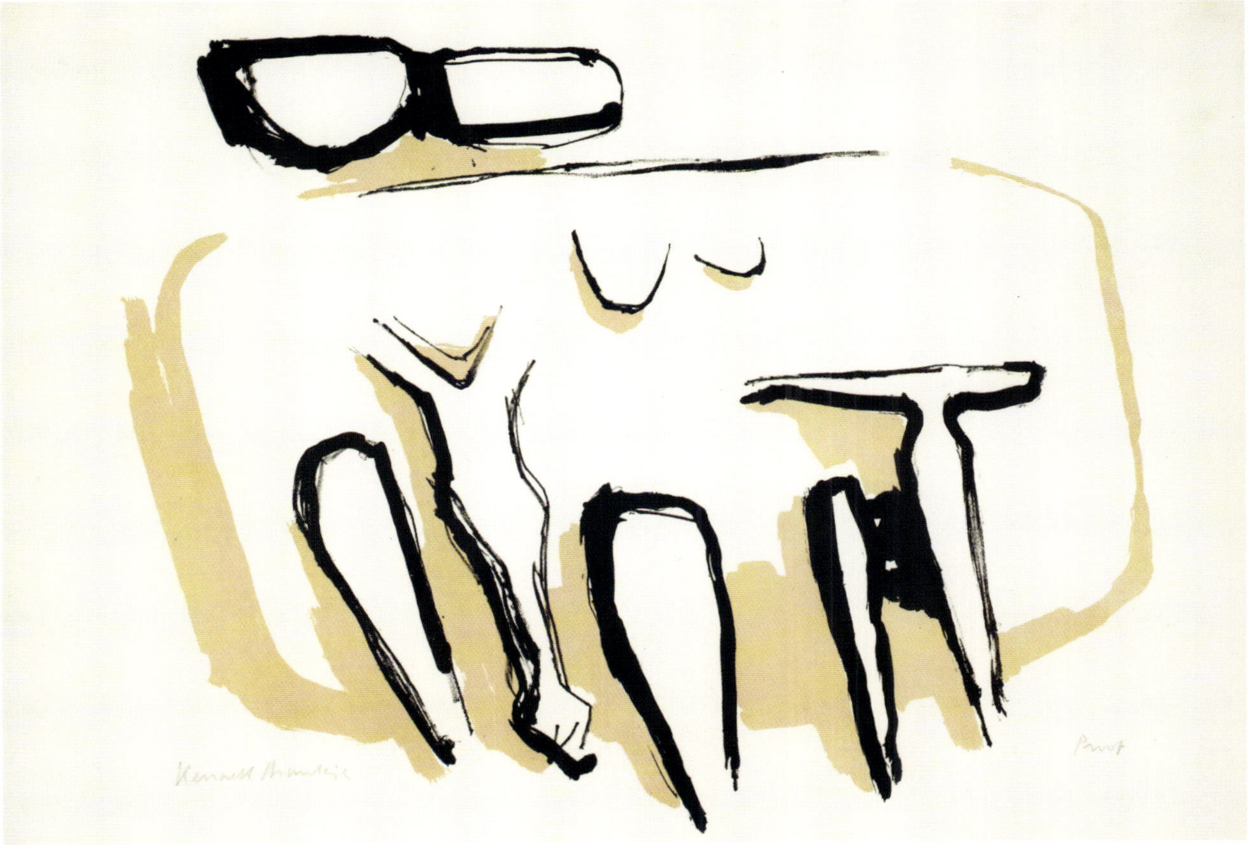

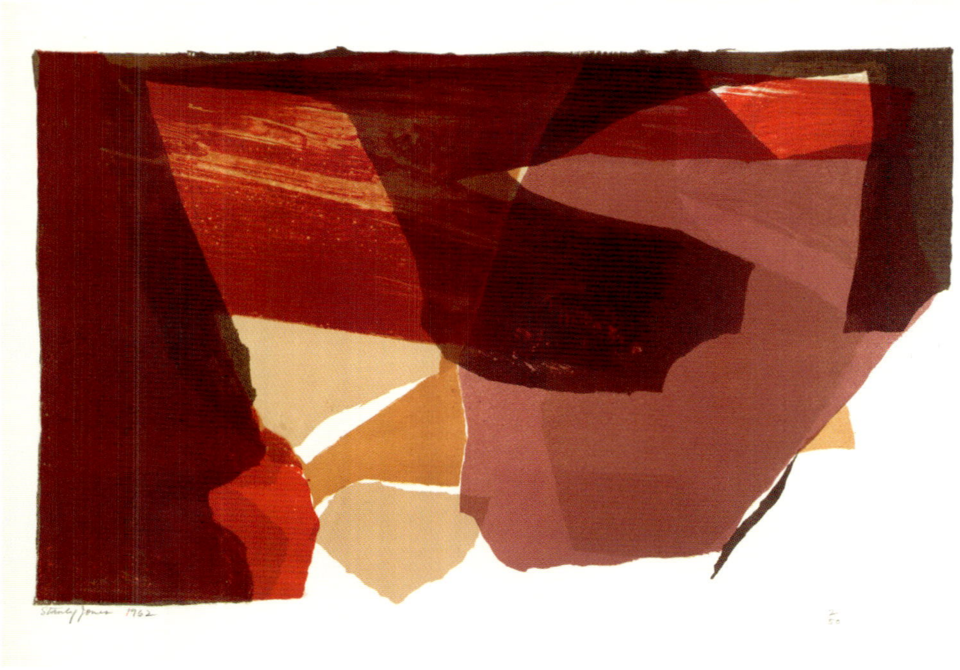

92
Stanley Jones,
Essex Landscape,
1962

93
Philip Sutton,
San Francisco,
1966

introduced to a work culture unlike that of a conventional print shop, involving almost continuous small infringements of the demarcation rules that, in other circumstances, might have led to strikes or disciplinary action against union members. Disasters were averted, but the wage scales were higher than those expected by art school graduates working as printers in the original studio. Over time, the total overheads of the Studio were only with difficulty balanced against the income from artists and publishers.

The premises, reached down a flight of stone steps in Midford Place, had a pleasing bunker-like quality (fig.94). The space was divided by concrete columns, with bays around the perimeter used as carrels for artists to work on plates with a weak daylight coming through the glass blocks in the pavement overhead. The middle of the floor was partly occupied by plan chests and tables on which proofs could be inspected and, eventually, signed. While more experienced artists might take away sheets of grained film for home working, beginners were encouraged to work directly onto plate and experiment at no cost before proceeding to their main work. In this often-repeated induction, Stanley Jones's enthusiasm and love of the medium was always apparent. Artists were encouraged to try effects particular to lithography, especially the more accidental, such as floating a wash of dilute ink in lighter fuel which turned, as it dried, into a texture like marbled paper. For artists, it was necessary to learn how the work drawn on the plate in black-tinted media is only a partial guide to the eventual quality of the print. On white paper, rather than on the grey-toned zinc, the contrast is much stronger, and the delicacy of the work may have to be a matter of trust rather than visual evidence. Skill in 'etching' the plate and 'rolling up' the image with black ink, as applied by Jones himself in most cases, was a matter of judgement rather than routine.

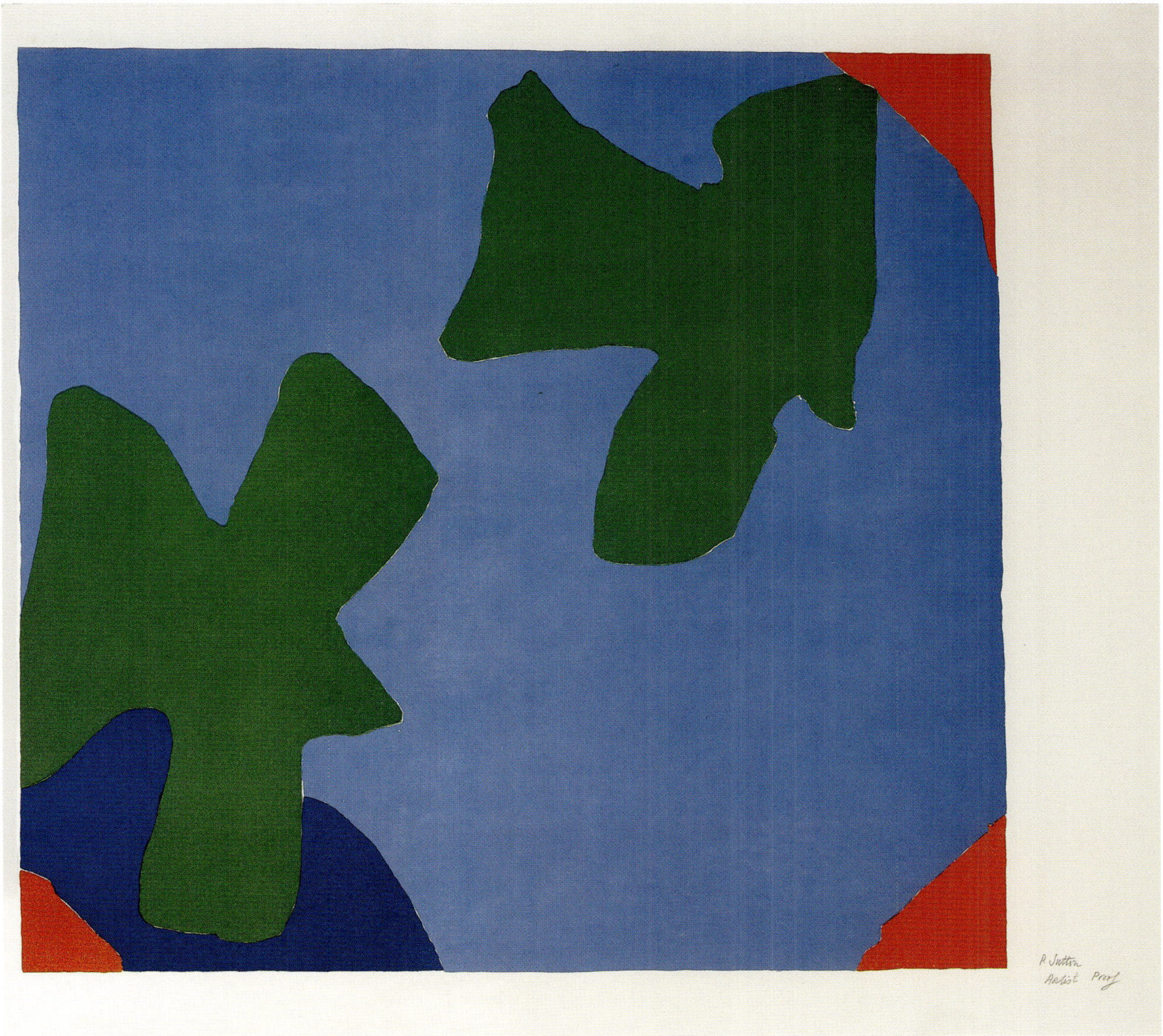
P. Sutton
Artist Proof

A standard scale of charges helped artists or publishers to calculate the costs involved in producing an edition, relative to the number of colours and the length of the edition run. These remained relatively modest. When a set of plates for a coloured image were ready, the work would be proofed, with specially mixed colours, and adjusted on the plate. Some artists, including Basil Beattie, came to the Studio to work on monoprints, using a plate on the bed of the proofing press as the basis for building up an image. The proofer, John White, taught part-time at Ravensbourne College of Art in the mid-1980s, and invited one of his students, Tracey Emin, to make monoprints at Midford Place.

Tea and coffee breaks were an important and inclusive ritual, contributing to establishing friendly contact between artists and printers. In the 1960s, Stanley Jones began to teach one day a week at the Slade, and always had an assistant in place to answer telephone calls and keep things going. Most of the 'goings on' were audible throughout the space, unless the press was running. Occasionally, publishers such as Peter Sampson of Merivale Editions would use the Studio facilities for artists to work on plates and have them processed, but take the printing elsewhere, in his case to Adrian Lack's Senecio Press at Charlbury in Oxfordshire, where there was a much faster-running modern machine with a smaller plate size, but capable of completing an edition of 500 in four colours during the course of a single working day. Such printers willing to handle hand-drawn work and make special colour mixtures became, however, rare to the point of extinction during the 1980s as machinery was relentlessly updated.

Limited editions printing and publishing in the 1960s

The move to Midford Place coincided with the creation of a new company, Curwen Prints Ltd, nominally separate from the parent press, although there were directors common to both boards. Apart from the Studio and its production, the company's activities included publishing, and the creation of the Curwen Gallery, initially housed in the ground floor and basement of a recently built infill terraced house at 21 Colville Place designed by Max Neufeld. It was a modern environment of the kind that the prints might be expected to be found in. Robert Simon decided to withdraw from his role at Plaistow and focus on Curwen Prints Ltd, together with Rosemary Simmons, who was Oliver Simon's assistant before leaving to live in India. On her return in 1965, she became a well known authority in the print world and helped Stanley Jones with the running of the Studio while putting on almost monthly exhibitions at the Curwen Gallery. Timothy Simon ceased to play an active role when he moved into his career in book publishing at the same time.

As publishers, Curwen Prints dealt almost entirely with work produced in the Studio, although the Curwen Gallery showed a wider range of work, still predominantly in the form of limited edition prints. The bottom drawer of the plan chest in the gallery housed the pre-war pattern paper designs by artists such as Paul Nash and Claud Lovat Fraser, which could

94
The Curwen Studio, entrance in Midford Place, W1

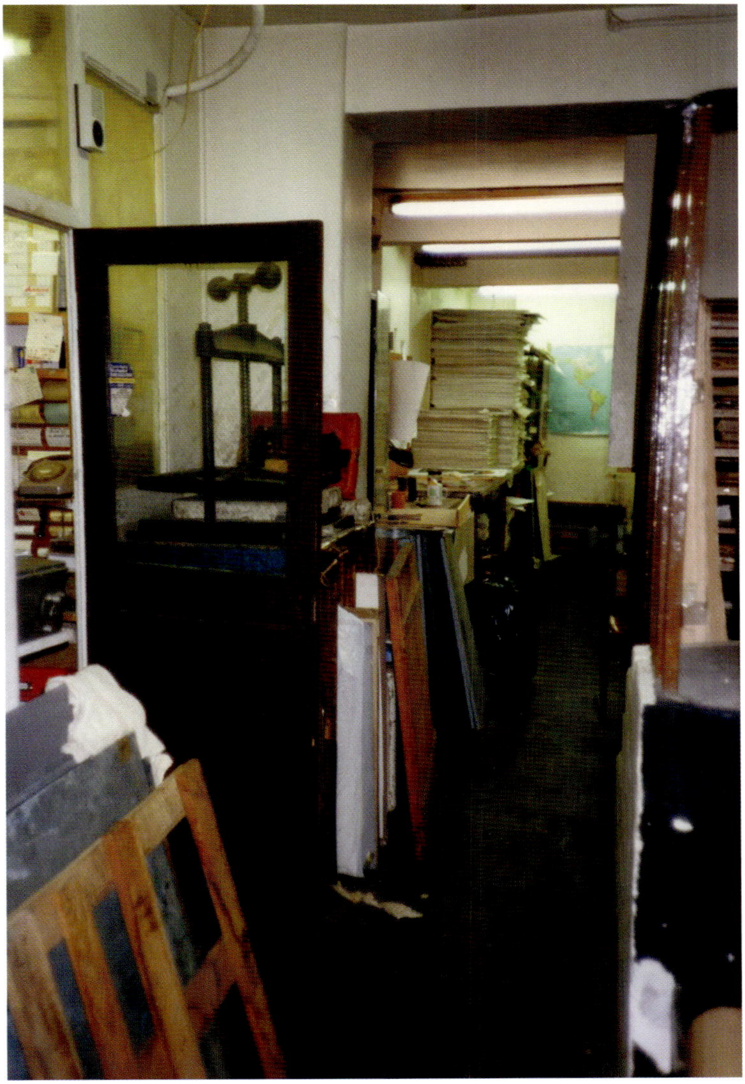

still be bought, and some of the later designs by Elisabeth Friedlander were reissued in brighter colours by a giftwrap and card company, Hunkydory, making their appearance on tin trays and other housewares.

Up to the early 1970s, the impetus of the print publishing boom was still apparent in a diverse range of activities, from international print exhibitions, such as the Bradford Print Biennale, to the interest shown by some of the major contemporary London galleries, such as Marlborough and Waddington, in publishing prints by the artists they represented. A significant manifestation was the creation of a new publishing company, Editions Alecto. Rather like St George's Gallery, it owed its beginnings to student enthusiasm, with Paul Cornwall-Jones and Michael Deakin commissioning prints from John Piper and others, targeted at school and college alumni. Two lithographs by Piper of *Westminster School*, 1961, were his first collaboration with Stanley Jones.
In London in 1962, the two founders of Editions Alecto were joined by Joe Studholme, a refugee from a City career.[43] Alecto was more focused on publishing and sales than Curwen, although it later developed its own studio. Its financial footing was in some respects stronger than Curwen's, and Alecto was successful in supplying the American market. In 1963 Robert Erskine decided to hand over his existing stock in a merger, and return to his previous interest in archaeology. Editions Alecto caught the mood of the emergent London art scene, and made bold commercial decisions, such as paying David

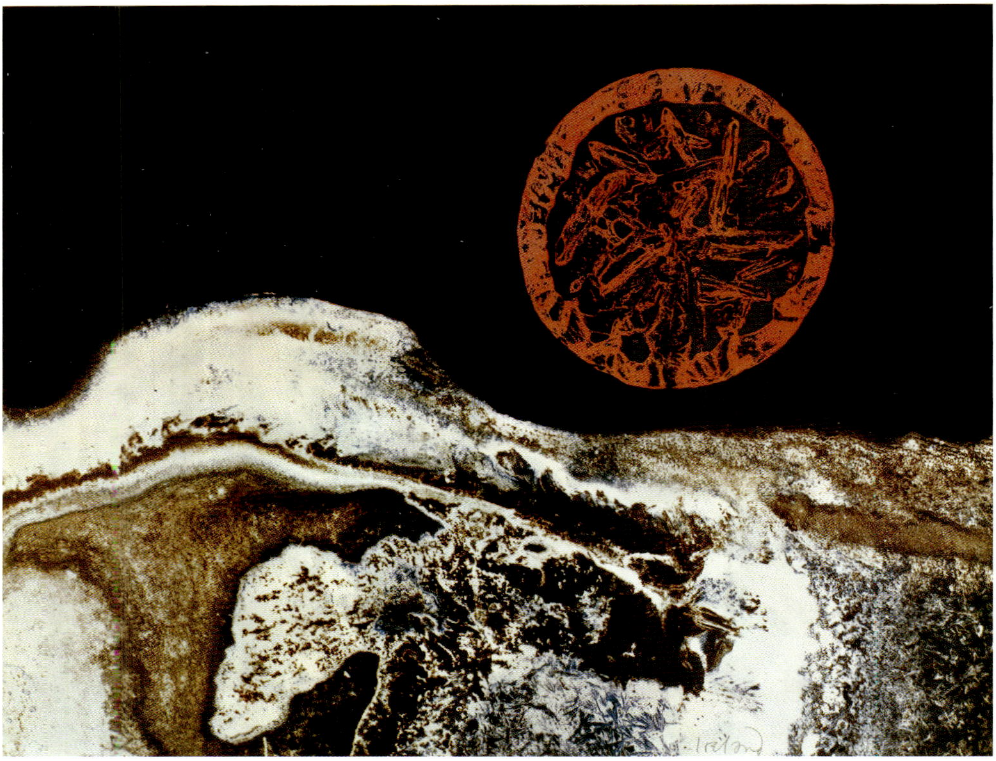

95
Geoffrey Ireland,
Sagres, 1965

96
Richard Bawden,
Telford's Bridge, Conway,
1965

Hockney £5,000 for the publication rights of his *Rake's Progress* series in 1963.

There is no doubt that Alecto outshone Curwen from this point onwards, so far as its international selection of artists and the smartness of its presentation were concerned. In Britain and America, limited edition prints became, not entirely to their benefit, a form of financial speculation when, as the critic Benedict Nightingale noted in 1967, the *Rake's Progress* set offered at £250 was already reaching £700. In his article in the radical-liberal magazine *New Society*, Nightingale investigated the relatively novel concept of the limited edition of a work to which, physically, there was no necessary limit, since, from a technical aspect, the print run could be extended almost indefinitely. He commended Curwen for maintaining a moral high ground by publishing certain prints in unlimited editions, 'about 60 of them so far, priced at 52s 6d [£2.62 1/2] a copy', by artists such as Geoffrey Ireland, Richard Bawden (fig.96), Edward Piper and David Gentleman. These, he noted, 'tend to be more conventional than those in the limited editions, but it is something that they are freely and cheaply available to all.'[44] This was true of the latter three artists, each the son of an artist active in the 1930s and, in the case of Edward Bawden and John Piper, significant in the Curwen story. Geoffrey Ireland (fig.95) an older artist, was more closely allied to figures such as William Scott or Ceri Richards.

In addition, Nightingale quoted 'a Curwen executive' on their policy of selling individual prints from suites and series, such as Elisabeth Frink's *Spinning Man*, priced at 165 guineas for eight lithographs, but individually at 20 guineas: 'We don't believe in selling in sets. The only customers who can afford them are institutions or rich collectors. We don't believe in high prices at all. Our basic philosophy is that original prints should be available to quite ordinary people.' A great deal of the missionary

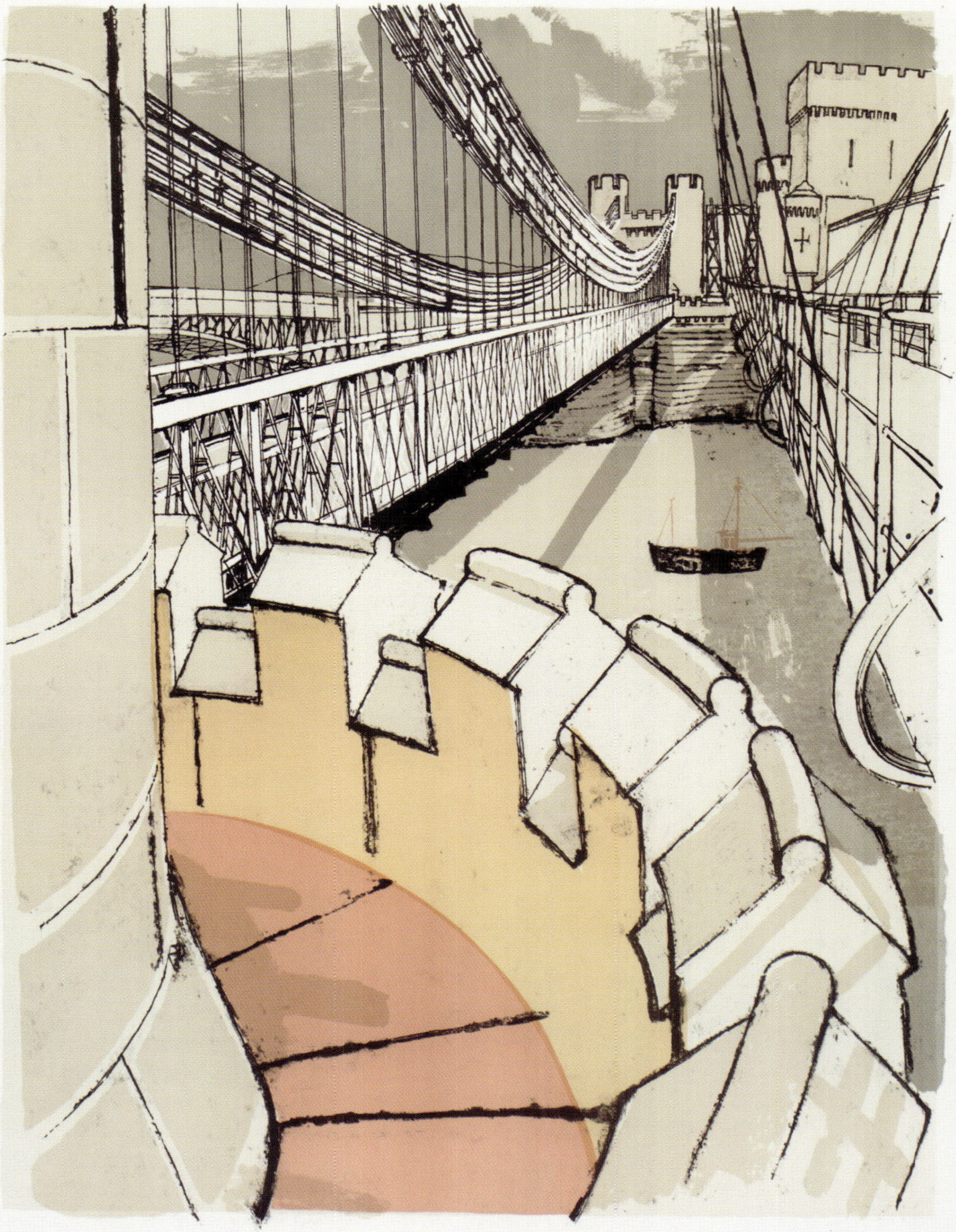

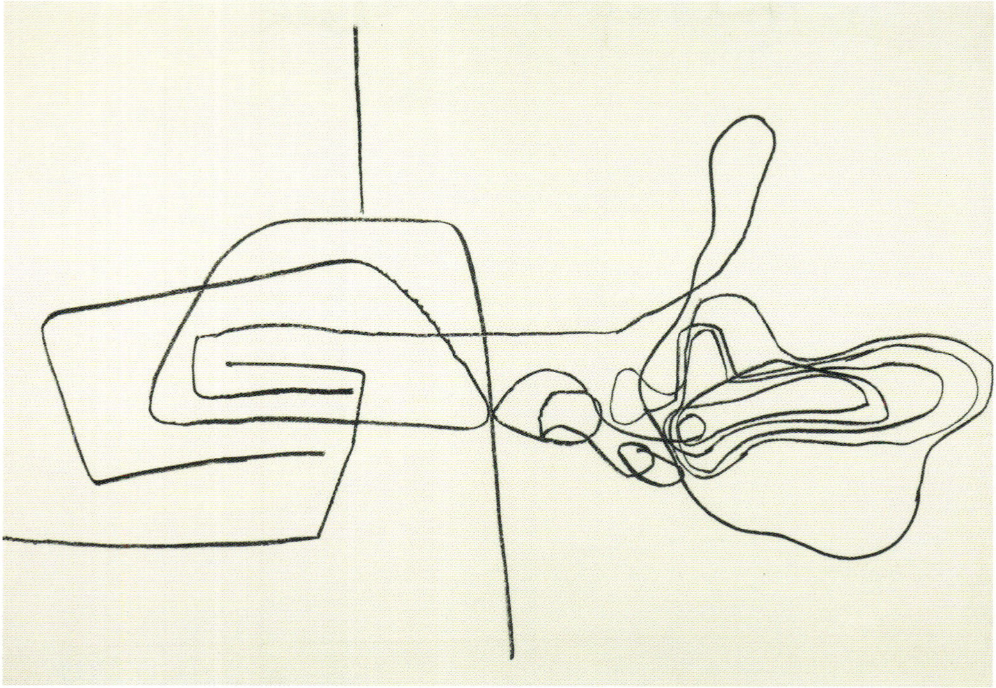

97
Victor Pasmore,
Points of Contact, No.3, 1965

98
Osip Zadkine,
Figure with Guitar, 1964

attitude of the Revd John Curwen was still apparent over a hundred years after he started his business. Alecto, by contrast, was at this time creating a new cult of the specially designed box for its print collections, and branching out into 'multiples' of three-dimensional art.

To begin with, Editions Alecto put work out to a variety of print studios in Britain and Europe, principally Curwen for lithographs and Kelpra for silkscreens. In the mid-1960s they acquired premises in Kelso Place, Kensington that enabled them to set up their own production facilities, including intaglio and silkscreen, but never rivalling Curwen's technical expertise in the field of lithography and never providing facilities for artists to work autographically, since the work was all processed photographically. To some extent, silkscreen took part of the potential market for lithography from the 1960s onwards, owing largely to Chris Prater's skill in making it a more suitable medium for reproducing effects that artists of the period were trying to achieve. Many artists who worked once or twice at Curwen, such as Eduardo Paolozzi or Allen Jones, printed their most significant body of print work at Kelpra, including such famous landmarks as Paolozzi's 1965 *As is When* portfolio for Alecto, with its poster-like solid colours and complex applications of photographic imagery.

Technically, once the principle of photographic imagery had been pioneered in lithography by John Piper and Stanley Jones, there was no essential difference in the effects that each medium, either silkscreen or lithograph, could generate. The tactile quality of working directly on plate or stone, although this was not necessarily employed by all the Curwen artists, was, however, not available when working with silkscreen. When making silkscreens, the printer could take a larger role in his collaboration with the artist, working in some ways more like the old-

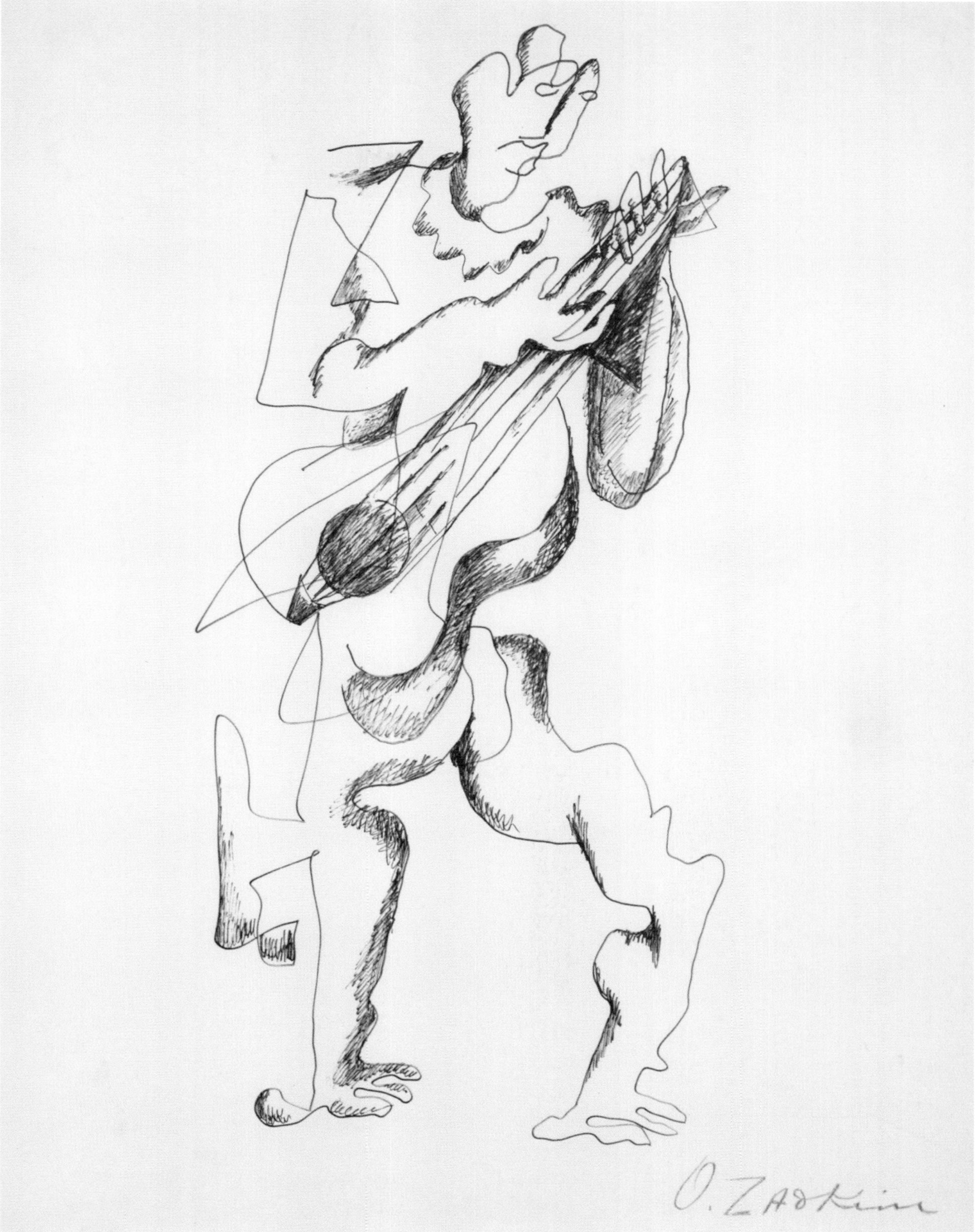
O. Zadkine

99
Duncan Grant,
Washerwoman,
1972–4

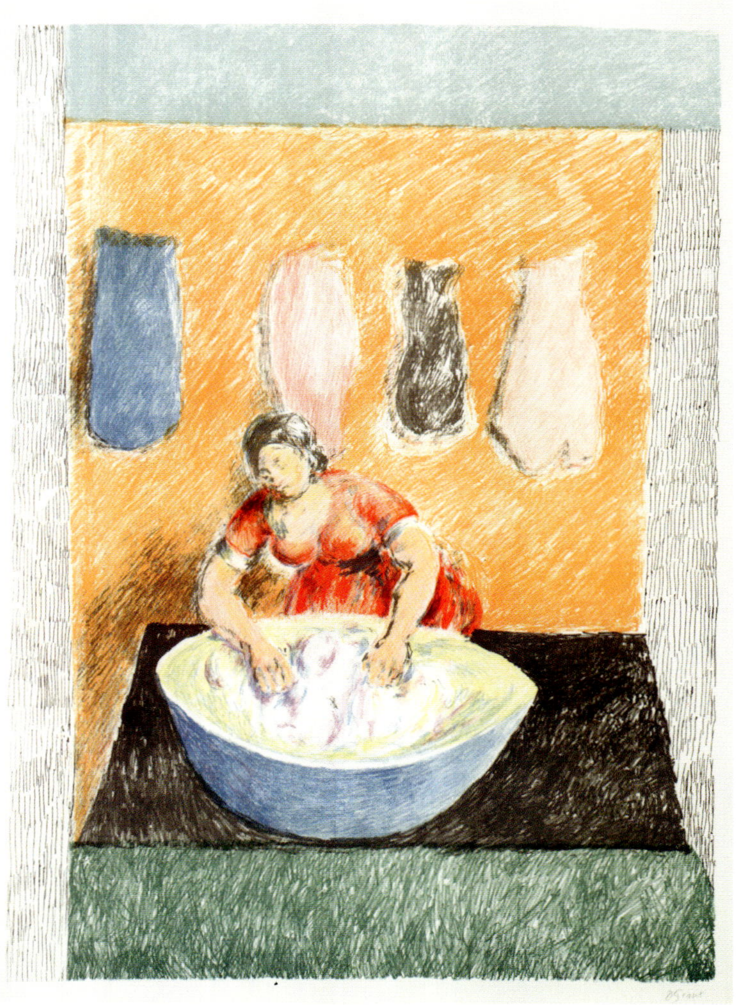

fashioned litho studio artists of pre-war days, interpreting a piece of artwork as colour separations. While this process was considerably more skilled and time consuming than mechanical four-colour reproduction, the original touch of the artist (not a factor much valued by Pop artists in the 1960s) was easily overlooked. When work by the same artist in the two media is compared, there is a loss of subtlety in silkscreen to offset the gain in strength, notably in the contrast between Piper's lithographs and his screen prints, the latter commissioned by Marlborough and derived from gouache paintings notable for their strong colours, but lacking the personal involvement that Piper had shown in his earlier work at Curwen.

There were many similarities between Curwen and Kelpra, where Chris Prater's skill and personality were equivalent to those of Stanley Jones, but Prater did not make provision for the continuation of the workshop and it closed just before his death in 1996. Editions Alecto survived until the early 1980s, but Paul Cornwall-Jones left before then to set up Petersburg Press, where he produced Hockney's *Grimm's Fairy Tales* etchings.

Artists of the later 1960s and early 1970s

With the presence of rival studios and alternative printmaking media, Curwen Studio diversified in the early years at Midford Place, responding to a variety of stimuli. Artists such as Moore and Frink created a regular flow of work. Some older artists began to make prints in new ways. Edward Bawden started to print and publish a series of linocuts himself from

100
Arthur Boyd,
Butterfly Man (Red),
1970

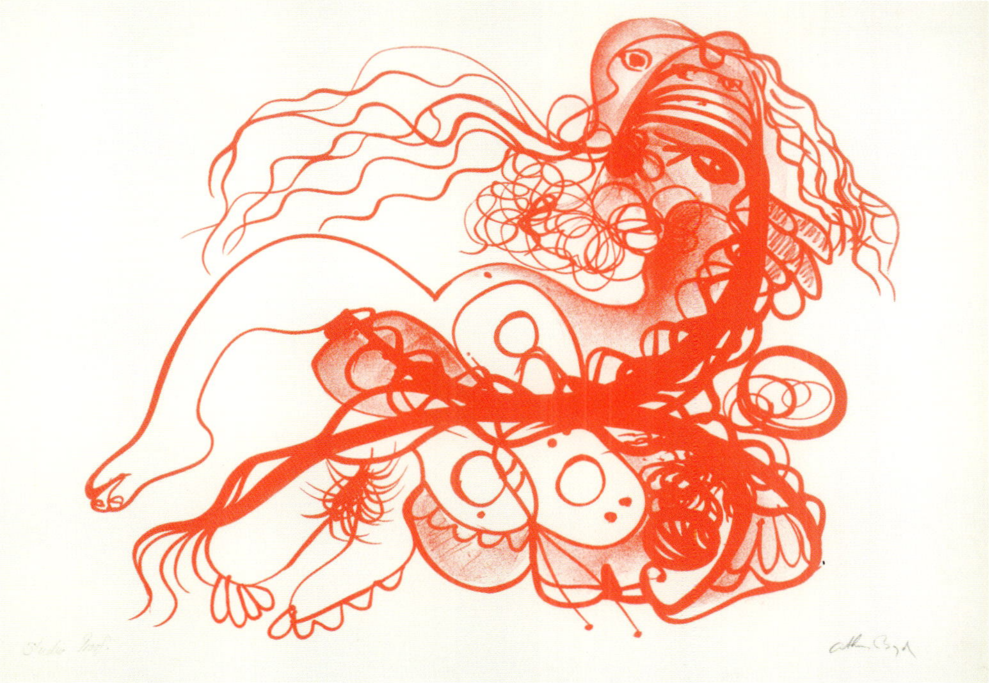

101
Howard Hodgkin,
Arch, 1970–1

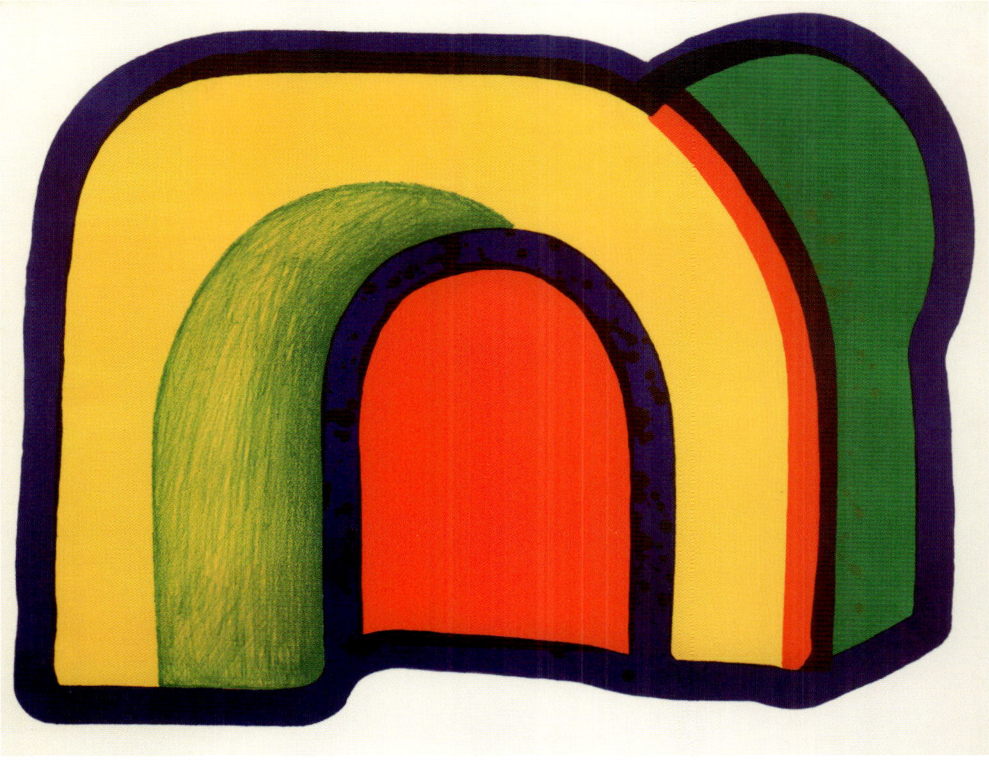

102
Derrick Greaves,
Vase and Falling Petal,
1971

103
Terry Frost,
Red and Black Solid,
1967–8

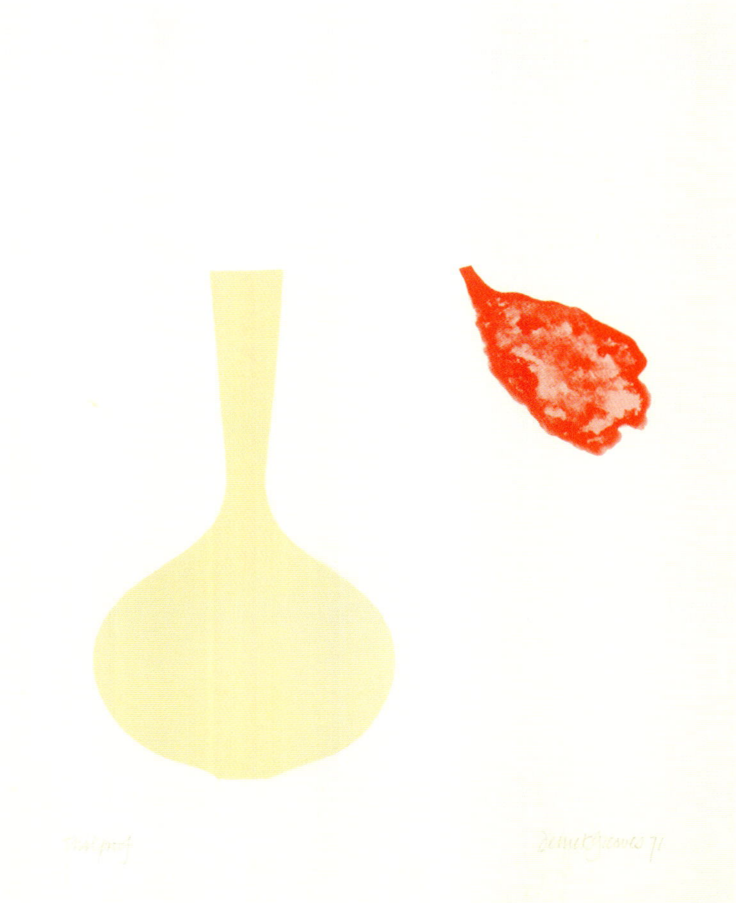

1950, as well as occasional lithographs, including *Three Financial Institutions*, 1963, commissioned by Editions Alecto and printed by Richard Bawden. In 1966, Alecto commissioned *Nine London Monuments*, printed as linocuts, which may have stimulated Curwen Prints to revive their successful pre-war practice of transferring Bawden's linocut images to zinc plate. Stanley Jones successfully did this for *Six London Markets* in 1967 under Bawden's close supervision, accurately rendering the broken and 'starved' textures that occur in his linocuts, but which could not easily be produced simply by drawing on plate or stone. In 1983, the Curwen Gallery commissioned two further prints of *Kew Palace* (fig.105) by the same method to celebrate Bawden's eightieth birthday. Other prints followed from other publishers, and Bawden and Piper together still constituted a link with pre-war Curwen well into the 1980s.[45]

Man Ray (fig.104), an international figure from the 1920s, made two prints at Curwen in 1969 for Consolidated Fine Art, New York, a company that rode the crest of the print boom. The prints combined lithography and screenprint, with the illusion of string connected to a luggage label. An even greater celebrity who was guided to Midford Place by Ed Newman of Consolidated Fine Art in the same year was John Lennon, with his new wife Yoko Ono. Lennon, seeking new activities as the Beatles fell apart, had previously worked on transfer paper and liked the resulting prints. Amid high secrecy, he worked over several days on zinc plates for the first time, on erotic images for a portfolio, *Bag I*, named

104
Man Ray,
Untitled I, 1969

105
Edward Bawden,
Kew Palace, 1983

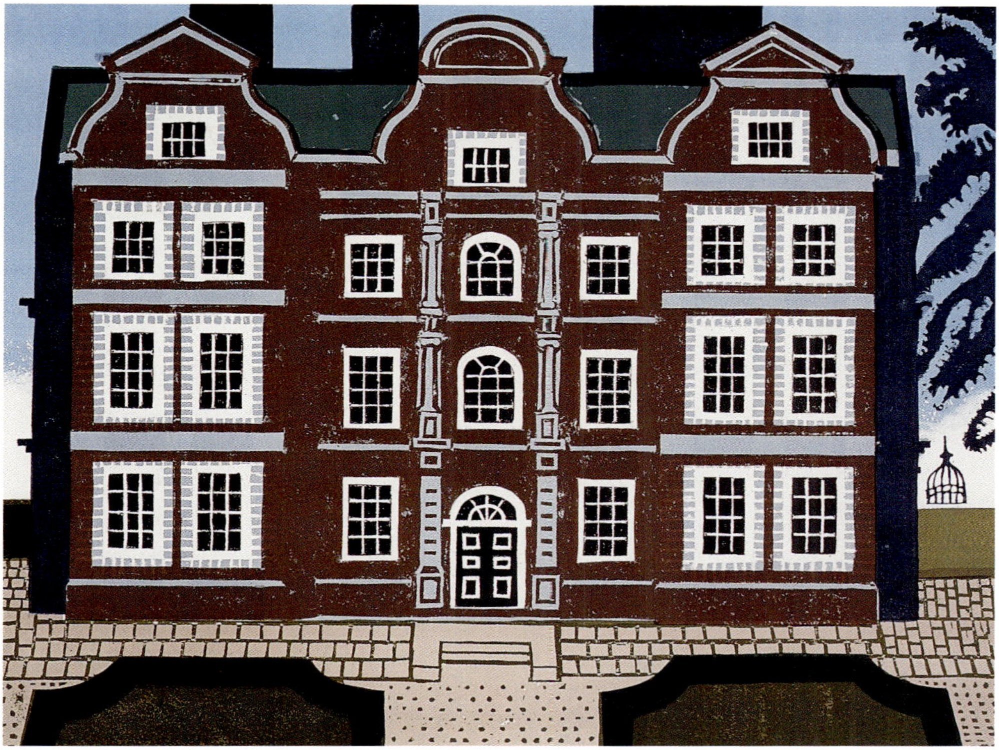

after Ono's Bag Publishing Company. Stanley Jones and his team worked with him. Lennon's assistant Anthony Fawcett recalled: 'While there, he created the image for the frontispiece, a simple sketch of himself crouched on the ground holding Yoko, which he drew directly onto a zinc plate. John was fascinated by the huge Heidelberg [*sic*] presses and watched intently as one of his own plates was put on for proofing. He had written a long alphabet poem, beginning "A is for parrot which we can clearly see", as an introduction to the portfolio, and he laboriously copied it out onto another zinc plate so that the poem itself would become a lithograph.'[46]

Herbert Simon had a special interest in industrial archaeology and canals which influenced the print publishing commissions that he initiated in the 1970s, including a number by David Gentleman (fig.106), who to some extent inherited the mantle of topography from John Piper, without striving to be particularly modern about it. Gentleman produced considerable amounts of book illustration, jackets and stamps, often using wood engraving, before turning to limited edition prints from 1970 onwards, with a series *Ten Topographical Prints*, all based on buildings of his choice. These tend to be frontal views without any landscape context, and some, such as *Little Moreton Hall, Cheshire*, play on the decorative quality of the building itself. They were indicative of an expanding interest in cultural tourism within the British Isles of the kind promoted before the war by Shell lorry bills, and in the 1970s by excellent guidebooks issued by Reader's Digest. In 1972, Gentleman's *Charleston Suite* extended the range to the southern United States, while the *Covent Garden Suite* of the same year recorded the existing buildings and spaces of this area, still only just emerging from the threat of a disastrous redevelopment and poised to become a centre for the arts. A further set of prints of

106
David Gentleman,
Kelmscott House, Chiswick, 1970

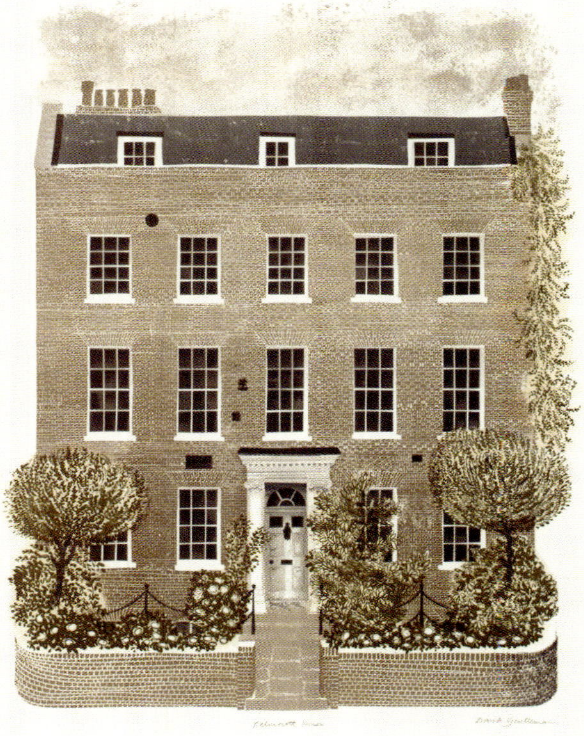

Bath followed in 1975, published by Curwen Gallery, and intermittent prints followed in the 1980s up to his latest in 2005. Gentleman expressed a desire to work more freely, but found this hard to achieve. His best effort at self-liberation came when Stanley sent him out with a plate to draw on location in Covent Garden. Other topographical artists, such as Albany Wiseman, brought work to the Studio, often in the form of commissions from institutions such as hospitals or Inns of Court for prints for sale to their own supporters and members.

Curwen Studio's mixed portfolio called *Follies* in 1971 referred, knowingly or not, to a Shell theme of the 1930s, although on this occasion most of the buildings depicted were quaint and curious structures in landscape saved by the Landmark Trust, founded in 1965 by Sir John Smith. Among them was *Pineapple House*, depicted by Barbara Jones, author of a classic book on follies, and *The Gothic Temple at Stowe* (fig.107) by Leonard Rosoman, an artist who had himself made a Shell lorry bill, *The Tower, Tutbury*, in 1936. In 1971, mini-skirted, thighbooted picnicking girls sprawl provocatively in the foreground, placed perhaps to lure the boys of Stowe School.

These prints, while seemingly retrogressive in terms of a narrative of modern art, were none the less an accurate reflection of the print market of the time and of a new enthusiasm for old buildings and conservation that formed part of a reaction against modernism in architecture and the environment. European Architectural Heritage Year was 1975, and from the ruins of collapsing industry and its

107
Leonard Rosoman,
The Gothic Temple at Stowe, 1971

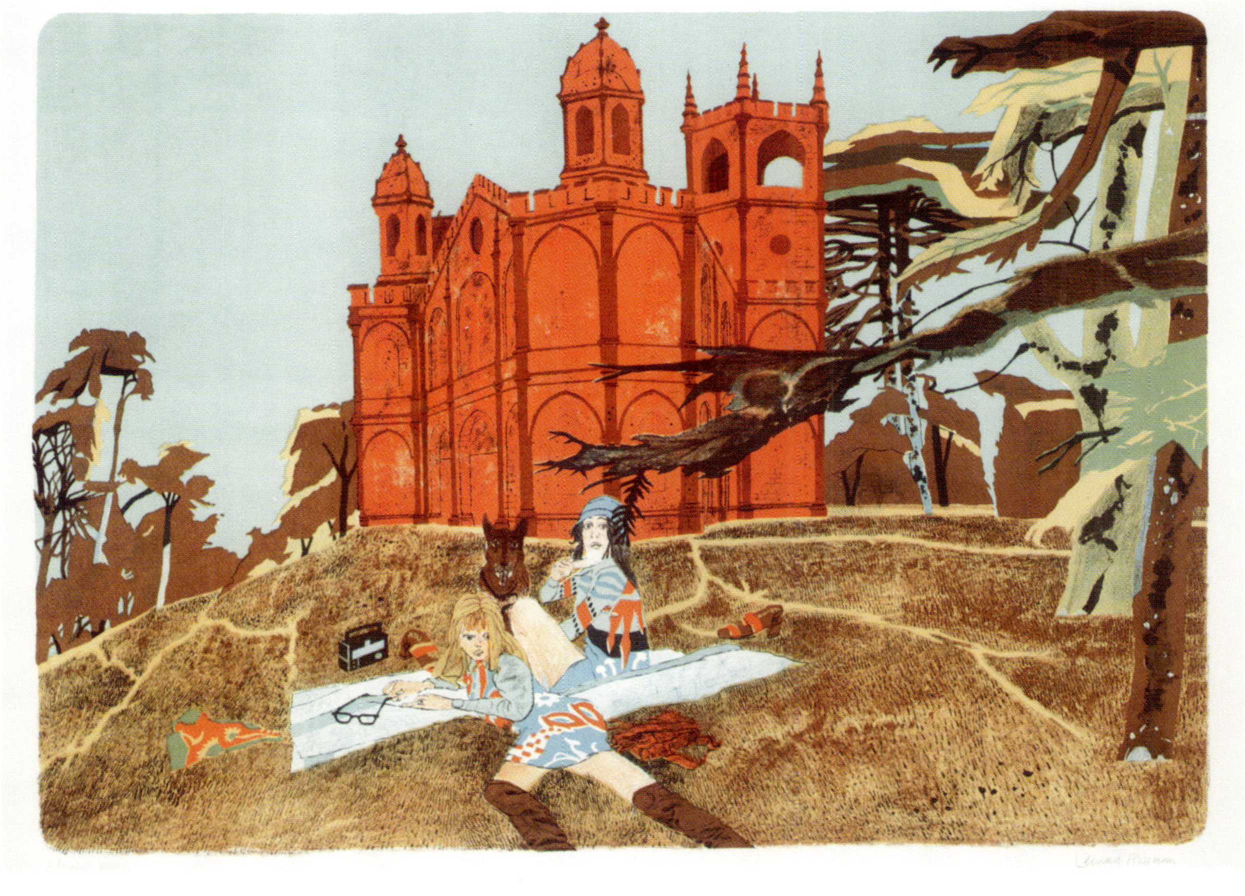

108
The Ratcliff press
at Midford Place

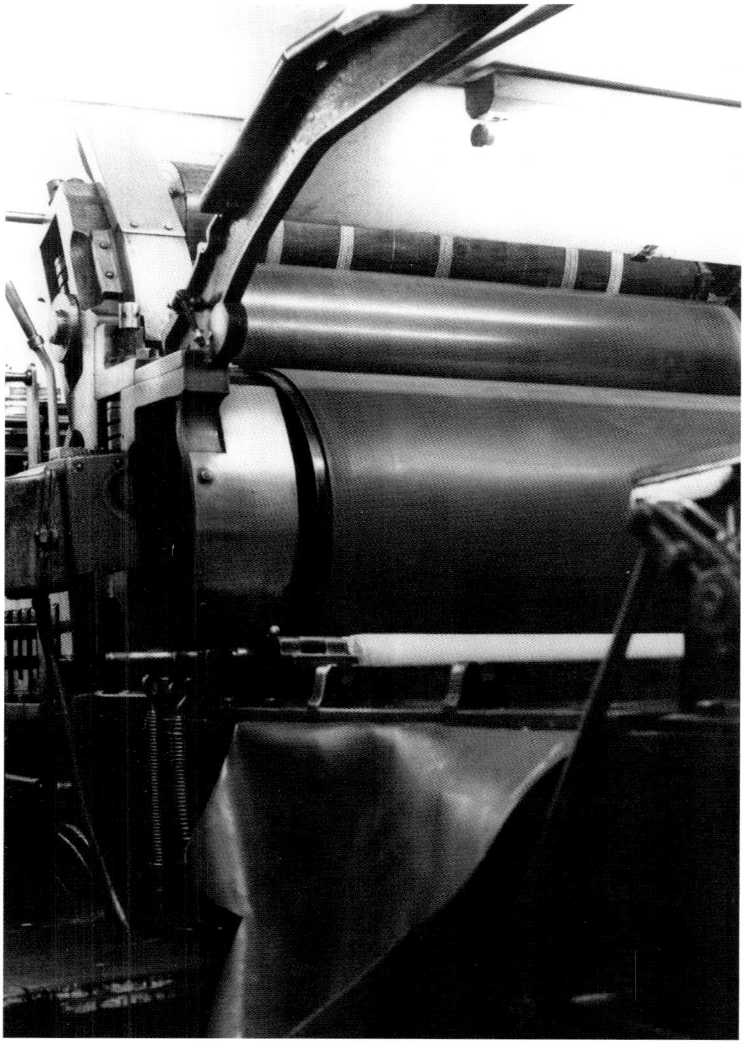

infrastructure arose a new form of populist romantic vision of the past, which Gentleman's Covent Garden prints accurately embodied. Stanley Jones himself acknowledges the importance of architecture in his home town of Wigan in his dawning visual awareness, with its worn and textured brick walls that lie behind his search for texture in his own printmaking. The heritage concept was perfectly matched in the marketplace by the idea of a printing technique that belonged to the age of steam, with the cast iron Ratcliff press (fig.108) clanking away in the Midford Place basement. A significant part of the market for print editions lay with architects and interior designers who might specify a suite of images for a hotel, office suite or some other semi-public space, where something reassuring and visually undemanding could still add distinction. Another part of the market was reached through advertisements in the weekend colour supplement magazines that were launched in the mid-1960s and often carried stories about heritage, collectables and costume drama films. The *Observer*, which re-introduced the School Prints series to a new generation through mail-order marketing, was especially geared to the world of prints.

There were more subtle approaches to the past evident in the transformation of an artist such as David Hockney, who veered in the early 1970s towards an academic style of drawing reminiscent of Picasso imitating Ingres. 'The purists think you're going backwards', he said in 1980, 'but I know you'd go forward. Future art that is based on appearances won't look like the art that's

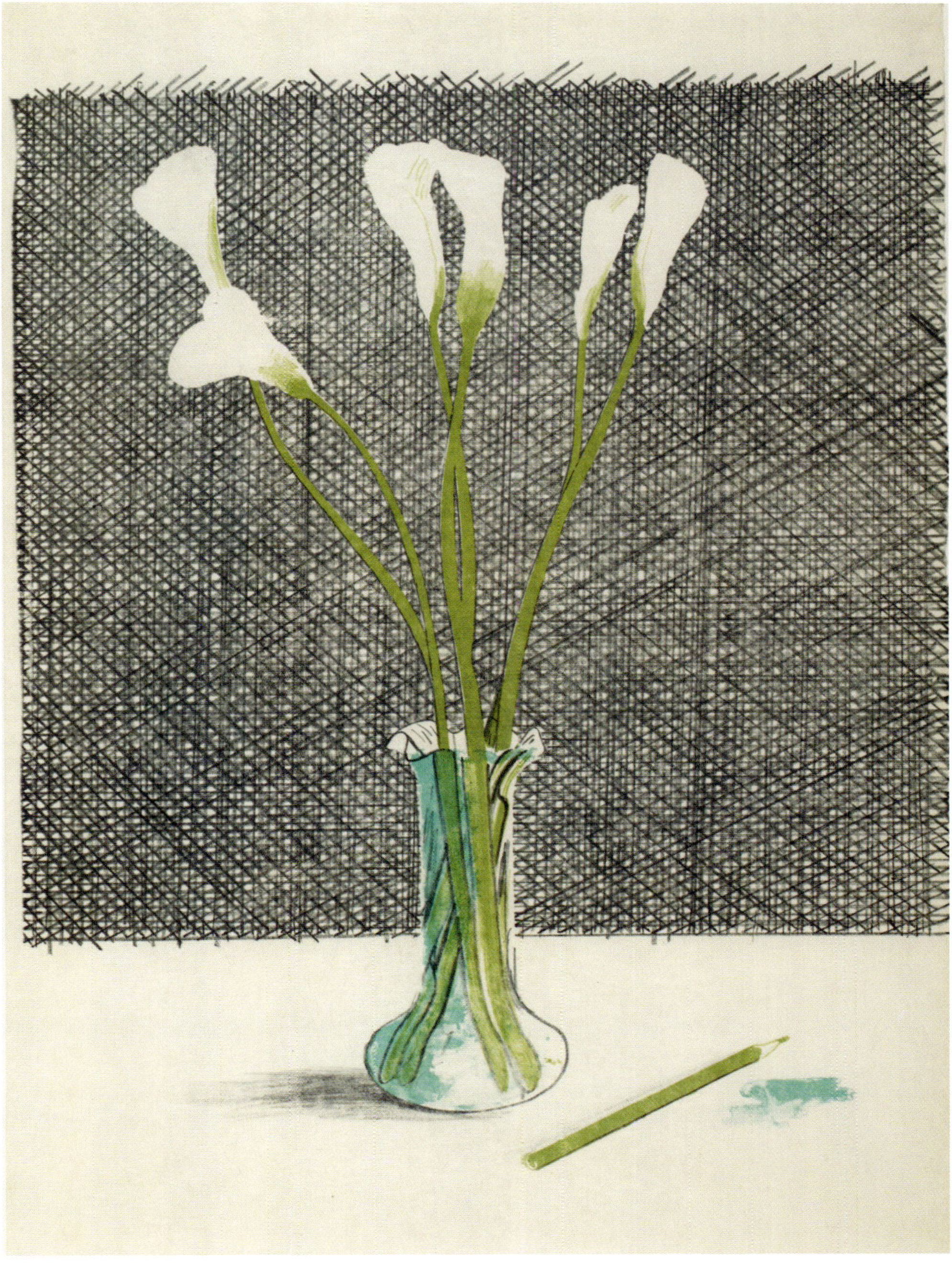

109
David Hockney,
Lilies, 1970–1

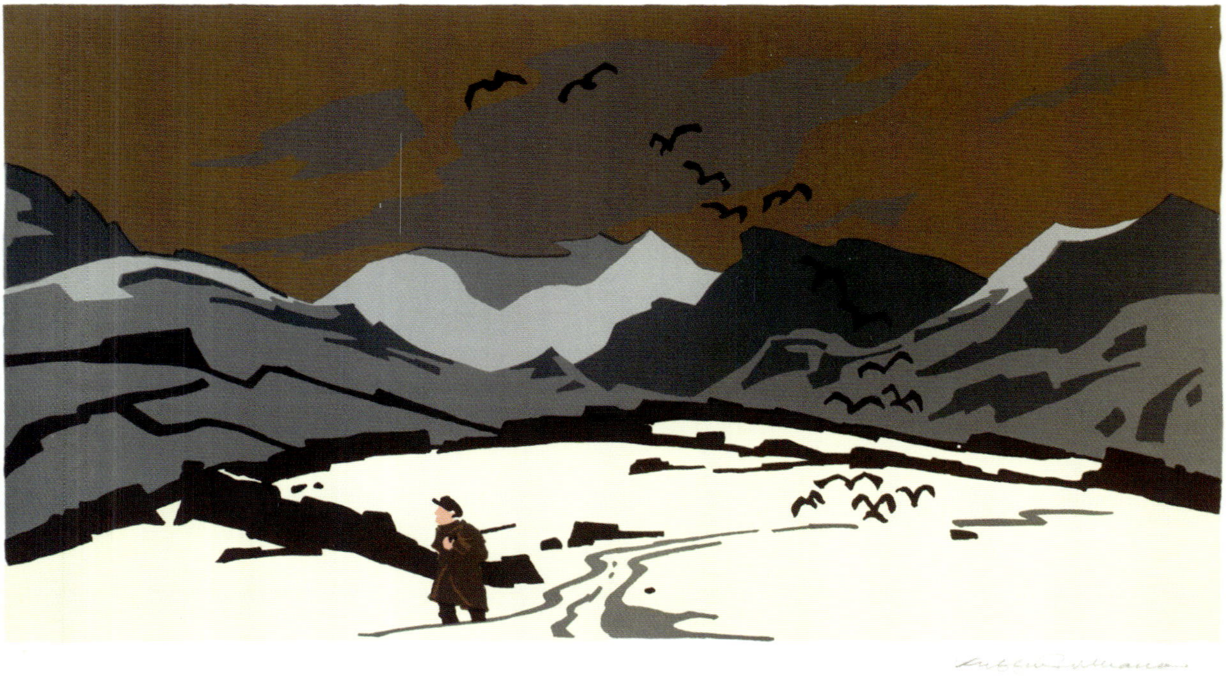

110
Kyffin Williams,
Pontllyfni in Snow,
1974

gone before.'[47] Inspired partly by his discovery of photography as a reference for painting, Hockney began a series of portraits in the late 1960s that signalled a new direction. His lithograph for Petersburg Press, *Flowers Made of Paper and Black Ink,* 1971, with its counterpart in colour, played with the difference between representation and reality. With its cross-hatched background and uncomplicated subject, the print showed, as Marco Livingstone has written, Hockney's 'delight in ornamental beauty and in the old-fashioned theme of simple still life ... almost in conscious defiance of current practice.'[48]

Hockney made three prints at Curwen: *Connoisseur*, 1970, for Petersburg Press; *The Print Collector*, 1970–1, a portrait of Felix Man, for Europaeische Graphik VII; and a 'pretty' still life, *Lilies* (fig.109). They do not compare in technical innovation with the coloured paper pulp *Paper Pools* series that he made with Ken Tyler in the USA in 1978, but belong rather to the gently nostalgic vein of his work that left a lasting impact on English artists such as Glynn Boyd Harte. Boyd Harte graduated from the illustration course at the Royal College of Art in the early 1970s and developed a fascination for lithography, not surprising, perhaps, in one whose childhood home in Rochdale had its garden path paved with litho stones from his grandfather's print works.

For another print-obsessed publisher, Jonathan Gili, whose 'day job' was as a documentary film director, Glynn Boyd Harte produced an artist's book around extracts from Betjeman's script for the television film *Metroland*, in 1977. A certain almost deliberate and naive clumsiness seen there in the rendering of 'found' images from postcards and similar sources began to change in *Temples of Power,* 1979, a swan-song for the vision of an integrated Curwen world of lithography and letterpress fine editions. The author, artist and publisher

111
Ralph Brown,
Embrace, 1978

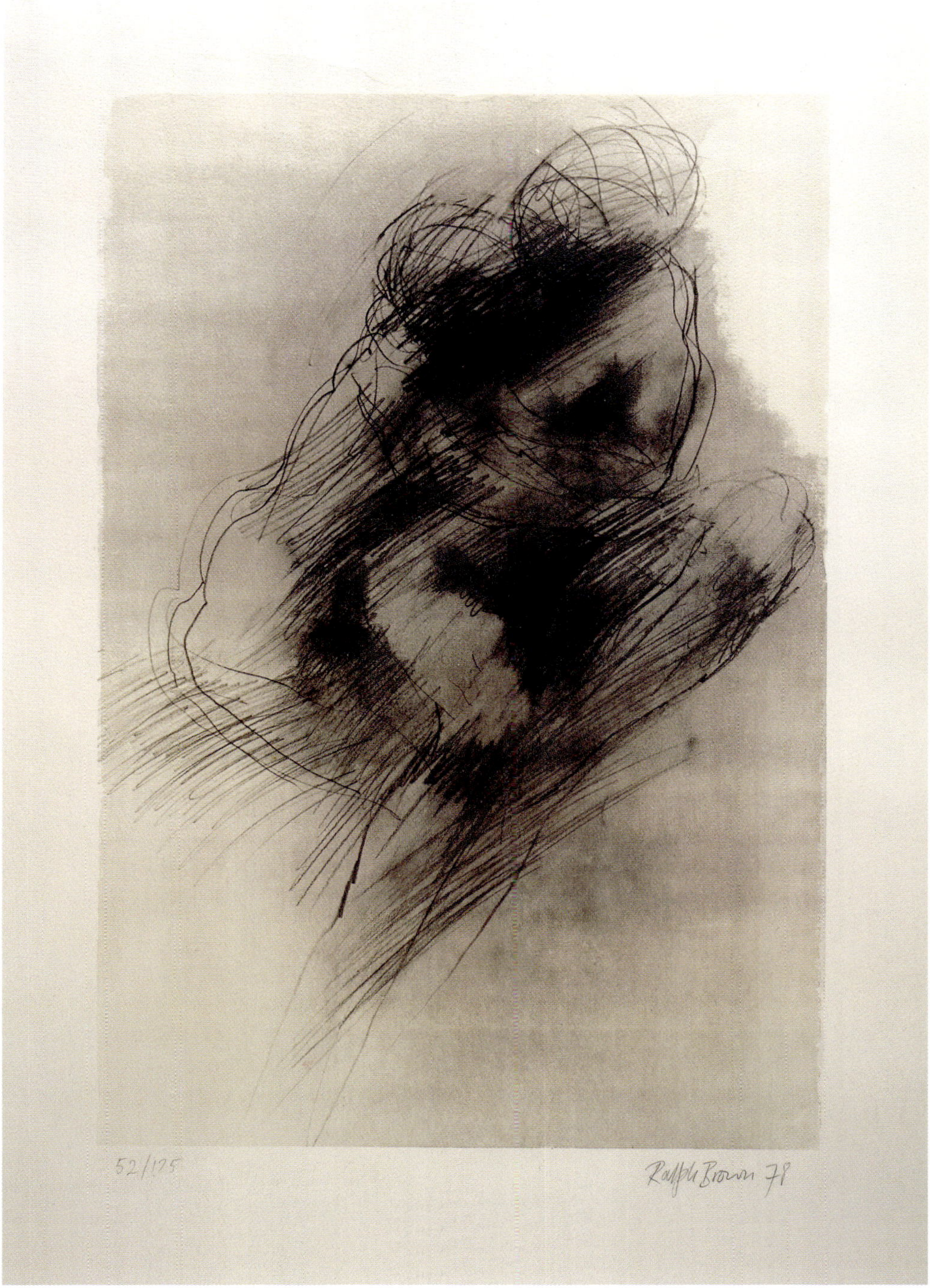

112
Glynn Boyd Harte,
Mr Dodd's Auricula,
1979

were prominent in the fashionable London 'young fogey' movement of the time, dressing in old-fashioned clothes and starched collars. In addition to these architectural subjects, Boyd Harte produced crayon drawings of still life assemblages, surpassing Hockney's efforts in their referential contents, with an emphasis on retro packaging and products, and these were translated into lithographs with ease and a developing skill (fig.112). Boyd Harte was influenced by the Curwen artists of the inter-war years, and Pat Gilmour's 1977 Tate exhibition on the Curwen Studio was inspirational for him. By the early 1980s he added watercolour to his repertory, and this was reflected in a new series of architectural prints with skilful colour separations.

Boyd Harte himself appeared, with the co-respondent shoes that he always wore, in a BBC Continuing Education television series in 1981, drawing a still life on zinc plates in his Islington home. He later appears in the Curwen Studio, still immaculately dressed, watching his plates being proofed. In the text of the book that accompanied the television series, Pat Gilmour wrote: 'Although it's true to say that his prints are essentially conceived as coloured pencil drawings the artist relishes the luminosity and the unification of various different drawing materials that lithography offers.'[49] The other lithographs represented in the programme, by Brendan Nieland, were photo-realist architectural subjects, a kind of flipside to Boyd Harte's work, printed by Alan Cox of Sky Editions. The juxtaposition shows that there were alternatives to the Curwen Studio for lithographic printmaking, as well as a range of artistic styles tending at this time to rather stylised representation in the manner of illustration. While Nieland's stencil-based images could well have been produced by silk-screen, however, the tactile handling of pencils and ink by Boyd Harte could not have been matched by any other medium.

Transitions in art and business

In 1970, Herbert Simon retired as Chairman of the Curwen Press, taking on the title of President for the remainder of his life. He sent his reluctant son Robert back to duties at Plaistow, and himself enjoyed a few years directing the Studio, having lost any of his initial scepticism towards it, and becoming, in Stanley Jones's words, 'a complete convert.'[50] After Herbert Simon's death in 1975, Curwen Prints Ltd acquired a new Managing Director in Stephen Reiss. He had been general manager of the Aldeburgh Festival, which included exhibitions in its annual programme, as well as commissioning distinguished artists such as Piper and Ceri Richards to design programme book covers. Reiss hoped to market prints more widely, and also to generate commissions from 'companies, colleges, clubs, local authorities etc.'[51] This initiative held an attraction for people outside the arts who were drawn to the possibility of contact with artists and with the pleasant bohemia of the Studio. In consequence, the National Trust commissioned prints from John Piper, David Gentleman, Graham Clarke and Michael Warren. This was done in association with Christies Contemporary Art, an offshoot of the London auction

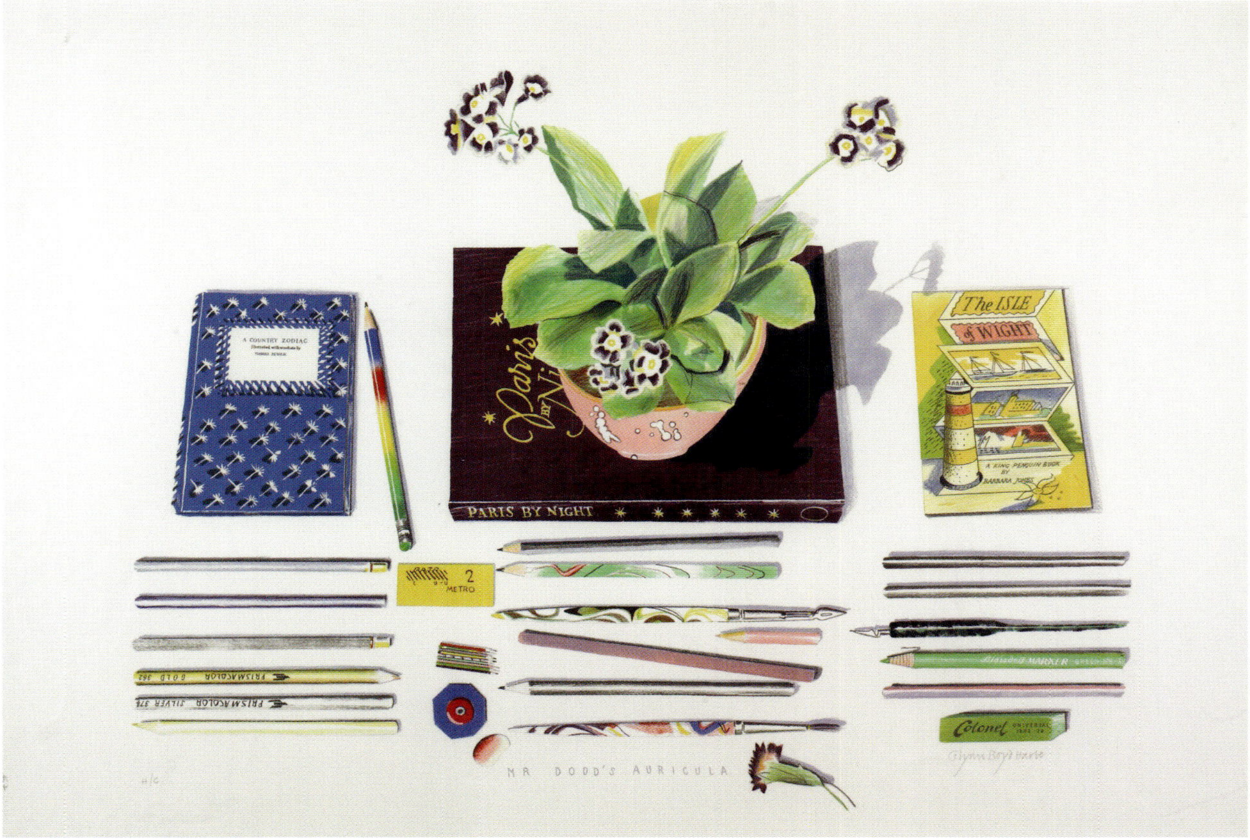
A COUNTRY ZODIAC
PARIS BY NIGHT
The ISLE of WIGHT
A KING PENGUIN BOOK BY BARBARA JONES
2
METRO
PRISMACOLOR GOLD
PRISMACOLOR SILVER
MARKER
Colonel
MR DODD'S AURICULA
Glynn Boyd Harte
H/C

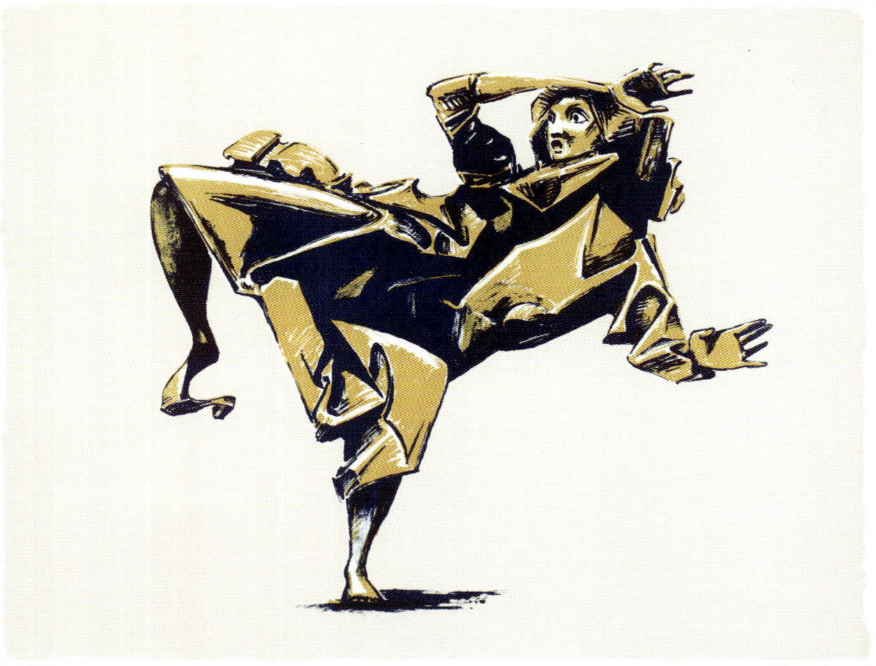

113
F.E. McWilliam,
Women of Belfast,
1973

house founded in 1972 which was responsible for commissioning a large part of the Studio's output over the following years.

In 1977, Reiss and the Chairman of the Curwen Press, John Hutchings, proposed a new 'shop window' for Curwen through the Business Art Gallery at the Royal Academy, another venerable institution driven to innovate by the uncertainty of the times, and gaining a new audience through the genial presidency of Sir Hugh Casson. As Reiss wrote to John Piper, 'For Curwen some kind of expansion has become a necessity. It is interesting (without I hope giving away any secrets) that Chris Prater at Kelpra has found himself in exactly the same predicament. A fully professional print-making studio by itself is an uneconomic proposition these days, just as classical music of a professional standard is uneconomic. The killer is not lack of demand, but the cost of production. The low standard, mass-produced object is so much easier to make. The studio is also at the mercy of the publishing situation. If the publishers have all the stock they want, a studio can be more or less abandoned for months, even years. An attempt had been made by Curwen to find protection by becoming a publisher itself but with insufficient understanding of the issues involved. Stocks were increasing relentlessly, at the rate of up to 1000 a year, and the overdraft rising correspondingly, until the point had been reached where the parent company was no longer able to contain the position.'[52]

Reiss had come to the conclusion that Curwen's own marketing could not compete with newcomers like Christies, with their established name and capital backing. He described to Piper the impossibility of getting support from official bodies: 'I did try first the Arts Council. I tried to persuade *them* to become

114
John O'Connor,
Kersey Church, 1976

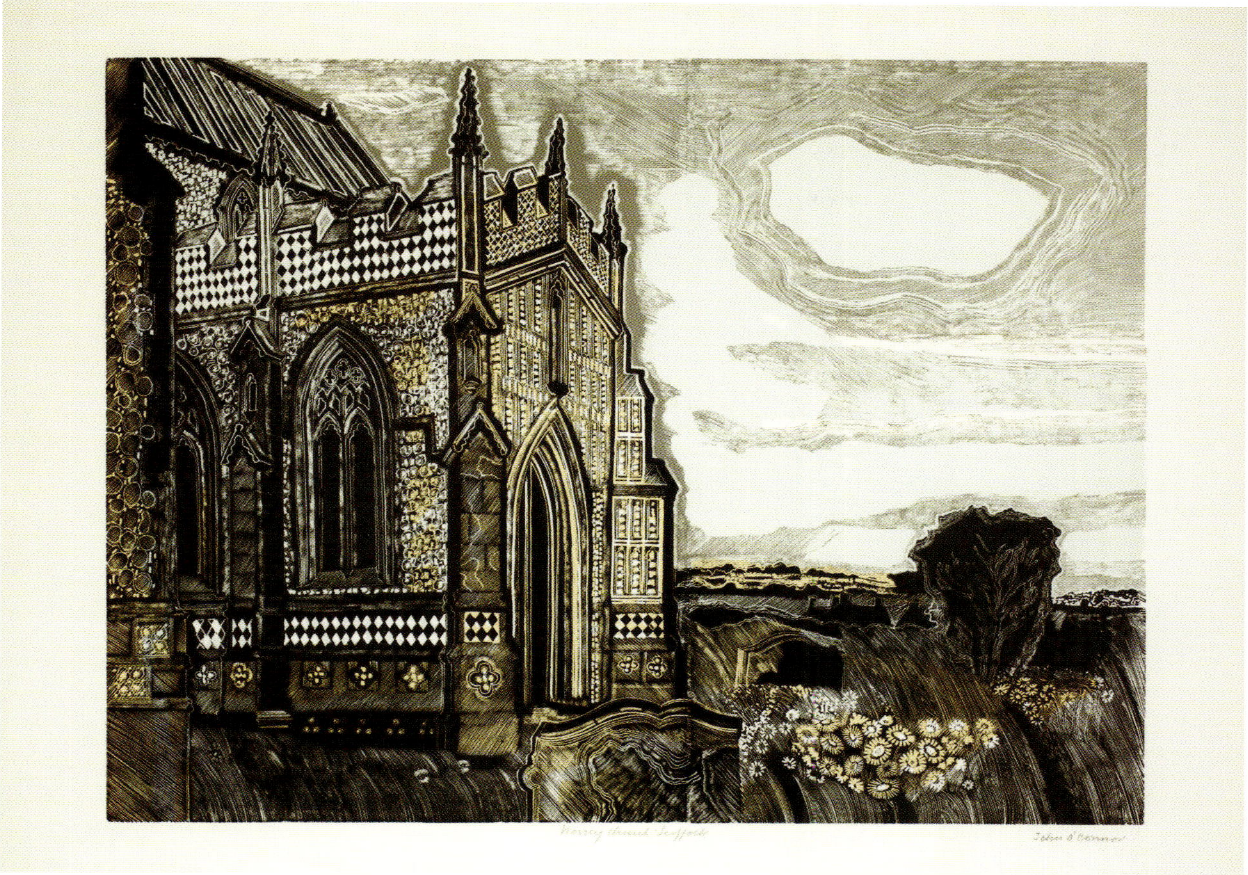

115
Bernard Leach,
Drawing for a Pot,
1973

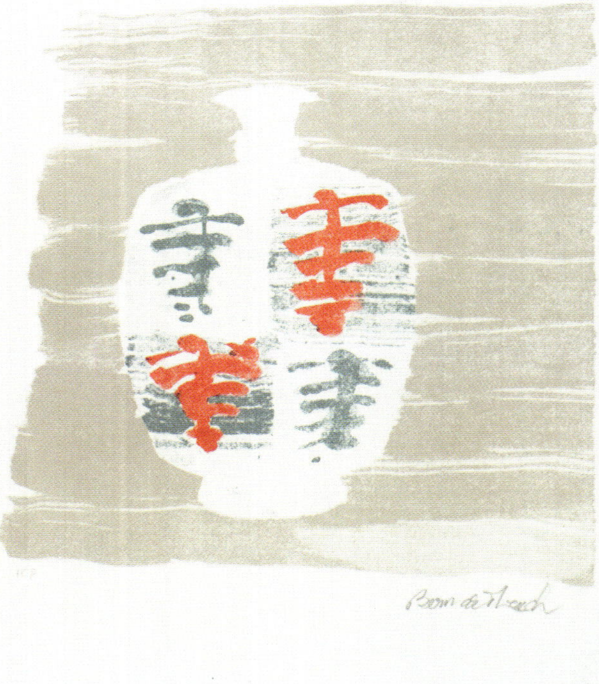

the sponsoring body for a nation-wide print marketing scheme, but I think they were put off by the fear that it might make money. I also considered the Tate Gallery, but suspected that their official, civil-service status would create too many administrative problems. The Royal Academy therefore seemed the obvious, if not the only, answer. One knows by the millions who visit Burlington House that it still remains for the average person, the symbol of quality in art. Moreover, the Royal Academy has a clearly defined obligation to foster the work of contemporary British artists, and what could be a better way of doing this than helping to commission and market new editions of original graphics.'[53]

Piper, who with his contemporaries retained a pre-war disdain for the Royal Academy's conservatism, was deeply suspicious, and Reiss admitted: 'I am not saying that everything we sell will be of the highest standard, simply because there is not enough of the highest standard to go round. At the same time, we are obviously relying on the fact that people like you and Henry won't boycott us.'[54] The predictions were right on all counts. The Business Art Gallery, its name well framed for the entrepreneurial 1980s, when it was the first of several art enterprises based on selling to companies and organisations, proved a commercial success. It occupied the old Diploma Galleries at the RA, before these were transformed into the Sackler Galleries in the late 1980s. It also fulfilled the need to keep the Curwen Studio ticking over with a regular supply of work.

John Hutchings, an accountant by training, joined the Curwen Press in the

116
Bill Jacklin,
Night Light, 1975

117
Michael Rothenstein,
Sunrise at 36,000 ft,
1973

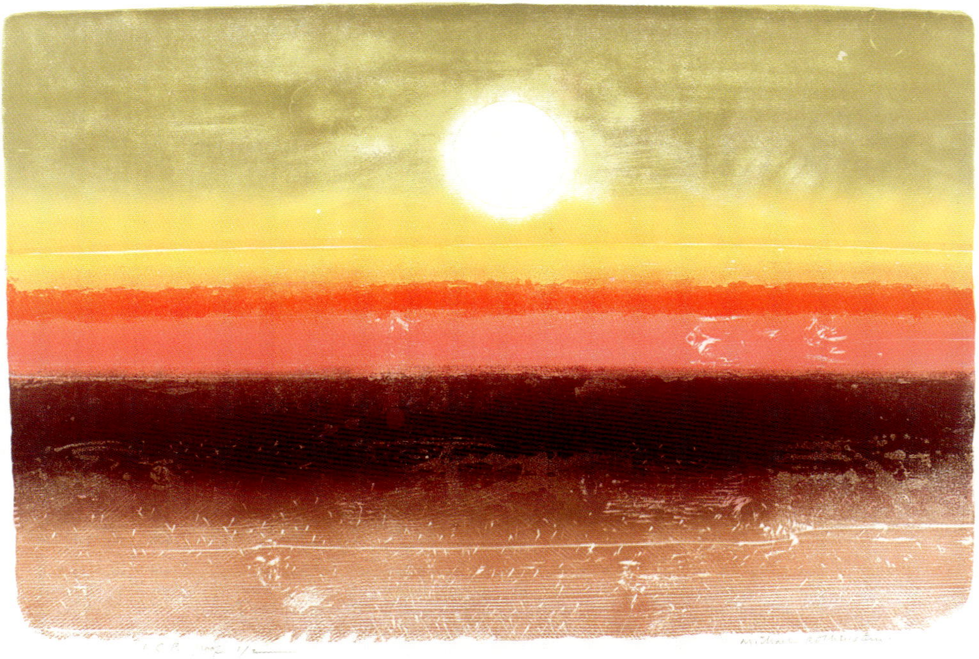

1960s as a financial advisor. Foreseeing that the parent company might suddenly be taken over, as eventually happened in 1983, he bought the Studio and Gallery in 1982 to preserve their independence, with Basil Harley's blessing. In 1987, the Business Art Gallery moved to premises in Windmill Street, with the name New Academy Gallery, not far from the Curwen Studio in Fitzrovia and opposite the new site of the Curwen Gallery, which had already gained more space than at its first home in Colville Place. In 2005, the two galleries were unified in one space as the Curwen and New Business Gallery, still under John and Jill Hutchings's direction. Exhibitions of original work are held, and a stock of prints, many from the Curwen Studio, is available, together with a commission service and an art hire arrangement.

Tate, the Institute of Contemporary Prints and Artists at Curwen

The *Artists at Curwen* exhibition in 1977 marked the occasion of a substantial gift of prints from the Curwen Studio to the Tate Gallery. This in itself is an interesting story, as it did not happen in isolation. The rise of artists' printmaking in the post-war years exposed the random manner in which prints were acquired for national collections. By tradition, the Prints and Drawings collections of the Victoria and Albert Museum and the British Museum acquired new works, but the Tate had only a handful of prints to put alongside paintings or sculpture by major artists. There has never been an equivalent in the print world to the British copyright deposit obligation for book publishers, although in France (where the political mischief making of artists was historically more feared than that of writers), a *dépôt-légal* exists for prints. As a result, the collector and benefactor Alastair MacAlpine created the Institute of Contemporary Prints in 1972, under the direction of Stewart Mason, a former Chief Education Officer for

118
Gerald Scarfe,
Students of the Revolution, 1969

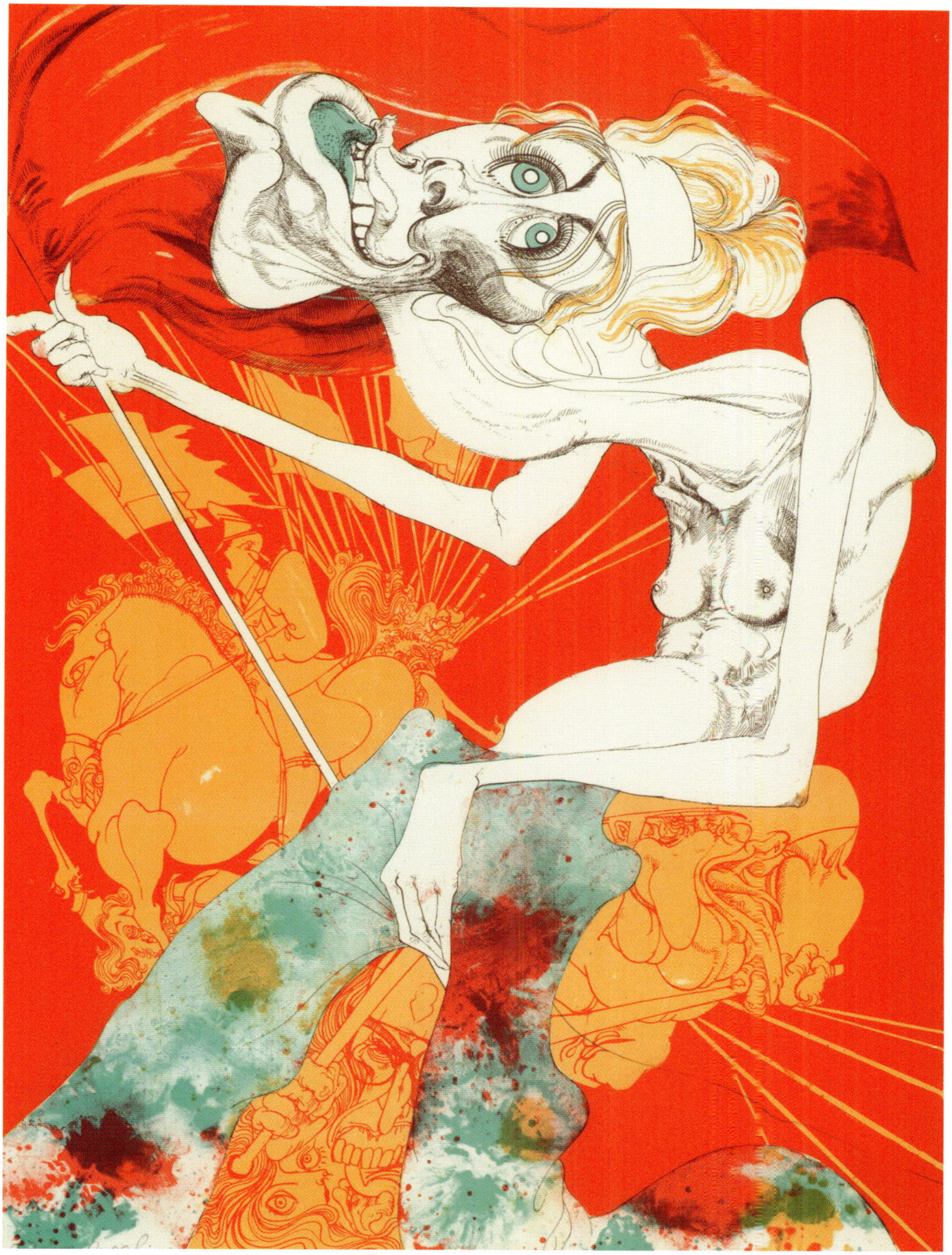

119
Leonard Rosoman,
Window Image, 1979

Leicestershire, where he commissioned works for schools and built up a notable modern collection.

Owing to the generosity of print studios and gallery publishers such as Leslie Waddington, 3,000 prints had been given to the Institute of Contemporary Prints by 1975. Kelpra gave 1,500, and Curwen 650, representing virtually all the significant work done since the Studio's foundation. The ICP and the Tate, who had established a formal relationship, decided not to select from these gifts, but to accession them in their entirety into the Tate Collection. In 1974, Pat Gilmour was appointed to a new Tate post as Assistant Keeper with a responsibility for contemporary prints, immediately setting new standards for conservation and storage. The Tate's director, Sir Norman Reid, was highly supportive, and, despite severe space restrictions, not only were the new collections housed in the Millbank building, but a dedicated display space was also created in the basement. As Pat Gilmour has written, 'initially, the department mounted small shows in a corridor leading to the coffee shop. Although close to the gurgle of the basement lavatories, the *force majeure* that drew people to the basement won greater attention for prints than the more salubrious hangs upstairs!'[55]

A show of Henry Moore's prints in 1975, placing them in the context of sculptures and drawings from the Collection, reinforced the message that printmaking was an integral part of many major artists' activity (something that has not been carried on with such consistency, partly, perhaps, owing to the increasing demand for low light levels when exhibiting works on paper). *Artists at Curwen* was the culmination of this trend. The exhibition was brought forward to fill a gap at the beginning of 1977, with selection, framing and a book-length catalogue all achieved in the space of a month. The show covered the Curwen Press from the 1920s as well as the Studio, bringing 'applied art' in the form of wallpaper, menus and other ephemera into the gallery, with the reasonable pretext that they were original prints. The exhibition was very popular, riding on a wave of revived interest in the 1930s and Art Deco, so that its closure was delayed by several weeks. It was followed by a Kelpra exhibition, by which time Pat Gilmour had moved on to teaching and freelance curating. Meanwhile, the Tate decided to purchase prints individually rather than continue the informal *dépôt-légal*.

Moving to Chilford Hall: 1989 to the present

The Curwen Studio was cushioned to survive the dissolution of Curwen Press, and the stability provided by Stanley Jones, now more widely appreciated since the *Artists at Curwen* show, was reassuring. The day-to-day financial situation was still precarious, however, and the high overheads were inseparable from the inherited situation involving the employment of union members, as well as the health and safety requirements presented by the basement location, with its restricted ventilation and means of escape. The mid-1980s saw the crisis for the print unions in Fleet Street, with the defeat of cherished but obsolete and expensive technology at

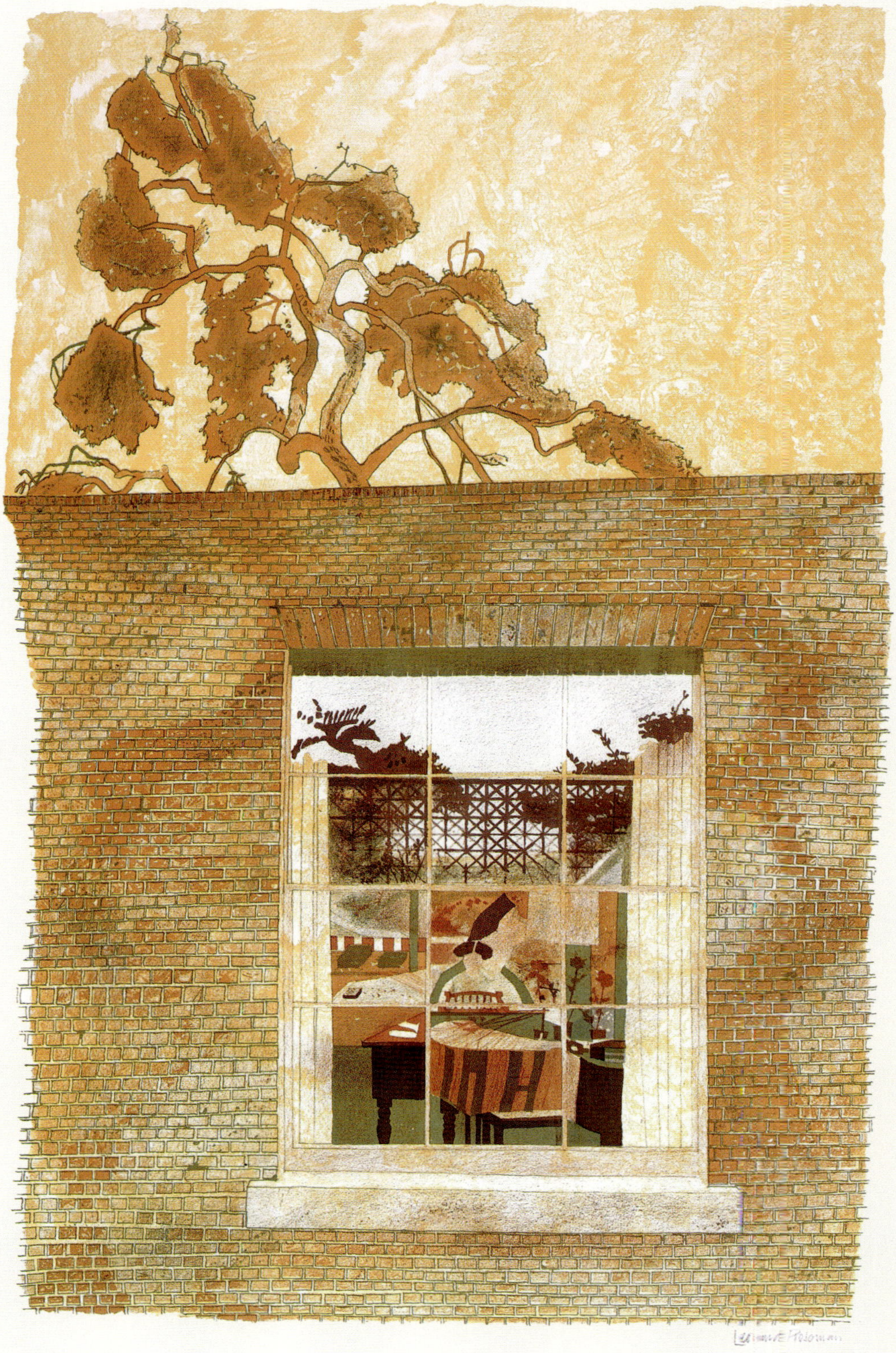

120
Anthony Green,
Tent and Mary Cozens-Waker's Box,
1988

the gates of Rupert Murdoch's new newspaper printing plant in Wapping, which was run by electricians who received copy from journalists electronically. Posters affirming solidarity with the Wapping strikers were hung incongruously in the Midford Street basement in the summer of 1986, but in vain.

While conveniently located and atmospheric, the disadvantages inherent in the Studio set-up as it had evolved over the course of its first thirty years became increasingly apparent as external conditions changed. When the lease became due for renewal in 1989, a search was undertaken for an alternative building in London, but nothing suitable could be found with an affordable price during this period of high property values.

At this point it would have been easy to give up. That this did not happen is due, above all, to Stanley Jones's determination that such a unique facility, having survived longer than any comparable organisation, should not fade away.

During the course of the property search, Sam Alper, the owner of Chilford Hall near Cambridge, made contact with the Curwen Studio.[56] Alper built up a business making caravans in the post-war years, cleverly adapting surplus military materials to create the Sprite, a product at about a third the cost of existing models. His genius for publicity was equally remarkable, and in the 1960s Caravans International, along with his other interests in travel and leisure such as the roadside Little Chef restaurants, were highly successful. After Caravans International went into receivership in 1982, Alper transferred his entrepreneurial energy to his immediate surroundings at Chilford Hall, where, disillusioned by conventional farming, he had a vineyard and a conference centre. In 1982, he founded Chilford Hall Press, a fine-art silkscreen printing studio run by the printer Kip Gresham. Its approach was on the same lines as Curwen, Kelpra and other studios. Curwen was invited to move in, and John Hutchings sold much of his shareholding to Sam Alper, retaining a minority interest.

Moving any enterprise of this kind is difficult. For Curwen, it precipitated a 'restructuring' that was, perhaps, overdue in any case. The most significant aspect of this was that the existing unionised workforce of three, while they would have liked to continue their employment, took voluntary redundancy as they did not wish to relocate so far from London. Curwen was left as a two-person organisation, with Stanley Jones assisted by Serena Castle, who had worked for some years in Midford Place as an administrator. For technical reasons, it was decided to dispose of the big Ratcliff offset machine, which, having been dismantled in order to extract it from beneath the pavements of Tottenham Court Road, found its way to Jarrolds Printing Museum in Norwich. Henceforth, the printing of editions was done on proofing presses, technically more dependable, but not capable of working at high speeds. Among the benefits of the new premises were ease of delivery for supplies, freedom from the arduous health and safety provisions, a larger floor space, and the potential for expansion. With the lofty space of a converted Dutch barn replacing the low ceilings, the atmosphere remained

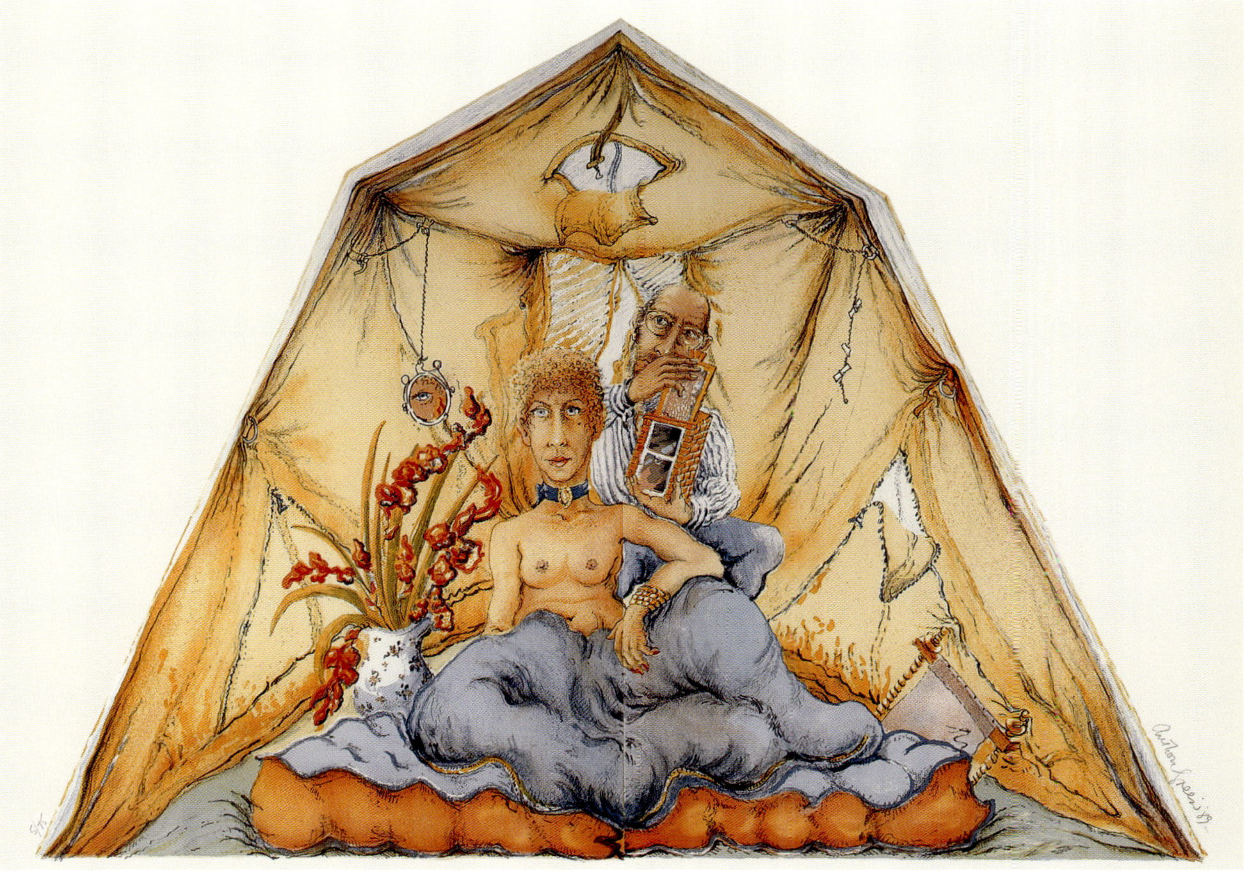

121 A–L
Bernard Dunstan, *Musicians in the Courtyard*, 1994, progressive states

A

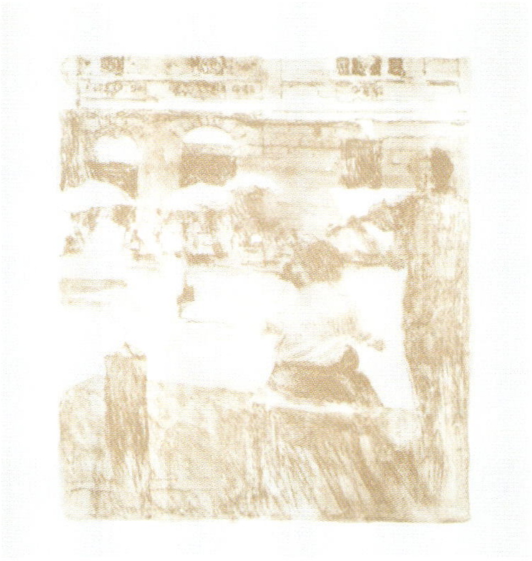

B

C

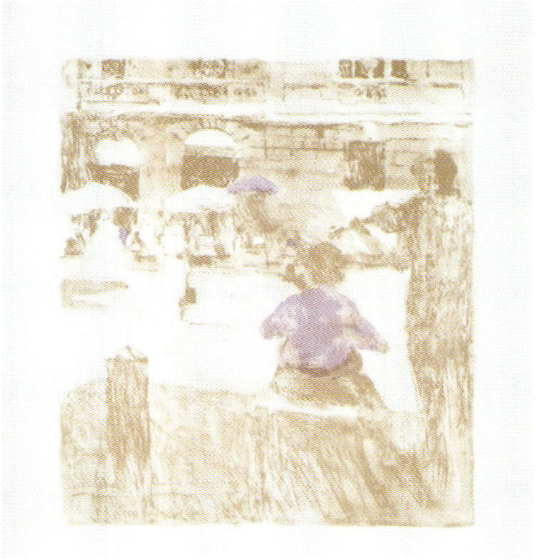

D

E

F

G

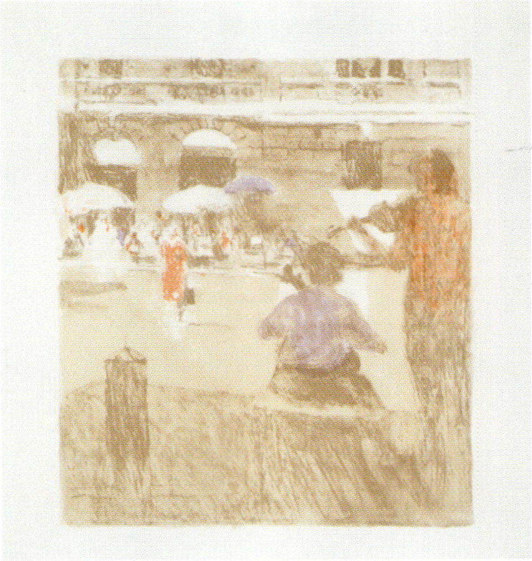

H

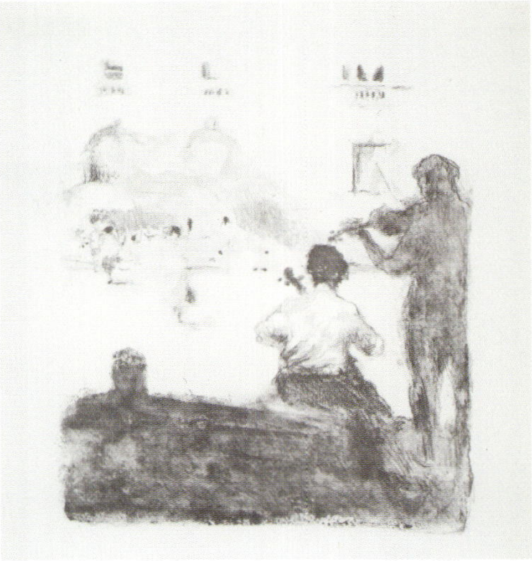

I

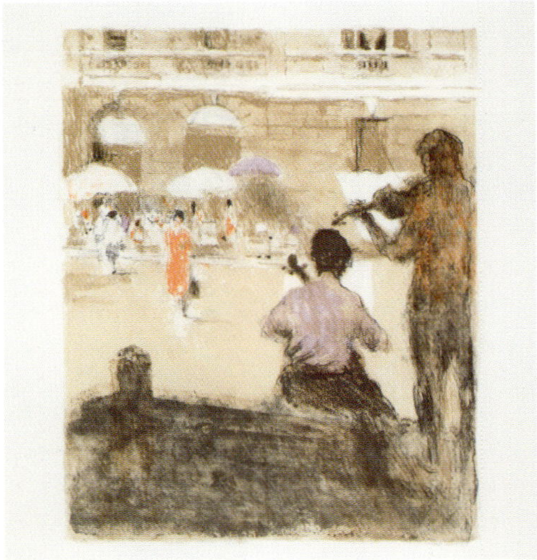

J

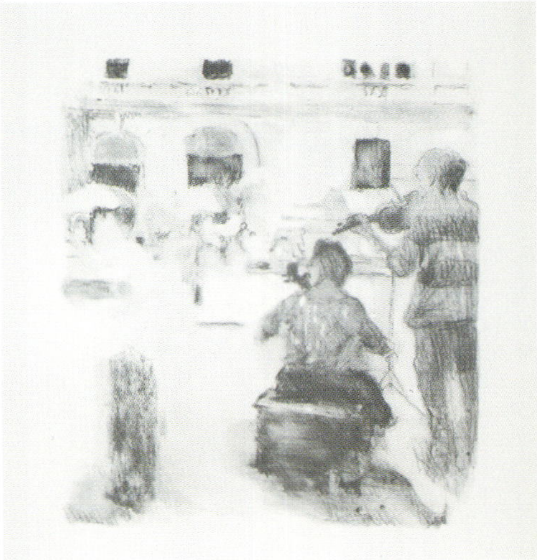

K

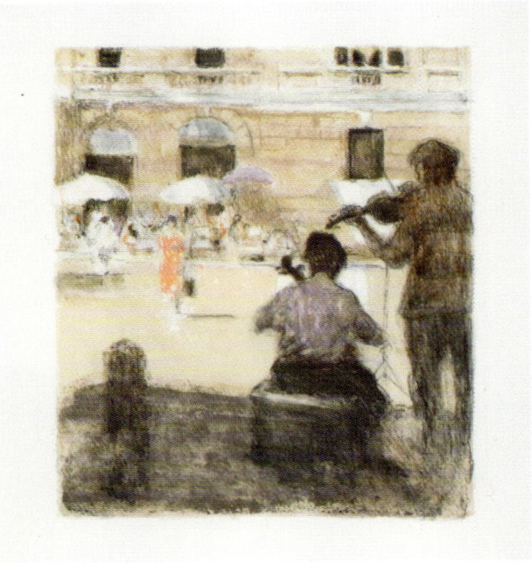

L

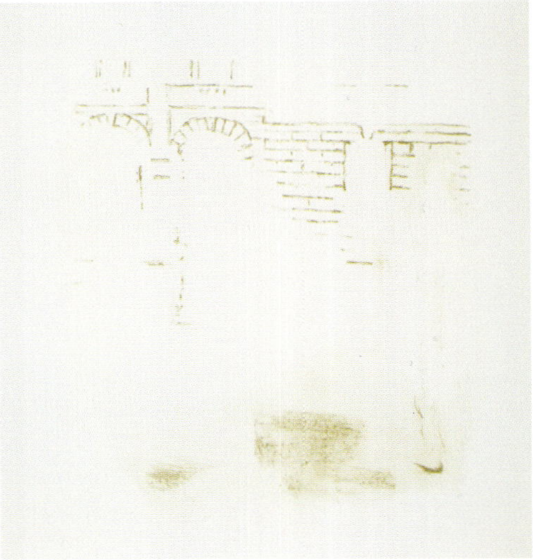

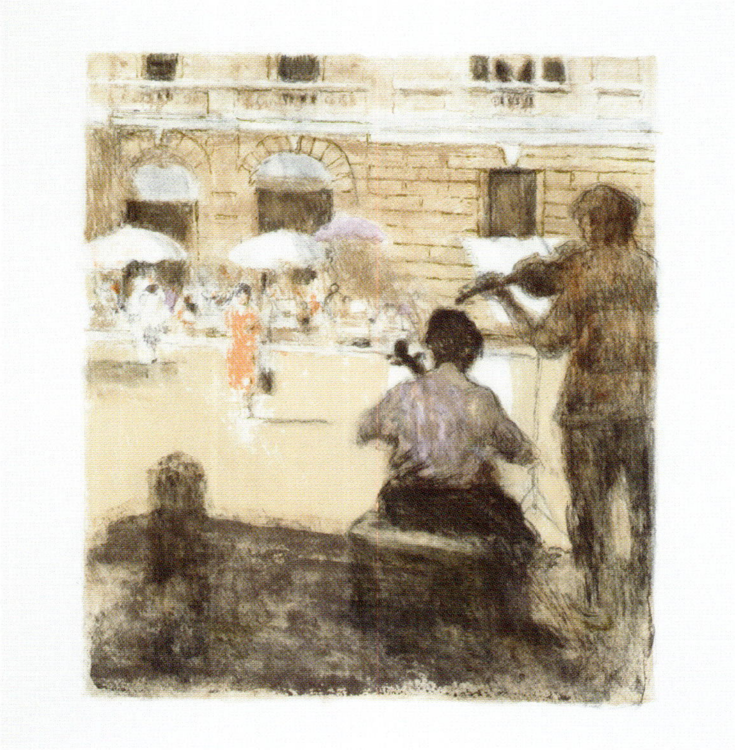

122
Bernard Dunstan,
Musicians in the Courtyard, 1994,
completed print

123
Bernard Dunstan,
Room in Viterbo, 1974

in other ways surprisingly unchanged. The same combination of hard work and sociability has meant that many visitors still drop in unannounced.

Stanley Jones's continuing involvement, as he entered his sixties, was essential, and the commute from his home in Woodford Green, Essex, up the M11 (opened at the beginning of the 1980s) was easier than the journey to central London had been. For a few years, he worked with Serena, who learned the job of printing and became highly proficient. For a Royal Academy exhibition catalogue in 1995, featuring new work by Bernard Dunstan, she provided the technical notes on lithography. Dunstan (figs.121–3) is a figurative artist whose technique would have been recognised by Walter Sickert or the Impressionists, using broken touches of colour and tone to create softly lit interiors with people. His set of prints of different parts of Burlington House were far removed from the hard graphic edges found in the work of Glynn Boyd Harte, David Gentleman or even Edward Ardizzone. There was a resurgence of interest in the painterly tradition to which Dunstan belonged, however, which satisfied art lovers who might feel excluded by other Royal Academy activities such as the *Sensation* exhibition of 'Young British Artists' that opened two years later. Despite the earlier activities of Tracey Emin at Curwen, the idea of carefully crafted lithographs was alien to the iconoclastic, if market-driven, art world. Even screen-printing, once the more radical alternative to lithography, lost its appeal to the newly fashionable cohort of the anti-academy.

The experiment of running silkscreen alongside lithography at Chilford Hall Press, as it was initially called, was relatively short-lived, owing to Kip Gresham's desire to pursue his work independently. This left more space, and Alper worked with Curwen to establish the Curwen Print Study Centre, an educational charity that promoted printmaking, and lithography in

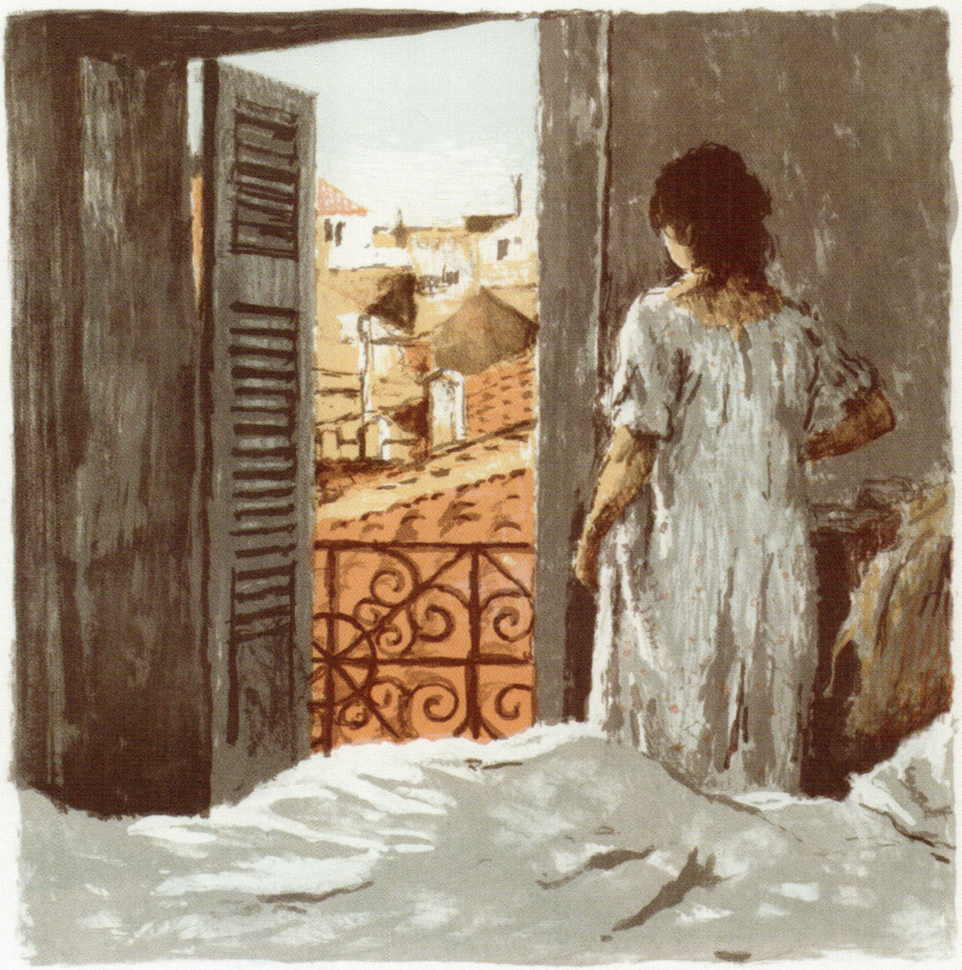
Bernard Dunstan

124
John Bellany,
Celtic Maiden, 1998

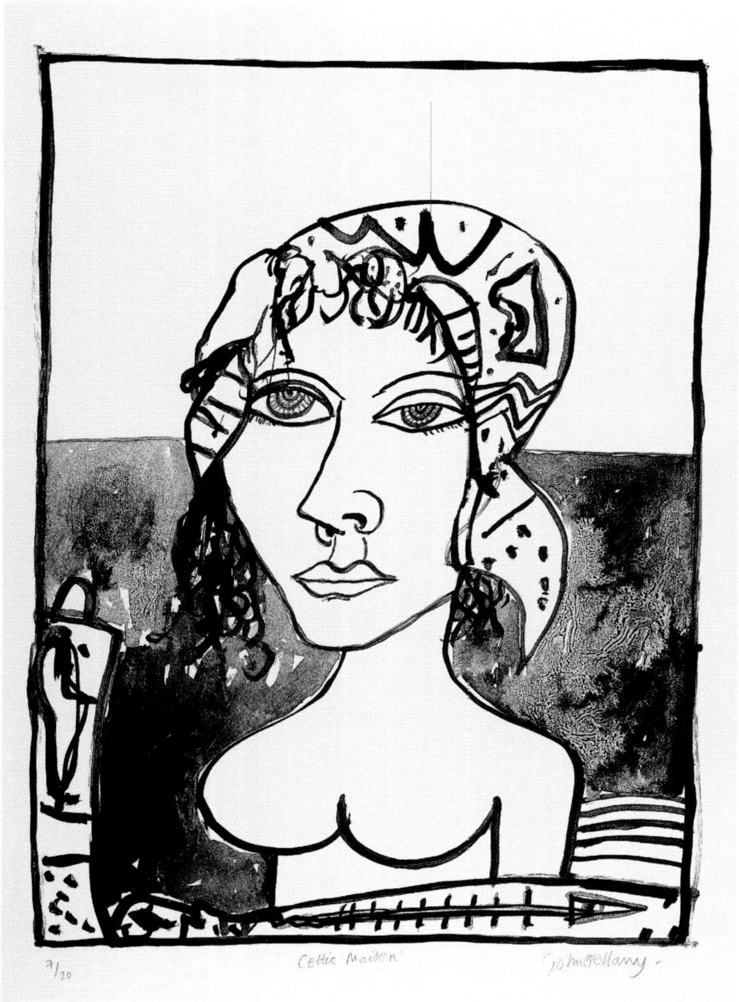

particular. The centre was a response to the decline of printmaking in art schools, which has meant that fewer students have a practical background in the subject, and therefore cannot pass on their skills as they had done before. The Study Centre provides courses for school children, students, artists and teachers, offering direct experience of all the major printmaking media in a way not available anywhere else.

In 1999, Jenny Roland joined the company in one of the most surprising of the many coincidences that mark the Curwen history. She is the granddaughter of Herbert Simon and daughter of Robert Simon, and although well aware of the Curwen Story, had no adult role in it before seeing an exhibition at the John Russell Gallery in Ipswich which rekindled her interest. She moved with her family to the village of Linton, near Chilford Hall, taking on the recently vacant position of administrator and bringing a fresh enthusiasm and commitment. By this time, the Studio had a regular staff of two printers, trained by Stanley Jones, of whom Tom Martin, who joined in 1998, is the current Studio Manager. Sam Alper died in 2002, but his son, Simon, was already a member of the board, and Jenny took on his role as Managing Director.

The Studio has its own publishing programme as well as making editions for publishers and for artists themselves. The physical distance from London still allows for an easy day trip, and has been compensated by the instant global communication of the internet.

It is no easier to tell the story of Curwen in the past fifteen years in terms of 'big

125
Paul Hogarth,
Santa Monica Beach,
1992

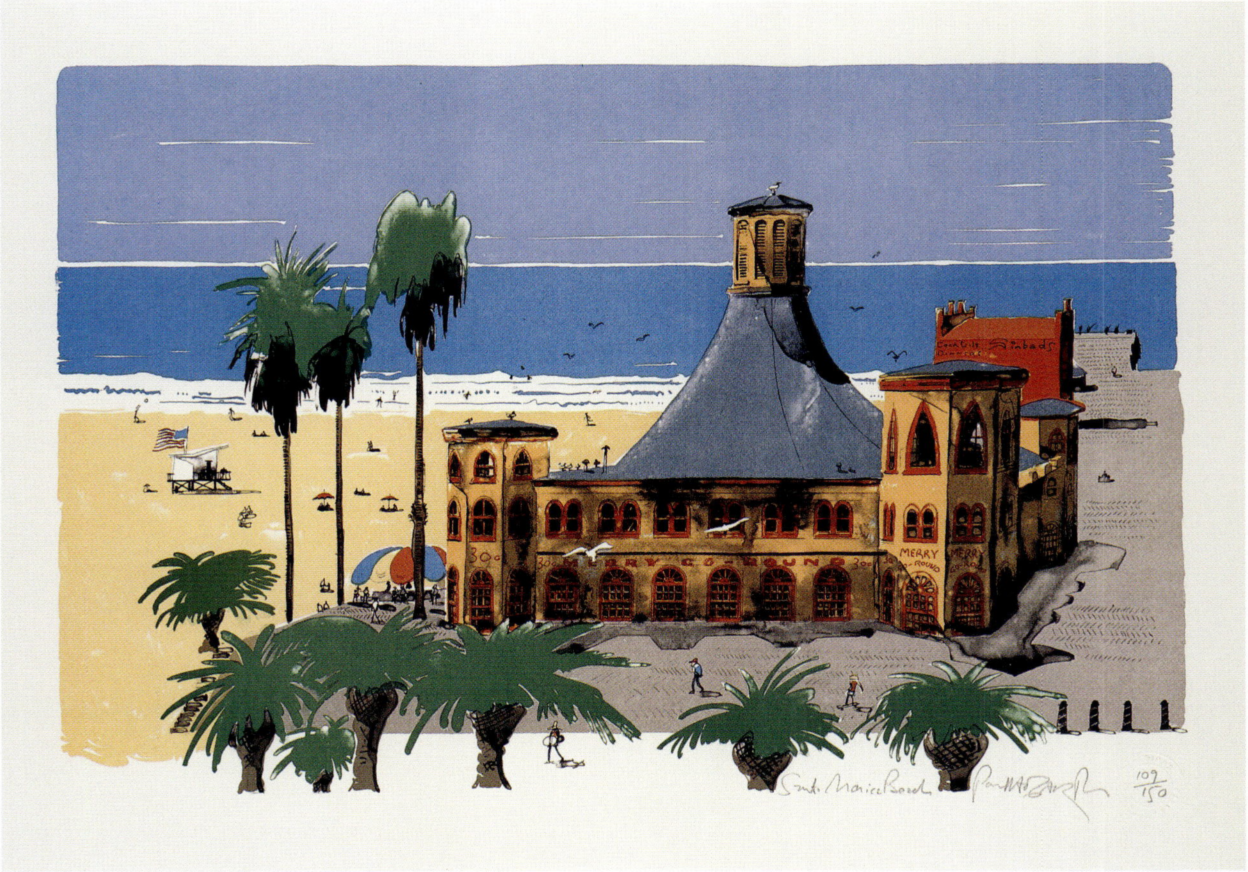

126
Paula Rego,
Jane Eyre, 2002

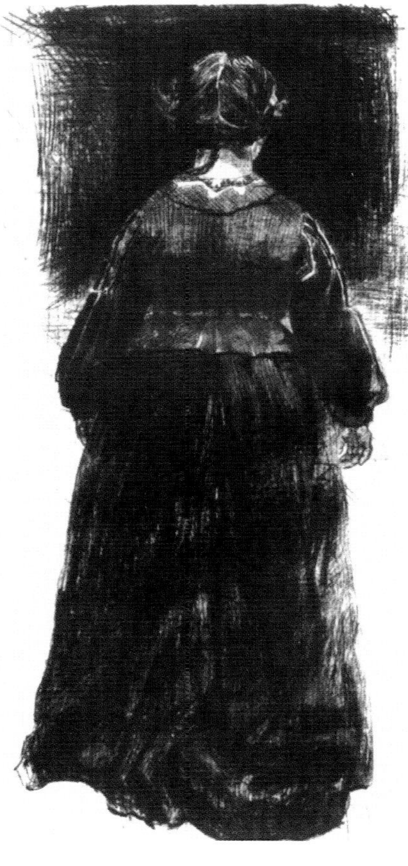

name' artists than it was from the mid-1970s onwards. This is not because big names have been absent. The selection made for a 1998 exhibition by Jill Hutchings and Stanley Jones of one print for each of the forty years of the Studio's history brings up an impressive list of names for the early Chilford period: Basil Beattie, Prunella Clough, R.B. Kitaj, Wilhelmina Barns-Graham (who made one of the early prints in St Ives), John Hoyland, Ana Maria Pacheco, Paul Hogarth, Richard Deacon, Peter Randall-Page and Patrick Heron.

Among contemporary artists, Paula Rego is the one who has made lithography a central part of her work in the past ten years, and has found at Curwen the facilities and working atmosphere conducive to her practice. Her large-scale prints display her skill in drawing in a direct and unmannered way that is rarely seen today in the contemporary sphere, yet make full use of the quality of the medium (figs.126–7). In Rego's words, 'I want them to work biff-bang.'[57] While Rego made many etchings and intaglio prints from her time at the Slade, contemporary with Stanley Jones, and more intensively from the later 1980s onwards, her initial experiences drawing on film for lithography were less satisfactory. As T.G. Rosenthal describes, 'She overcame the problems that some artists have with commercially made transfer paper by using a special transer paper developed by Jones himself. The technical results of her work with Jones in the Jane Eyre sequence are extraordinary, and show that she has mastered lithography as subtly and as comprehensively as etching.'[58] Rego's work on stone gets the

127
Paula Rego working at the Curwen Studio, 2008

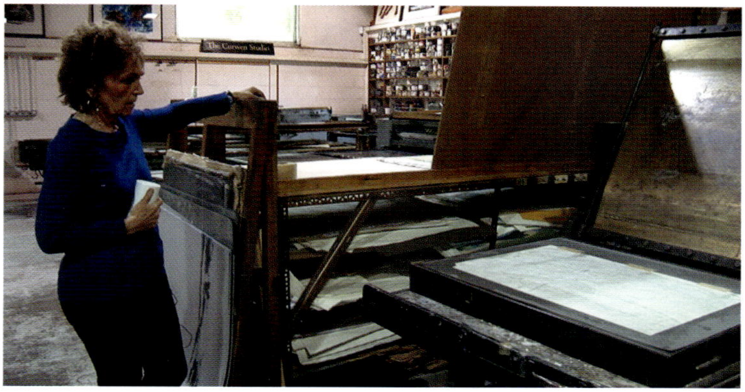

most intense quality of black, matched by an intensity of imagination almost unknown in current traditional and academic work. She likes working with texts, and her prints using lithography and intaglio have been used as book illustrations, thus making a neat circle back to pre-war Curwen and the three artists whom Oliver Simon commissioned to illustrate *Wuthering Heights*, with a commentary by Kenneth Clark in *Signature*.

The location in East Anglia connects the Studio with artists and other arts institutions in the region. The Fry Art Gallery at Saffron Walden, for example, is home to the North West Essex Art Collection, which exhibits artists who lived in and around Great Bardfield from the 1920s onwards. Of these, Eric Ravilious and Edward Bawden are the most notable, both with strong historic connections to Curwen. In addition, some of the less well known artists, such as Bernard Cheese, Sheila Robinson and their daughter, Chloe Cheese, who grew up in Bardfield, all made prints at Curwen at different times. Younger artists who have associated themselves with the graphic manner of Ravilious and Bawden, including Colin Wilkin and Mark Hearld, have also made prints at Curwen which have been sold at the Fry.

Slightly further afield, the Aldeburgh Festival has historic links with several Curwen artists who designed sets and costumes for Benjamin Britten's operas. John Piper is the foremost, but Ceri Richards was the designer for *Noyes Fludde* in 1959, and both he and John Nash made

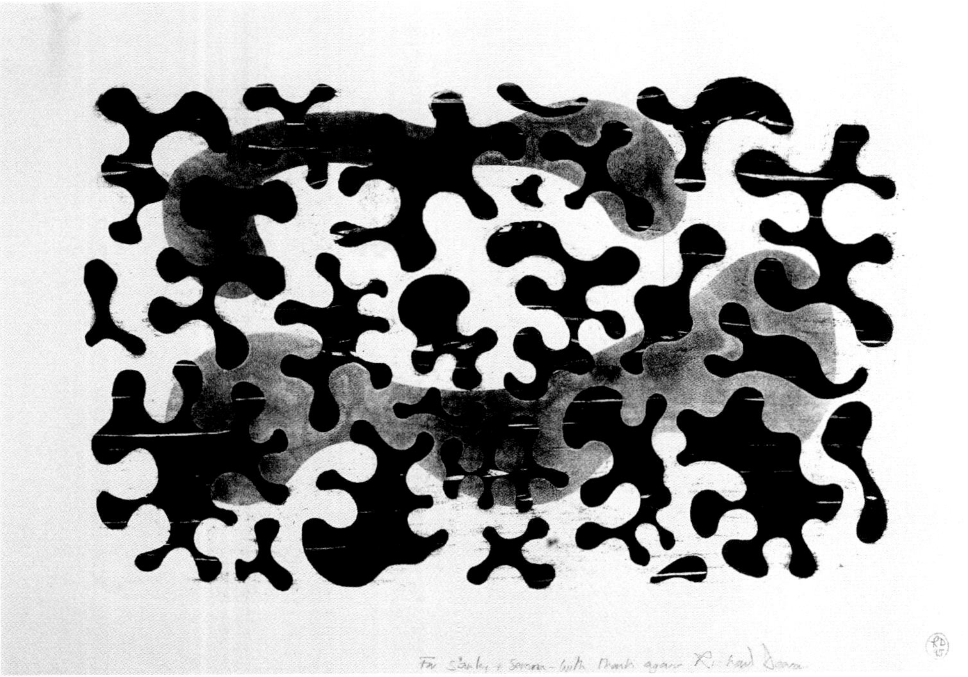

128
Richard Deacon,
Tomorrow, 1995

drawings for early Festival programme books printed at Cowells. In 2005, Aldeburgh Productions published a set of lithographs made at Curwen of local topographical subjects by David Gentleman (who has longstanding Suffolk connections), which were exhibited in the gallery at Snape Maltings Concert Hall.

In addition to continuing the tradition of hand drawing on plate or stone, the Curwen Studio has further developed its use of continuous tone lithography as a medium for printing photographs. The Photographic Contone process, which is currently subject to a patent application, allows for the multiple printing of an image equivalent to a platinum print, historically the gold standard of photographic printing from a negative. This follows in the steps of Stanley Jones's adventurous use of photography in artists' prints in the 1960s in defiance of the orthodoxy that defined an original print at the time. Photographers who have used the process include Mike McCartney, John Claridge, Noel Myles, Nicholas Sinclair and Julia Hedgecoe. Institutions that hold important photographic collections from which they want to generate reproductions of the highest quality, such as Royal Institute of British Architects and Liverpool City Archive, have also made use of Photographic Contone.

To enable an enterprise such as the Curwen Studio to explain its purpose to the outside world, it is still important to make clear distinctions between an artist's original print and a reproduction. Back in the 1950s, it was relatively simple to explain the distinction between an autographic image and a photomechanical reproduction, and to justify the special expertise and costs required for the creation of the former. By 1970, the distinction was less clear, owing to artists and printmakers choosing to cross the boundaries of purity and adopt photomechanical means, often with exciting and worthwhile results. Had this

129
Patrick Procktor,
View of Greenwich,
1989

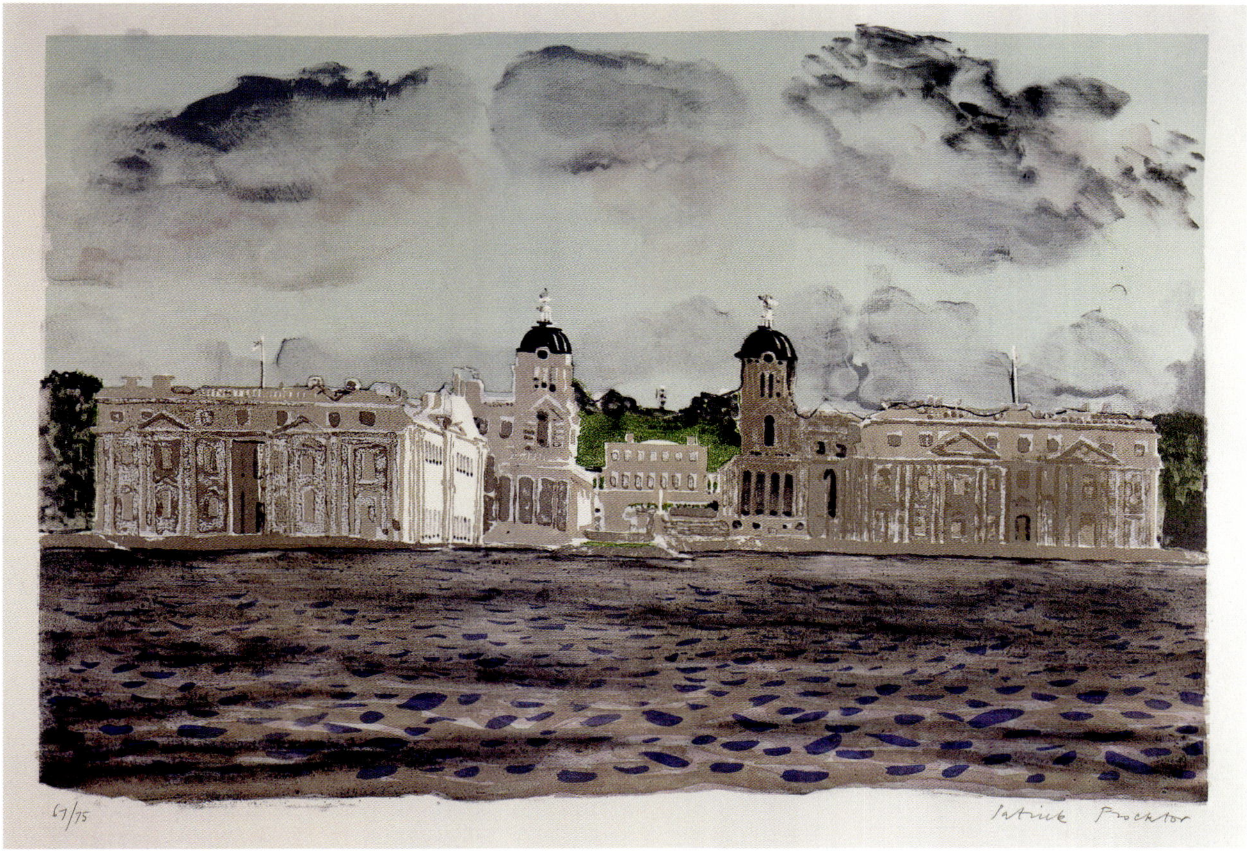

130
Ken Kiff,
The Giant Tree,
1999

131
Victor Pasmore,
Beyond the Eye, 2,
1995

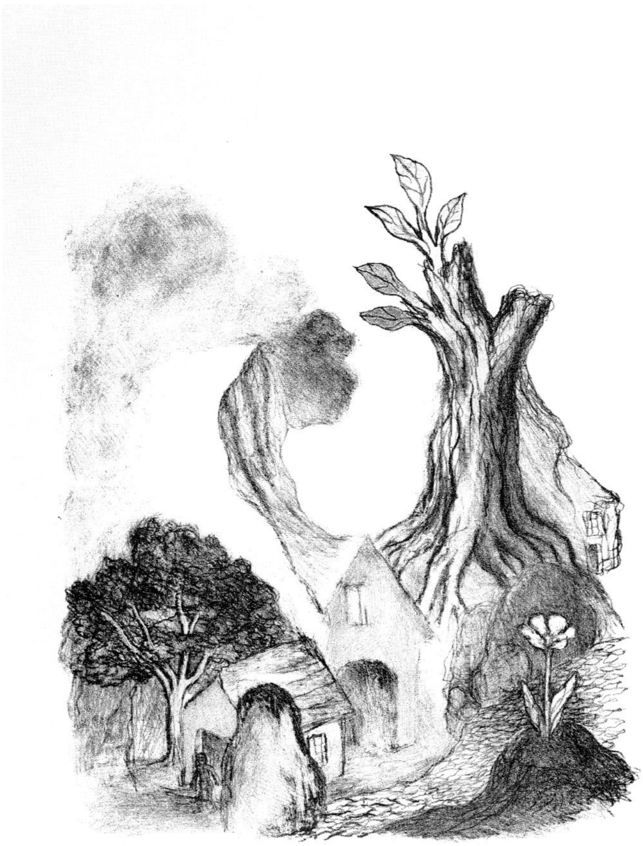

blurring of boundaries not occurred, the current situation would undoubtedly be simpler, but artistically poorer, and there is no going back.

With the invention of the giclée print (the French name for a tomcat's spray), the art lover may well be confused. Giclée, a form of computer printing from a scanned image, is currently much proclaimed as the equivalent of a traditional artist's print. The quality is the best available in this medium, and the benefit for a publisher is that prints can be run individually without any cost penalty. By contrast, a lithograph edition is normally printed all in one go, with a lower unit cost, but a higher overall risk that copies may not sell fast enough. The inks are different, and so is the paper. Despite the high technical achievement of giclée, the collaborative work encouraged at the Curwen Studio now as in the past is something totally different. It allows for an originality that goes beyond the interpretation of the reproduced image, the same quality of discovery through a medium that excited printmakers in the 1940s and 1950s. Everyone involved in printmaking has a role to play in explaining the difference between the demands of lithography and the convenience of technical solutions such as giclée to a justifiably confused public, and this is an area in which the Print Study Centre can play a significant role.

At a time when many households have their own in-house printmaking facility in the form of a colour inkjet printer, the idea that printmaking achieves something more demanding and subtle can potentially engage a greater number of people rather

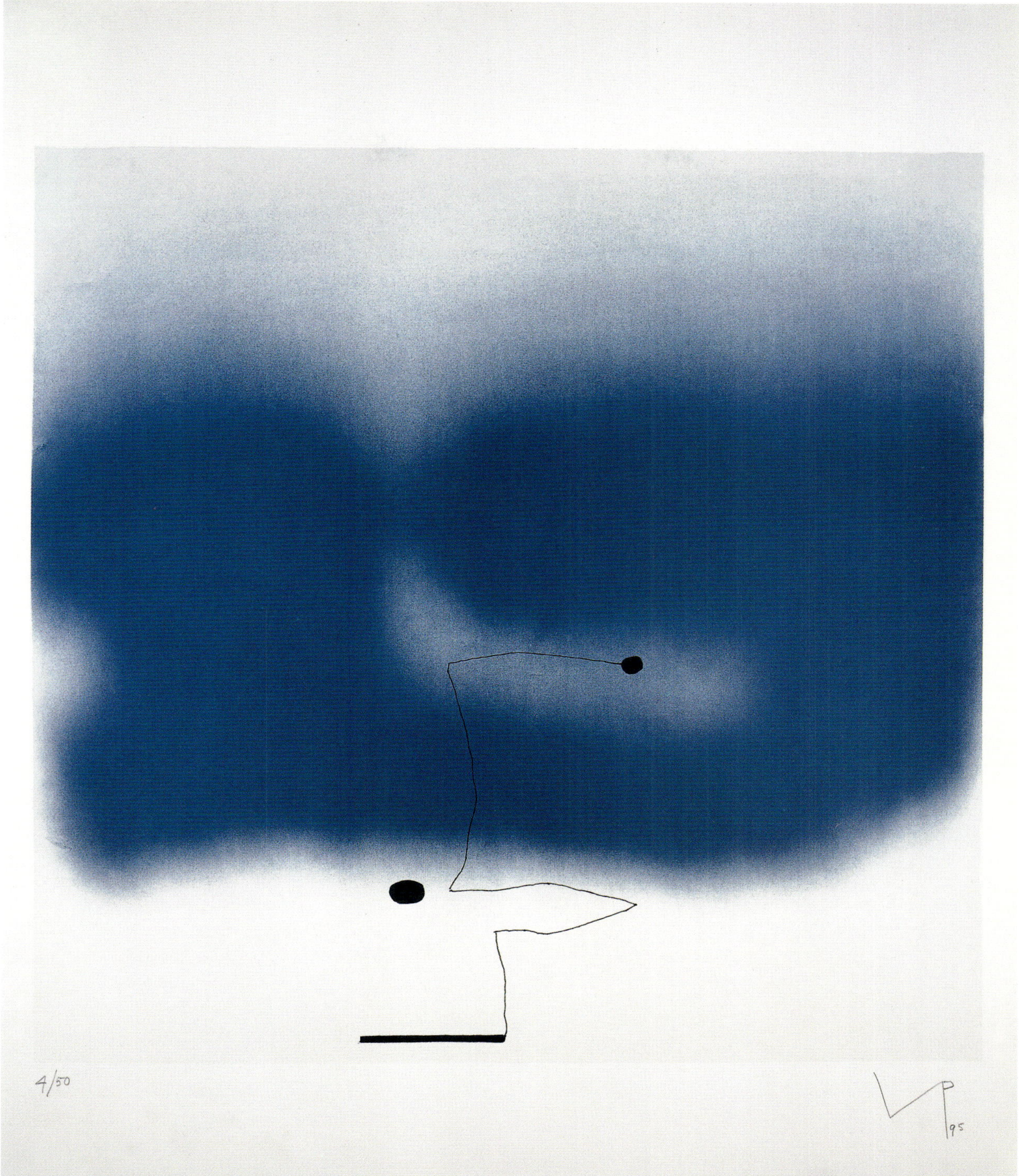
4/50
95

132
Michael Rothenstein,
experimental print, 1993

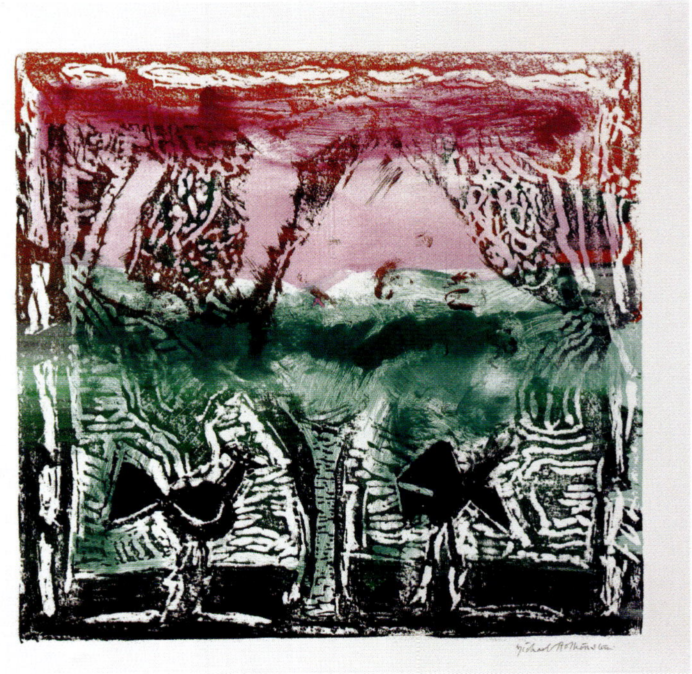

than fewer. It is especially regrettable that, at a time when the printed image is generated more widely than ever before, the specialist art schools should have wound down their printmaking facilities, owing largely to the cost of specialist staff and premises, as well as to the residual belief that printmaking is an activity of secondary significance, a prejudice that museums do too little to dispel.

Looking back over the period from Harold Curwen's joining John Curwen and Sons a hundred years ago, one sees that the best results in printing have rarely come from the cutting edge of technology, but from its opposite, the penumbra of obsolescence. This may be a reflection on the direction that most technology has taken since the nineteenth century, away from human control and towards a 'perfect' and consistent product. A giclée print is the workmanship of certainty to the extent that to call it workmanship is almost misleading, while a lithograph, far from being diminished by the risk factor it involves, owes its life and soul to living in a world of experiment and adventure. So long as artists value and understand the workmanship of risk, they will prefer such life-giving processes to the totally predictable ones.

At fifty years, the continued health of the Curwen Studio is something to be celebrated, with a staff who are dedicated to the concept of original print collaboration and to developing the medium of lithography. Jenny Roland says, 'we still view lithography as an evolving process. As new products come on the market we are able to adapt them in a more experimental way than they were intended

133
Geoffrey Clarke,
Search, 2000

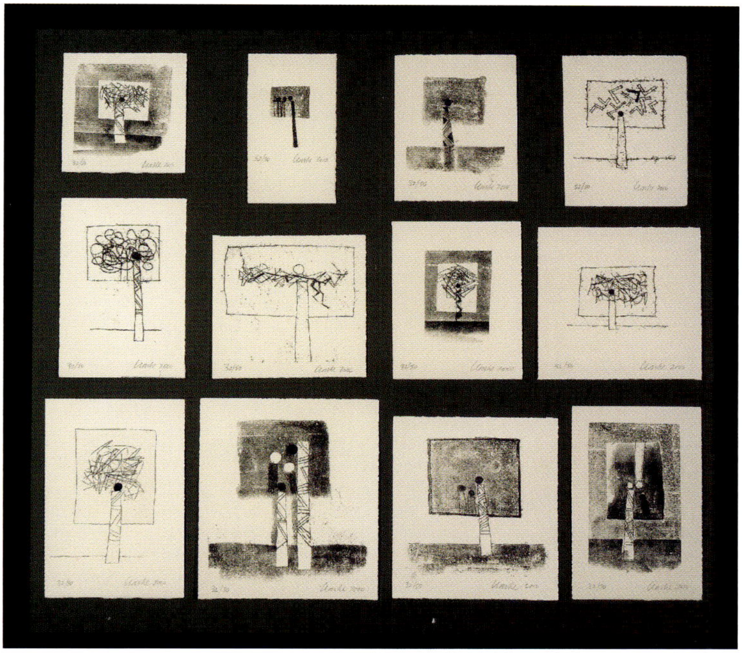

for in the commercial sector. Artists being artists are always looking at things from a different perspective and therefore encourage us to find ways of pushing the boundaries of lithography.'[59]

Tom Martin, as Studio Manager, has in Jenny Roland's words, 'brought new life to the process following his foundation gained from Stanley's knowledge, partly through his own artistic endeavours, but also through the desire to explore what contemporary lithography can offer to artists. Lithography isn't solely about drawn lines, washes, etc. You can use stencils, even objects, and mono printing is extremely versatile and easy to practise.'[60] Martin's own work covers a variety of techniques and genres, including brightly coloured prints with the vigour of Alan Davie, more subtle one-off images showing the potential of lithography for building up transparent overlays of colour. In addition, Martin has devised a range of cut out models and miniature model theatres in the Victorian tradition. These began as amusements for his own pleasure, but now extend to souvenirs for properties such as Kettles Yard, Cambridge, and the Crooked House, Lavenham.[61]

The ethos of the Studio combines, as it always has done, a strong belief in the value and excitement of plates, paper, ink and presses as a means to creating original images.

NOTES

THE CURWEN PRESS

1 Grace Lovat Fraser, *Claud Lovat Fraser*, exh. cat., Victoria and Albert Museum, London 1969, p.16.
2 *Commercial Art*, no.54, December 1930, p.264.
3 See Oliver Green and Alan Powers, *Away we Go ...*, Norwich 2006.
4 Oliver Simon, *Printer and Playground*, London 1956, p.8.
5 Herbert Simon, 'A Note on Oliver Simon', *Penrose Annual*, vol.51, 1957, p.68.
6 Holbrook Jackson, *A Cross-Section of English Printing: The Curwen Press 1918–1934*, The Curwen Press, Plaistow 1935, p.6. The same text appears in the *Curwen Press Newsletter*, no.9, March 1935.
7 Harold Curwen, undated typescript letter to the press, Cambridge University Library (CUL) Morison XXVII 121.
8 Paul Nash, *Room and Book*, London 1932, p.97.
9 Paul Nash, 'The Stencil Process', *Curwen Press Miscellany*, 1931, p.113.
10 Collotype is a form of screen-less photographic printing, in which an image is laid onto a gelatine base from which prints can be taken. It was widely practised in the nineteenth and early twentieth centuries, but the results were sensitive to humidity at the time of printing, and it was generally superseded by the more dependable photogravure, for which dot screens of a much finer grade could be achieved than with normal process blocks.
11 Barnett Freedman, 'Lithography: A Painter's Excursion', *Signature*, no.2, March 1936, p.13.
12 Losses were recorded in 1915–16, 1918–19 and 1922–3.
13 CUL Morison XXXVII 20.
14 CUL *General Minute Book*, Morison XXVII 21, 23 April 1934.
15 Ibid., 14 May 1936.
16 Simon 1956, p.68.
17 Graham Sutherland to Pat Gilmour, 11 November 1976, Tate Archive, TGA 92/316/20.
18 See Ruth Artmonsky, *Art for Everyone: Contemporary Lithographs Ltd.*, London 2007.
19 Some of the second series of Contemporary Lithographs, launched in 1939, were printed at the Baynard Press. Piper's double panorama of the seaside was printed at Waterlow and Son, as it required an extra-large press. Piper recalled that he had to be smuggled into the printing works owing to lack of union cooperation with outside artists.
20 Lynton Lamb to Pat Gilmour, 24 October 1976, Tate Archive, TGA 92/316/13.
21 CUL General Minute Book, Morison XXVII 21, 19 July 1943.
22 [Basil Harley,] *The Curwen Press: A Short History*, Plaistow 1970, p.25.
23 See Nicholas Ardizzone, *Edward Ardizzone's World: The Etchings and Lithographs*, London 2000, pp.130–2.
24 *The Times*, 11 May 1970.
25 CUL Minutes of Board AGM, Morison XXVII 21, 25 July 1963.
26 *The Times*, 11 May 1970.

THE CURWEN STUDIO

1 Denys Sutton, 'Nicolas de Stael', *Signature*, new series, no.17, 1953, pp.23–30.
2 David Pye, *The Nature and Art of Workmanship*, London 1971.
3 S.W. Hayter, *New Ways of Gravure*, London 1948, pp.267–8.
4 Ibid.
5 Brian Robb, 'The Engraver and his Techniques', *Signature*, new series, no.18, 1954, p.63.
6 John Piper, Preface in John Buckland Wright, *Etching and Engraving*, London 1953, p.12.
7 Daniel-Henry Kahnweiler with Francis Crémieux, *My Galleries and Painters*, London 1971, p.119.
8 Jean Adhémar, *Twentieth Century Graphics*, London 1971, p.193.
9 *Sunflowers at Marignac*, 1956 and *Sunflowers*, c.1957, nos.103 and 104, in Orde Levinson, *John Piper: The Complete Graphic Works, catalogue raisonnée*, London 1987.
10 Stanley Jones, Preface in Mel Gooding, *Ceri Richards Graphics*, exh. cat., National Museum of Wales, Cardiff 1979.
11 Bryan Robertson, 'A Background to British Printmaking, 1946–1976' in *Out of Print: British Printmaking 1946–1976*, London 1994.
12 See Ruth Artmonsky, *School Prints: A Romantic Project*, London 2006.
13 See Diana Miller, *The Ladies of Miller's*, exh. cat., Eastbourne 1989. The quote is from Robertson 1994.
14 See Christopher Allan, *Artists at Harleys: Pioneering Printmaking in the 1950s*, exh. cat., Hunterian Art Gallery, Glasgow 2000.
15 Robert Erskine, 'St George's Gallery', in Charles Spencer, *A Decade of Printmaking*, London 1975, p.20.
16 Ibid.
17 Ibid.
18 G.S. Whittet, 'Newer London Galleries: The St George's Gallery', *Studio*, vol.163, May 1962, p.193.
19 Pat Gilmour, *Modern Prints*, London 1970, p.124.
20 Stanley Jones, 'Artists' Lives' Interview, National Life Story Collection, National Sound Archive (interviewer Linda Sandino, 2004), F15066A.

21 June Wayne, Preface to G. Antreasian and C. Adams, *The Tamarind Book of Lithography: Art and Techniques*, New York 1971.

22 Gilmour 1970, ibid.

23 Fritz Eichenberg, 'American Artist Printmakers', *Penrose Annual*, vol.53, 1959, p.14.

24 Robert Erskine, '"Poor man's paintings," My foot!', *Studio*, vol.157, 1959, p.107.

25 In her biography of Hepworth, Sally Festing suggests that Marcus Brumwell, a director of Stuart's Advertising and a major Curwen client and supporter in the 1930s, was responsible for introducing Hepworth to the Simon brothers at that time. She also attributes a role to Brumwell (who had a holiday house on the Fal estuary) in suggesting that Curwen Studio should come to St Ives. Sally Festing, *Barbara Hepworth: A Life of Forms*, London 1995, p.282.

26 This paraphrase of Lundgren's words is taken from Nobert Lynton, *William Scott*, London 2004, p.234 Lundgren's review of a touring exhibition, *Thirteen British Artists*, was published in *Arbeterbladet*, 10 November 1961.

27 Roberto Sanesi, *The Graphic Work of Ceri Richards*, Milan 1973, p.71.

28 Mel Gooding, Introduction to *Ceri Richards Graphics*, exh. cat., National Museum of Wales, Cardiff 1979, p.60.

29 Catalogue note for *William Scott, Works on Paper: Gouaches, Drawings, Prints*, exh. cat., Curwen Gallery, London 1988.

30 Pat Gilmour, *Artists at Curwen*, exh. cat., Tate Gallery, London 1977, p.103.

31 Stanley Jones in conversation with Christopher Allan, quoted in Christopher Allan, *Elizabeth Blackadder Prints*, London 2003, p.19.

32 Herbert Simon to Piper, 10 December 1958, TGA. 200410/1/1/42.

33 Anthony West, *John Piper*, London 1979, p.50.

34 John Piper, 'Book Illustration and the Painter-Artist', *Penrose Annual*, vol.43, 1949, p.52.

35 Stanley Jones, 'John and Curwen', in Geoffrey Elborn (ed.), *John Piper: A Celebration for his Eightieth Birthday*, London 1984.

36 Pat Gilmour, *Henry Moore: Graphics in the Making*, exh. cat., Tate Gallery, London 1975, p.15.

37 Stanley Jones, Note to catalogue *Moore: 80th Birthday Exhibition of Graphic Work*, exh. cat., Curwen Gallery, London 1978.

38 Telephone conversation with Pat Gilmour, 26 October 1976, quoted in Gilmour 1977, p.107.

39 See Matthew Gale and Chris Stephens, *Barbara Hepworth Works in the Tate Gallery Collection and the Barbara Hepworth Museum, St Ives*, London 1999, Appendix A, pp.275–6.

40 Pat Gilmour, *Kelpra Studio: The Rose and Chris Prater Gift, Artists Prints 1961–1980*, Tate Gallery, 1980, p.21.

41 Stanley Jones, 'Lithographs', in Caroline Wiseman, *Elisabeth Frink Original Prints*, catalogue raisonné, London 1998, p.38.

42 Pat Gilmour, 'Forty Prints from Forty Years', in *Forty Years at Curwen Studio*, 1958–1998, exh. cat., Curwen Gallery and New Academy Gallery, London 1998, p.13.

43 See Tessa Sidey, *Editions Alecto Original Graphics, Multiple Originals*, 1960–1981, Aldershot 2003.

44 Benedict Nightingale, 'A Licence to Print Originals', *New Society*, vol.9, 7 February 1967, pp.206–7.

45 Orde Levinson's catalogue of Piper prints concludes in 1983. In 1989, Curwen printed an image of Inglesham Church by Piper, published by the Society for the Protection of Ancient Buildings in an edition of 100, in tribute to John Betjeman, who loved this unrestored church. Anthony Fawcett, *One Day at a Time*, New York 1976.

47 David Hockney interviewed by Marco Livingstone, in Marco Livingstone, *David Hockney*, London 1981, p.112.

48 Ibid., p.129.

49 Pat Gilmour, *Artists in Print: An Introduction to Prints and Printmaking*, London 1981, p.73.

50 In conversation with Alan Powers, 18 June 2007.

51 Stephen Reiss to John Piper, 13 October 1975, Tate Archive, TGA 200410/1/1/42.

52 Stephen Reiss to John Piper, 14 December 1977, ibid.

53 Ibid.

54 Ibid.

55 Pat Gilmour, 'Setting up Departments – I: Prints at the Tate Gallery', *Print Quarterly*, no.2, vol.22, 2005, p.161.

56 See Peter Frost, 'Samuel Alper (1924–2002)' in *Dictionary of National Biography*, online supplement.

57 Quoted by John McEwen in *Paula Rego*, 1997, p.179.

58 T.G. Rosenthal, *Paula Rego: The Complete Graphic Work*, London 2003, p.166

59 Jenny Roland, email to Alan Powers, 6 March 2008.

60 Jenny Roland, email to Alan Powers, 6 March 2008.

61 See http://www.thomasmartin turnpiece.n